STEPPING STONES

STEPPING STONES OF UNGAVA AND LABRADOR

To Alec, Sharon Hannah and Jeremy Happy Adventures! Nigel Foster June 2010

NIGEL FOSTER

Outskirts Press, Inc.
Denver, Colorado

Outskirts Press, Inc.
http://www.outskirtspress.com

ISBN: 978-1-4327-4528-8
ISBN: 978-1-4327-4555-4

Outskirts Press and the "OP" logo are trademarks belonging to Outskirts Press, Inc.

PRINTED IN THE UNITED STATES OF AMERICA

To Kristin Nelson, my wife.

Contents

Acknowledgements

I would like to thank those who offered inspiration, support and hospitality while I planned and completed the kayaking trips, then researched and wrote this book. I will mention here or in the following chapters a few of the many who helped, but thank you all.

A heartfelt thanks to my parents, Peter and Elizabeth, for instilling in me a sense of adventure tempered by a process of risk assessment. Relating to the trip from Iqaluit to Labrador, thank you Sharon for helping make that happen. Thanks also to the British Canoe Union for travel and freight expenses, Graham and Bob Goldsmith for the Vyneck kayak, Alistair Wilson of Lendal for paddles, Tony of Alpine Sports Brighton for rain gear. Thank you Peter Beril and Naudla (and Jim and Brent) for taking care of me in Iqaluit, and to the officers of the tanker Eastern Shell for picking up and caring for a hitch-hiker.

Relating to the Ungava and Labrador journey, my special thanks go to Kristin Nelson, the dynamo behind the trip and the perfect person to travel with. Thanks to Kristin's parents Richard and Alice for renting us an emergency satellite phone, Jen Kleck for the loan of laser flares, Mountain Surf for spray skirts and waterproofs, Seaward Kayaks and Norway Nordic.

"*Nakoumek*" (thanks) to Larry Watt and Sarah Airo in Kuujjuaq for the loan of firearms, David and Suzie from George River who with family and friends welcomed us into the shelter of their tent beside a tidal rapid, Eli and his staff at Inuksuq Lodge, Louis Le May and his team at Saglek, the reconstruction group at Hebron, Jim and Helena from Nain, and Tom Goodwin at Atsanik Lodge.

In writing this book, thanks to Wayne Moye for your endless encouragement, and Joel Rogers and Ed Reading for advice and editing. Thanks to Millissa Probart of Outskirts Press. Finally, to Kristin Nelson, thanks for your patience, untiring help and support throughout.

CHAPTER 1

Going East

We all explore. Whether into the back of a desk drawer, astral physics, or the insect world hidden beneath the roses, we all explore. We are motivated by curiosity, by challenge, and by our own questions. Exploration is addictive.

With Kristin beside me I took the first turn at the wheel of the Jeep. The Seattle skyline shrank behind us as we dropped down onto the floating bridge and crossed over Lake Washington. Our eyes focused ahead on the Cascade Mountain forest, selectively editing-out the clear-cuts and the patches of stumps and rock. As we climbed toward the summit, rivers of ice-melt cooled the air in the shade alongside the road. Over the top, with the engine idling, we descended sweeping curves into eastern Washington, the green forest now displaced by blue-gray sagebrush. Here and there were ochre-yellow dots of flower heads. Hot herbal scents buffeted us through the open windows. The outside temperature indicated mid-90s Fahrenheit, and the road shimmered with mirages of puddles and pools above the searing tarmac. My eyelids began to droop. Kristin rapped my leg and began talking, incoherently to me. Then she said abruptly, "Nigel, pull in over here—I want to get some water."

We drifted off the road into tree shade at a small store at George. George, Washington. We had only just crossed the Columbia River and had 4,000 miles ahead of us. I closed my eyes; my head pulsed with the heat. I was exhausted. We had been preparing this kayak trip to Labrador for months, yet we were up late last night, still dealing with details. Now that we were finally on the road, it seemed important to cover some distance to prove we had started. It seemed hardly believable that after 23 years I was returning to finish a trip I had started in 1981. My decision to take Kristin with me was tormenting me—I barely survived the first attempt.

Kristin is self-sufficient, independent, bulletproof, yet really as dependent and fearful as the rest of us. She maintains a happy exterior largely because she rationalizes well, turning life's knocks to her advantage with a flippant, "If it doesn't kill me it'll only make me stronger." If I had left her behind, gone alone or with friends, yes, it would have made her stronger, but she was strong enough to come with me. Kristin is a ceramicist, but like most artists she gets her inspiration outside the studio. She skis and kayaks, peers into flowers, and watches bugs. She's curious. I met Kristin at a sea-kayaking symposium. She was ordering her first sea kayak, having started kayaking on white-water rivers. That was maybe seven years ago; her skills have advanced.

Kayaking began for me when, still a teenager, I was attracted to its challenge and its serenity, its physical effort and its relaxation. I was free to explore the endless wilderness on the water. After circumnavigating Iceland in a kayak at age twenty-four, I cut my kayak in half to fit it on a flight to Newfoundland, to paddle there. I took a ferry from England to paddle in Norway. I crossed France from the English Channel to the Mediterranean in a tandem kayak. I paddled through the tumultuous tidal rapids around the Faroe Islands, where ten-knot currents run beneath 2,000-foot cliffs. Looking up into dense clouds of circling seabirds, I wondered if anything could exceed this feeling of awe. Addicted to sea kayaking, I used those early years to gain the British Canoe Union's Level 5 coach award, and became a teacher at a residential outdoor activity center, but in an economic downturn I chose to go exploring.

In Newfoundland in 1979 I had become intrigued by photographs I had found of the rugged Labrador coast. The island of Newfoundland sits at the eastern end of the Gulf of Saint Lawrence. Its northern finger points across Belle Isle Straits toward Labrador. The Canadian province of Newfoundland and Labrador extends more than a thousand miles from south to north, from forest into subarctic tundra. In Labrador the native Innu, which are the mostly inland-dwelling Indian tribes, and the Inuit Eskimo people have mixed with people from Britain, France and Newfoundland and their descendants. Labrador is divided into north and south by the Melville Inlet, with the northern section predominantly populated by Inuit and Innu. Both groups used to migrate with the seasons to hunt for their subsistence. The Inuit relied on sea mammals, the Innu on caribou. Inuit once roamed the entire coast of Labrador, but in the last fifty years the Canadian Government has systematically relocated these people into towns farther south. I felt a special affinity with the Inuit because they used kayaks, but I was also intrigued by stories I read about the Innu, who ranged freely across the interior. They did so until the caribou herds were so decimated by fur-trading that the Innu could no longer survive by their traditional means. Now, roads, railways, mining projects, logging and hydroelectric projects have begun to divide up the land.

Labrador's remoteness enticed me, promising mountain ranges that rise abruptly from the sea, and wild tidal rapids around the icy northern tip. In 1981 I made plans with friends to bring kayaks by coastal steamer to Nain, the northernmost town. By sharing camping gear we could free up enough space in the kayaks to carry food for four weeks. We thought four weeks would take us from Nain to the Button Islands off the northern tip and back to Nain, a round trip of 700 miles in uninhabited territory. But my friends were unable to take enough time off work to do the trip. I would have to go solo. This would leave me less room for food, so I began to eye an alternative route that would cut the distance by fifty miles. This more challenging idea thrilled and frightened me.

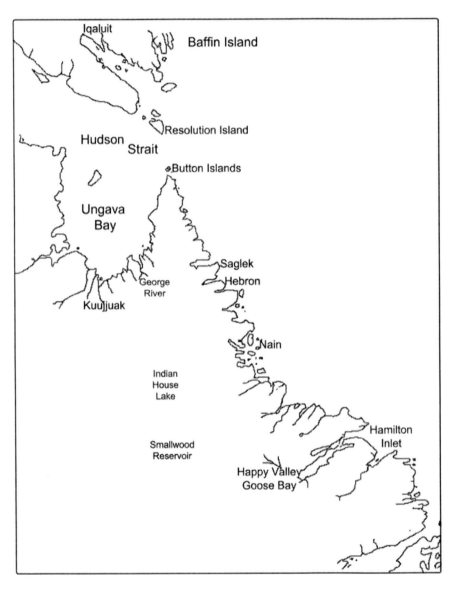

I would start at Frobisher Bay on Baffin Island, the vast island that lies sixty miles north of Labrador across Hudson Strait, at the town of Iqaluit. The sea there had tides with a range of forty feet. At mid-cycle such a tide will rise two inches per minute, so that—from dry feet at the water's edge—one will have water to the knees in less than ten minutes while several hundred yards of beach will be inundated. This can make camping difficult. The 150 to 200 pounds of laden kayak cannot be carried up rock ledges single-handed, so the kayak must be unloaded quickly and the contents, and then the kayak, carried clear, while one races the rising water. This exceptional tidal range also creates currents that run to seven knots, which is faster than I paddle. The practical paddling season here is short: just one month. Frozen through winter, the sea ice breaks up around mid-July. From then until early August the current sweeps the floating ice about, sometimes jamming it between rocks and islands to create barriers against which the current piles still more ice. Vessels much larger than kayaks have been swept into the ice jams and crushed. Early August seemed a safe time to leave, but offered only a brief window before the storms began to lash the coast in early September. Daunting as these challenges seemed, they paled beside the Hudson Strait itself. Forty miles across at its narrowest, between Resolution Island to the north and the Button Islands, with tidal currents up to seven knots and extensive tidal rapids, the strait experiences fog one day out of two. The Button Islands target forty miles away seemed relatively small. I felt tormented over the decision to launch from Iqaluit and tormented more so afterwards. Yet I began preparing my Vyneck, the sea kayak I had designed with a friend a few years earlier, adding both a foot-operated bilge pump and a fixed hand pump. If my kayak filled with icy water I must have a way to empty it. I fitted a compass to the deck and bought a backup to carry in my pocket. I laminated charts. I continued my research.

In July, a few weeks before departing, I loaded the kayak with food and equipment and air-freighted it to Iqaluit. In August, after a delay for a bomb scare at London airport, I flew to New York to find my baggage had not arrived, and I missed my onward flight to Montreal. While I waited overnight, 13,000 American air traffic controllers in stalemate over pay walked off the job. President Reagan sacked them all, and I was stranded. I went overland to Montreal and flew standby to Iqaluit. At Iqaluit, my kayak had not arrived either. Day by day I watched the daylight shrink from the 24 hours I enjoyed when I arrived to distinct days and nights as time went on. My carefully chosen window between the departure of pack ice and the arrival of September storms was shrinking while I paced the dusty town in frustration.

Two weeks later, when I was finally able to leave, I doubted that I could finish my trip as planned. I figured that if I could reach Labrador before September, perhaps I could still make it. If not, I would circle Resolution Island and return to Iqaluit, but I did not need to make that decision until I was in position to cross Hudson Strait and could see what the conditions looked like. With each day of paddling the Hudson Strait seemed more daunting and my anxiety increased. I passed the southern end of Baffin Island and paddled the stepping stones of the Lower Savage Islands to Resolution Island. Near the south end of Resolution Island I waited one whole day in fog and wind, resting, hoping for conditions that would make my decision easy. I passed the time painting with watercolors, something I enjoy doing when I have the time, and find relaxing and absorbing.

By the next morning the wind had dropped, so I left a quiet shore enveloped in fog and aimed out into Hudson Strait. To my dismay a wind sprang up and soon became strong. Conditions were difficult that day, and I was not certain I could make it across. After sixteen and a half hours of paddling I accomplished a wild, bruising landing in the dark on the Button Islands. I had frostbite in my fingers. The weather deteriorated. Strong winds blew almost every day for the next week. I made little progress. I might have shown more wisdom had I turned back before leaving Resolution Island, but by now I had crossed Hudson Strait and had no way to shorten the trip or abandon it.

One day, hugging the coast, I came upon an anchored oil tanker, pausing on its journey south and I begged a ride. Four days later we docked in Nova Scotia and I disembarked, knowing my journey had been incomplete. I spent that fall of 1981 in Newfoundland, before returning to instruct at the National Watersports Center in Wales. I kept an eye open for an opportunity to return to Labrador, but kayaking instructors are kept busy in summer. By 1986 I had started my own kayaking business, and later moved from Wales to the United States.

My desire to finish the Labrador trip smoldered, until I knew if I did not go soon, I never would. Canada was proposing a new National Park in the Torngat Mountains of northern Labrador. With that in place would I still want to go? I had found northern Labrador so powerful, so beautiful, and with a presence that seemed so ancient that I knew Kristin would be moved by it. So in 2004 I asked her if she would come with me. In the seven years we had been together we had paddled in rough conditions off the Pacific coast, had surfed kayaks in fifteen-foot breakers, had run the Grand Canyon in whitewater kayaks, and had made numerous self-contained sea kayaking trips of one or two weeks at a time. I knew how tenacious Kristin could be. I knew how well she rationalized fear when conditions were scary. I knew how easy she was to live with in a tent. Having experienced something of the conditions in Labrador already, I knew what to expect and I felt sure Kristin was capable, if she wanted to come.

She was hesitant. She said she had never been on such a committing trip. I told her how I had felt planning for Iceland in 1977, considering factors beyond my experience. I had set off to paddle around Iceland without being certain I could do it. I treated each day of paddling afresh. Sure, I kept the goal in mind, but it is difficult to match up the few miles of a day against the massive total of miles ahead. It is easier to think of going paddling for the day. The next day becomes the same, preparing to paddle for the day. Part of Kristin's hesitation was the remoteness. In Iceland I had had an escape route. There were coastal towns and villages. A road was completed across the south of Iceland in 1976, the year before my voyage. I was asking Kristin for a much more serious commitment. There are no settlements, no roads, along the section of Labrador we would paddle, and no people. This would make any trip serious. We would be beyond the range of VHF radio or cell phone and on our own for weeks.

Kristin cited a couple on a kayak trip in Labrador who had been hit by the intense offshore winds that spring up from the fjords with little warning. Although they reached shore, the woman was so terrified she could not continue. In the end they summoned a plane to carry them out. Would Kristin be able to handle the winds? Despite her doubts, she had not rejected the idea. She wanted to be able to come, so I pulled out the charts and we began to talk about it. We did not need to start on Baffin Island; we could stick to the mainland. The Labrador Peninsula juts north to form the southern side of the entrance to Hudson Strait. To the west lies the wide Ungava Bay, biting south into northern Quebec. The town of Kuujjuaq sits beside a river that enters Ungava Bay at its southern extremity. Maybe that would be a good place to start. From Kuujjuaq we could follow the coast of Ungava Bay east and north until we reached the place where I had boarded the oil tanker. Beyond that lay the unfinished section of the trip I had attempted in 1981. As we studied the chart and looked at details, I could imagine us being there together, I could also imagine enjoying our impressions afterwards, sharing the memories.

And so we had set out. Here we were in George, Washington, with 4,000 miles of interstate highway, two-lane blacktop, and gravel road ahead of us to Labrador.

"Nigel!" I could hear Kristin say. "Nigel!" She sounded far away. "Nigel! Take this—you have to drink water!" I felt hot, horribly hot and sweaty, and could not figure out what was going on. I wanted to sleep. "Take this Nigel! Come on, we'll drive and cool down the car! Move over, I'll drive." I felt drugged, but I moved over into the passenger seat so Kristin could drive. As she pulled out onto the road I sank down in my seat, the air conditioner began to cool us, and I drank some water. My sweat-soaked T-shirt started to chill me. I heeded her advice and drank more water. In time I felt comfortable again.

We were on our way.

"You were too hot, Nigel," Kristin said. "You would have been there all night— you have to keep hydrated." I stared out at the landscape of low rolling hills and fields of golden grain. It reminded me of where I grew up at the edge of the South Downs in southern England. As the afternoon wore on, shadows pooled in the hollows.

The heads of grain blurring the hills glowed as the sun sank. Dust devils swirled dirty columns into the sky, spiraling upward as they moved across the fields to either side of the road. I pulled out our trip plan to navigate but, as I flipped through the pages, I realized that we would be on this same Interstate 90 for at least another day. I relaxed, settling into the scenery without guilt, with nothing more challenging to consider than where to eat and where to camp. I looked to see Kristin alert and happy at the wheel, and I smiled. This road trip was a bonus for me, an opportunity to relax before kayaking, and to truly register where Labrador was in relation to Seattle. We would shift gradually from the city across changing time zones into wilderness, with time to ease into the right frame of mind, like sliding into a warm bath. As I began to relax, I missed subtle signs that Kristin was worrying more than she showed about the trip ahead.

Droning down the interstates by day and camping by night, we drove on through the Badlands of North Dakota, where we spotted bison grazing. We stopped in Medina at a burger joint squeezed between a ranch and the railroad, pinned our fluttering napkins against the vinyl tablecloth with the greasy saltshakers, and hoped our meal of buffalo burgers would not reduce the herd. We cheered at Brainerd when we crossed the Mighty Mississippi, as Kristin called the fledgling river that grows from here and hurries south to the Gulf of Mexico. Hours later we crossed the watershed beyond which water flows east through the Great Lakes to the Atlantic. We reached Lake Superior at Duluth. Huge grain elevators, storage hoppers for iron ore and copper, and vast brick warehouses towered above the enormous rail terminals and the ships being loaded on the lake. We did not stop, until in the evening light we parked overlooking the calm water of Lake Superior at the college town of Marquette.

The town bore its industrial past like a scar. Old wharfs and warehouses stood derelict along a rusted railroad and a brick-studded shore. A roughly cleared lot revealed old floor plans cast in concrete that sprouted weeds in every corner and every crack. I remember seeing the same scene at London's postwar bombsites, bright with fireweed and wallflowers. But there was another dimension to Marquette: a new yacht marina, cycle trails and waterfront parks that seemed to promise a rebirth in a more leisure-oriented future. We strolled through streets of brick houses to discover a pizza parlor, and carried our garlic-rich prize back to eat at the waterfront. Leaning against one another, we stared at ripples. Water lapped against the shore, the lake's quiet heartbeat almost smothered by the bubbling of a small motor pushing a sailboat from the marina into the world's biggest freshwater lake. The scene was seductive, but we were prepared for wilderness and here everything seemed civilized.

Next day we reached the eastern end of Lake Superior at The Soo, or Sault Sainte Marie. Twin towns with the same name straddle the waterway that constitutes the U.S.-Canadian border. Giant locks, sufficient to carry the huge freighters we had seen loading at Duluth, bypassed rapids that otherwise would stymie shipping between northern Lake Huron and Lake Superior. Each of the twin towns has its own set of locks, one Canadian, one managed by the United States. We wandered around the American town until the darkening sky opened to rain. Then we ran to the car and drove across the bridge. Waiting at the border, our passports and papers ready, I looked at Kristin. She looked unhappy. "Are you OK?" "I'm scared." "What of? It's just a border." "Nigel, I'm scared of going into Canada. When we cross the border it means we're really going to Labrador. Once we've gone across, it seems there's no turning back." I looked at her hard. She did look frightened. "You're going to be fine. We'll look after each other. You know you can do it." But my words of reassurance seemed too thin. Her hands clutched her passport, and her face was almost in tears. I reached across and hugged her tightly.

We reached Montreal on 20 July and found our way to Norway Nordic, a store that combines all the character of a ski lodge with a kayaking store. It gets its distinctive personality from its owner, Neils Hollum. Born in Norway, Neils is a skier and kayaker. When my eyes rose to a pair of slender wooden telemark skis mounted on the wall, he proudly divulged that he would soon be leaving for southern Norway to kayak through the district from which that distinctive style of skiing takes its name. Neils values his expedition time, often leaving the store to his assistant Kayle while he vanishes with a sea kayak or a pair of skis. I like his attitude.

Norway Nordic, the Montreal sales representative of my sea kayak designs, was ideally placed to help ship our kayaks. The model we had chosen for this trip, the Legend, was somewhat different from the Vyneck I used in 1981. The Vyneck was fast and tracked straight, while the Legend has more cargo space, more stability and maneuvers more easily. When our kayaks arrived, Neils escorted them to the airport to wait standby for air freighting to Kuujjuaq. He would store for us any gear we did not need for the remainder of our car trip. We would drop the Jeep at Goose Bay (or Happy Valley-Goose Bay, as it is now known), so we could have transportation home with our kayaks after our trip, then come back to Montreal to pick up the equipment for our flight north to the put-in point, Kuujjuaq.

We strolled the Saint Lawrence River waterfront with Neils for espresso and a bite to eat, and to relax for a short time. Kristin especially enjoyed this opportunity since we were traveling hard, camping each night and would soon be on our own. Here the open air dining was undeniably elegant, with good company. A procession of impeccably turned out women in long dresses and high heels, with straight-backed escorts in suits, strolled past along the promenade. Perhaps they were enjoying the warm evening air before heading to a restaurant, or perhaps to the opera.

Leaving Montreal the next day, we continued on now smaller roads along the north shore of the Saint Lawrence Seaway. After a day of driving, our journey took on a different nature when we reached Saguenay. There an exceptionally long fjord extends north from the Saint Lawrence to block the winding coastal road. Cutting through ancient rocks along what might have been a geological fault line, the Saguenay River adds something unique to the shore. Where the deep fresh water meets the salty tide, wildlife flourishes. We parked close to the lighthouse on the point in sight of the ferry unloading across the fjord and walked toward the cliff. Kristin spotted something in the water. "Beluga!" she cried. I caught the disappearing flash of something white. Other sightseers clamored around, jostling for a look. The small white whales, perhaps a dozen of them, swam toward the point on which we stood. We raced down the path, down the steps, for a closer view of the bright white bodies arcing repeatedly up through the surface. It was exciting to see beluga, whales I have always associated with the Arctic, for it heightened my anticipation for what lay ahead. We crossed the Saguenay River on the ferry, peering down from the deck into the clear water in the hope of seeing more whales.

Beyond Saguenay the road is more intimate, curving through small towns, past vacation homes and bed-and-breakfast signs. Silky tidal mudflats choke the narrow bays. Winding our way through low hilly country we distanced ourselves from the cities. But the coastal road ends 250 miles short of the border with Labrador. To reach Goose Bay we would turn inland at Baie Comeau along the Manicouagan River.

Baie Comeau grew up around the site of a paper pulp mill founded in 1937 by the Chicago newspaper magnate, Robert R. McCormick, who licensed logging rights around the Manicouagan River. I had come across references to McCormick in my studies of Labrador because he often used a Sikorsky S-38 amphibian plane to visit his mills in Canada, and in 1929 he had sponsored an attempt to fly a great-circle route from Chicago to Europe. That attempt was aborted in northern Labrador at the same place I abandoned my kayak trip in 1981.

The road from Baie Comeau follows the river through forest and shortens the journey that took the Innu two hard weeks by canoe and portage on their annual migration into the interior. The river is dammed in four places to harness hydroelectric power, most notably at the top where the multiple-arch and buttress dam of the Manic 5 station stands. Completed in 1967, the dam is said to be the largest of its kind in the world, rising to more than 700 feet as it crosses the broad valley in a series of elegant arches. Yet for all the massive presence of the dam above us as we climbed in low gear to its base and then up beside it, what fascinated me more was the lake behind it. The water fills an asteroid crater more than 60 miles in diameter that is almost filled by an island. The reservoir is large enough to be seen easily on an atlas map of Canada. The island is big enough to accommodate the city of New York and its 8.2 million inhabitants with room to spare.

We had been cautioned to fill up with gasoline at every opportunity between Manic 5 and Goose Bay, but with just a handful of developments along the road, each incorporating a gas station, it would be difficult to miss one. Between settlements were hours of rutted, slippery, gravel highway with another vehicle seen every hour or two. Behind us, our plume of dust drifted across the boreal forest, leaving a brown mist between the thin dark trees and across the pale open ground of yellow lichen, insipid as snow. We rattled along the washboard road onto causeways and bridges over string lakes and muskeg, motored up along outcrops, and rose over blind summits through blasted rock gateways. Slithering like a boat from side to side to find the smoothest ride between boulders and potholes, we checked our speed only when approaching the bends, where the loose gravel, like ball bearings, could send us over the roadside berm.

Near Fermont the Cartier Railway met the road and we ran alongside, the road dodging perfidiously back and forth across the sober track that carries the ore trains from the Fermont mines. We were forced to stop only once, at a warning sign, to let a long train rumble slowly past. Soon we reached signs of the opencast mines that had stripped the skin from the belly of the mountain and are now disemboweling it. Bright red water gushed beside the road, flowing into long bloody lakes. Dump trucks with tires almost twice my height appeared puny against the scale of the quarry workings.

These workings are relatively recent, given the deposits were first reported in 1892. Their inaccessibility prevented action until the 1950s, when a railroad was pushed 200 miles into the wilderness from the coast to haul away the ore. An airstrip was built so materials could be flown in to build the town. A hydroelectric plant was constructed at Twin Falls to provide power, and an ore dock was built at Sept Isles to take the ore from train to ship. Ore began to move in 1962 from what is now Labrador City. Rival mining towns sprang up at Wabush, four miles away, and at Fermont, across the border in Quebec, but the Labrador City mine is still the largest iron mine in Canada. In 2001 Labrador City and Wabush together, called "Labrador West," had a population of 9,638, more than a third of Labrador's population. Most came from outside the province, swelling the population at the border. Even with the additional people, the Labrador population numbers just 28,000. The Seattle Seahawks football stadium seats 67,000.

From Labrador City we rumbled along the gravel road for another 330 miles before reaching Goose Bay. We parked the Jeep next to the fence in a small lot and walked through the tiny airport building to an Air Labrador De Havilland Dash 8 twin-propeller airplane. We would not need our car again until our return journey. From here on we were at the mercy of small local airlines with sketchy timetables.

At Wabush, the first stop, we found our connecting flight delayed, then cancelled, with no alternative flights. The airline offered us meal tickets for the rest of the day, then a room for the night. Next day, after breakfast, we tried again. We flew to Sept Isles, site of the ore-shipping terminal, then Quebec City, and finally to Montreal, where Kayle collected us from the airport. At his house we repacked all the gear we had left at Norway Nordic on our drive east. We had almost everything we should need for the next five weeks. It seemed impossible it would all fit into our kayaks, but it had fit into identical kayaks in Seattle before we left.

Next morning we squeezed into Kayle's small car over our bulging bags and suffered a claustrophobic ride to the airport. After twelve days of hard travel, from Seattle to Goose Bay, then back to Montreal, we were now airborne for the final leg of the outward journey. We sat side by side as the First Air jet, a Boeing 727-100C, juddered and bounced through turbulence on its way north toward Kuujjuaq. Kristin hates air turbulence. "This isn't so bad, really," I said, "It's rather like the road to Goose Bay." Holding her hand seemed to help more than my wisecracks did.

CHAPTER 2

Kuujjuaq

"Ooh!" gasped Kristin. "This air is delicious!" I sucked in a lungful and clattered down the metal stairs after her. The air felt warm and fresh, clear and clean, and the low angle of sunlight was easy on my eyes. We followed the line of passengers across damp asphalt to a small single-story building. Mosquitoes carried in with us to where a dozen or more people were awaiting their baggage in the one public room that served as departure lounge, arrivals, baggage claim, and ticket office. It was an intimate space. I looked around, wondering what brought them to a place like Kuujjuaq. Did they live here? The group of men beside me, crusty, with unshaven chins and wild hair and clad in thick woolen jackets, explained they were from Montreal and were heading north and west to prospect for diamonds. Behind me an Inuit family sat motionless on a bench, their round brown faces relaxed and calm. They may have been local. A group speaking Quebecois clustered together, preparing to leave for a fishing camp, their nervous movements betraying excitement. This area, they explained, is renowned for its salmon and arctic char.

There was a loud crash and I turned to see a rucksack accelerating down the ramp of steel rollers that served for luggage delivery. A second bag flew through the hatch onto the ramp, and through the hole I could see men outside lifting bags from a cart. As each bag thumped onto the rollers and thundered down the slope onto the bench, it crashed into the previous one, leaving the metal cylinders spinning and jingling behind. The pile of bags backed up rapidly until a passenger took the initiative to offload some onto the floor. I watched for our bulging luggage, heaved each piece aside and shouldered a space for them in the crowd. Kristin leaned across the pile to tell me she had found out where to collect our kayaks: at the cargo depot, a short walk along the airstrip.

The kayaks weighed heavily in their armor of cardboard and Bubble Wrap as we carried them into open air. The sun was beginning to dry the runway, but the bare ground beside the cargo depot was sticky with mud and puddles. Gingerly setting our packages down, we slit open the wrappers and peeled aside the layers. Our kayaks emerged like butterflies from cocoons, gleaming with that deep shine you see only on a newly buffed surface. The decks were yellow, similar but not identical, and one kayak had a pale gray hull, the other white. Each had black trim, black hatches, and black deck rigging. We checked over the fittings, lifted the two together, and splashed back through the mud to the terminal building. With everything gathered together we stood beside a hand-painted board that read in Inuktitut (the language of the Inuit), French, and English "Welcome to Kuujjuaq." We hugged each other and smiled. A few yards away the diamond prospectors stood waiting beside their small bags, their boots and heavy clothing looking appropriately tough. They looked at our kayaks and asked how much they cost. As I glanced around I had a twinge of guilt about owning such a sleek new craft. But the moment passed. We had to get to the river, wherever that was, and our faces were already speckled with mosquitoes.

An airport pickup truck pulled up the dusty unpaved road from town toward us, its fat orange light on the roof suggesting something official. As soon as the man cut his engine and stepped from the cab Kristin headed him off. "We need to get our kayaks to the river..."

and she smiled. The man paused mid-step and looked sideways at her. She continued, "Is that the sort of thing you do?" He replied, "I work for the airport... but I can drive you down. Load your stuff on. I'll be back in a minute." As he slipped into the building I watched a cloud of mosquitoes shudder with the air as the door swung shut.

Our kayaks measured almost eighteen feet long. The length of the pickup bed was maybe six. We couldn't balance the kayaks with more hanging over than could rest on the bed, and we didn't want to ruin his gleaming black paintwork by propping them up on the cab. Even after trying it, we found they wouldn't balance anyway, so we set them sideways behind the cab. I had not seen any other vehicles on the road, so I hoped we would get away with an eighteen-foot-wide load. It turned out to be just a short, bumpy ride to a beach close to a short dock or pontoon. Two flat-bottomed barges were being unloaded, one onto the dock and the other via a ramp onto the sand. A truck and earthmoving equipment worked close to the water, while a few yards up the hill toward the airport stood a cluster of tall, silver, gas cylinders. Above the beach was an area of leveled ground that looked as if it served as a freight yard, or for sorting refuse. There was a stack of blue oil drums and several piles of metal and here and there charred circles where garbage had been burned on open fires. A flat stony area in the shelter of low bushes would serve for our tents. We offloaded, thanked our ride, and watched him drive back up the dirt road raising a cloud of dust along the hillside like a contrail.

We carried two tents, one to sleep in and the other to cook in, and right now we needed them both to organize our gear. We put them side by side with the kayaks and opened our bags, which had been packed in haste but well enough to protect the fragile things. Mounds of vacuum-bagged food, clothes, sleeping bags, mats, photographic equipment, and kayaking gear cascaded onto the groundsheet. In the torment of some of the densest clouds of biting flies I had ever encountered, I began sorting. Anything related to sleeping went into the sleeping tent. Valuables such as cameras followed. Kayaking gear went to the kayaks. Food and cooking hardware remained in the cooking tent. I paused. Kristin had located the insect repellent. When everything was under cover we bundled our empty luggage bags to mail back to Montreal and hiked into town.

Kuujjuaq lies just north of the border between tundra and taiga, on a tidal shore thirty miles upstream from the mouth of the Koksoak, or "Great River." The earliest written reference I could find to the Koksoak River dated from 1811. Two Moravian missionaries, Kohlmeister and Kmoch, sailed here from Okak, Labrador, that year. With the Moravians already well established in Labrador, they were ostensibly looking for missions farther afield. I think they were seeking adventure! I carried a copy of their journal with us to compare their observations to what we might see on our trip. Our starting place here at Kuujjuaq, Quebec, was the farthest west they had reached before returning to Labrador. They had found people camping here and described how the location was attractive to the Inuit because it was on the fall migration route of caribou: the then-massive George River herd. The river was full of fish and beluga, the white whales we had seen on the Saguenay, and there were trees for wood farther upstream. This might have been the ideal spot for a permanent settlement had it been closer to the coast and farther from the trees, for inland, and especially among the trees, was the domain of the Innu. Occasional fighting between the two groups kept them mostly to their own territories; Kuujjuaq was in the no-man's land where the groups occasionally ran into one another. The Inuit, they said, felt safer spending the winter back on the coast.

The Hudson's Bay Company learned from a missionary pamphlet that this area produced excellent furs, so in 1831 a party traveled overland from James Bay (at the south end of Hudson Bay where they had already established trading posts) to "take possession." They planned to build a trading post on the west shore of the Koksoak River, a short distance downstream and on the opposite shore from where Kuujjuaq now lies. The accommodations they managed to build with the limited resources available were so basic that the Hudson's Bay Company shipped materials from England in 1837 for something more substantial. Even so, the post operated under trying conditions until in 1842 it was closed, following post manager John McLean's recommendations. He reported that there were simply not enough furbearing animals around to sustain reasonable trade, hunting was too poor to feed the employees, there was no easy supply route through the interior to provision the post, and it was dangerous and costly to bring supplies by sea. Nevertheless, the company reopened the post fourteen years later, in 1866. Both Inuit and Innu resumed trading, although they cautiously made their camps at a distance from one another and either side of the post. When the geologist A. P. Low surveyed the Koksoak River in 1898, he described Fort Chimo, the Hudson's Bay Company's northernmost post, as a dozen small buildings made of imported lumber, the local trees being too short and thin to be of much use for building. He estimated that the total resident population numbered twenty-five, including the post officers, servants, wives and children.

In 1942, after the outbreak of the Second World War, the United States built an Air Force base known as Crystal 1 at Kuujjuaq. It operated until the end of the war, when the base was turned over to the Canadian government. Local people had settled around the base, so a Catholic mission was established in 1948, then a nursing station, a school, and a weather station, all around the airstrips. The Hudson's Bay Company moved its trading post closer in 1958, bringing to town the families that lived around it. In 1961 the local people formed a cooperative. Kuujjuaq had changed from a summer gathering place into a town. It is now a modern town of 2,400 people with a network of roads running between modest, loosely spaced houses. A dirt road leads in one direction to the airstrip, where passenger planes offer the only easy way in and out of town, and carries on farther to the communications towers. Another road leads in the opposite direction to a boat launch on a lake. These two most distant destinations together require no more than eight miles of road, so it is not possible to escape town by car, and it is easy to walk everywhere. The town itself sits beside the river, and apart from air freight, everything arrives by sea during summer in small freighters that anchor in deeper water downstream and offload cargo by crane into small barges that are towed to the landing where we camped. Ungava Bay is frozen much of the year. The navigation season stretches from July until October. But although Kuujjuaq is quite small and remote, it is clearly marked on the map of Canada in a world atlas. In the context of settlement in Ungava Bay, Kuujjuaq is the big city; it is Nunavik's largest community.

From the edge of town we could see rows of houses spread across a slope bordering treeless barrens. There were larger buildings but we had no way to identify them until we reached them, so we walked onward. Tidy single-level prefabricated houses were set in wild grass back from the road, which was bordered either side by low earthen banks. Bare ground or rough tracks between the houses offered access from one road to the next, and all-terrain vehicles (ATVs) and snowmobiles were dropped at the doorway of almost every house. We asked for directions and found the police station beside a tarmac road; I was surprised at how large and busy it seemed. Tired from travel, I was not as well prepared for the meeting as I was for the trip. Officers Giovanni Taddeo and Charles Boulianne tried to discourage us, probably because people like us have gone off on such trips and not come back. A yachtsman who left earlier that season called for help off northern Labrador when his sailboat broke up in ice. Adventurers setting off into Labrador to canoe and climb last year vanished, as did a small plane. So the police showed concern. They were not encouraging. They wanted us to be safe, and how could I assure them that we would be safe? We described our route and our timetable, left emergency phone numbers in case we failed to return, gave them details of our equipment, such as the color of our kayaks, tents, and clothing. They gave us a signal flare and directed us to the only place in Kuujjuaq they thought might sell us more. When we left my confidence felt thinner.

Kristin had phoned ahead from Seattle to find out what fuel we could buy in Kuujjuaq so we could take the right kind of stove. At the co-op we bought two gallons of white gas for five weeks of cooking. We would funnel it into our fuel bottles to stow in the kayaks. The Inuit girl at checkout yawned and chatted casually in Inuktitut with the girls at the other counters as she tallied. She admitted she was looking forward to finishing work that night. The store was about to close, but each time someone slipped out of the building, someone else burst in. The place seemed to offer respite from the mosquitoes. One man hurried in, stood for a few minutes near the door, then turned and hurried back out. When I said the mosquitoes seemed to be getting worse with evening, she said the town had recently bought six mosquito traps. They spew out carbon dioxide with an attractant called Octenol and suck in thousands of mosquitoes and black flies. I don't know where the traps were kept, or what the mosquito density would be like without them, but it was a reminder to buy more mosquito coils. We bought lots of them. Even a piece of one of the flat, green coils smoldering at the tent entrance is enough to make camp life easier.

Outside the store, ATVs were parked haphazardly on the hard-packed earth. One roared up with what looked like the whole family clinging together on top. Small children hugged the driver from behind, more sat on her lap and others hung on either side. They appeared to be a single compact aggregation, comfortable on the move, but as soon as the ATV jerked to a stop they exploded in all directions. An old lady with a time-wizened face climbed off a large ATV, her outsized parka bulking out her body, while her wiry legs protruded from underneath in narrow blue jeans. She grinned widely at me when I nodded hello, and scurried into the store.

One of our goals was to find Ida, a woman who had helped Kristin with her research for the trip. "Will you stop and say hello when you come to Kuujjuaq?" she had asked. We checked at the regional government building where she worked. The receptionist could not find her, so she phoned her at home. Kristin described where we were camped and Ida said she'd find our tent later. We trudged back to find two large dogs pulling our bags of food out of the tent. They had already spread our belongings wide. We chased away the dogs and rounded up our supplies. Most were intact.

With darkness approaching, no-see-ums crawled in my scalp. These tiny biting flies descend in clouds to nibble at your lips and into the corners of your eyelids and deep into your scalp where you cannot apply repellent. They pester first by crawling and biting and second by making you rub your eyes and lips, which then sting with the repellent from your hands. The mosquitoes seem almost pedestrian by comparison. I had to force myself to focus on our task: almost everything we needed for the next four or five weeks was assembled in this place. We would use some of it tonight camping; the rest could be stuffed into the little waterproof nylon dry-bags and sealed tight, ready for loading in the morning. We had a plethora of bags, and, familiar with the challenge of locating things in identical bags, we had made bags of many sizes from several different colors of fabric and with several different colors of webbing around the neck. If I could remember the color of bag that I used for my extra sweater I would be able to find it quickly.

Into the midst of this chaos came the sound of a vehicle approaching, and I looked up to see a car bouncing down the track; it stopped by our tents. Who would own a car when there are no roads out of here? Most of the local people seemed to ride ATVs all summer and snowmobiles in winter. Two women got out and introduced themselves as Ida, the woman we were hoping to see, and her friend, the broadly smiling Sara, who worked for the school board. They greeted us enthusiastically, examining our kayaks and asking to hear all our plans. But all of us were hopping from foot to foot, so intent on swatting flies it was difficult to converse. Ida said the bugs were particularly bad tonight and suggested we get in the car. There we systematically squashed all the mosquitoes we could see, and she drove us slowly around town. I reflected to myself that a car in Kuujjuaq was not such a strange idea after all if the summer bugs were always this relentless. It was dark before we returned. Sara begged us to sleep in the comfort of her house for the night, but, tempted as we were, we declined. We were far from being organized, and we would have to focus all our time on sorting our gear if we were to leave the next morning. We were also awaiting more visitors.

Our next visitor was the pilot who had flares we could buy. The place that might have sold us flares was closed, so the police had given us his number. We selected two orange and black plastic flare pistols, each strapped to a plastic clip holding six 12-gauge flare cartridges. Each pistol was sealed in a zipper plastic bag with instructions printed on the outside. When fired the pistol could send a red flare several hundred feet into the air. Kristin's father had rented us a satellite phone in case of emergency, in which case, assuming a connection, we had a way to call for help. If we saw people coming to our aid we could use the flares to pinpoint our position. That's a normal use for flares. Our main reason for taking them was to scare off polar bears. We had insufficient time to get licenses to buy guns and ammunition and carry them across the border, so we had given up taking a gun. We paid for the flares with the last of our Canadian currency.

The next visitor was the man from the freight office. His large pale dog leaped down from the back of his pickup and sniffed everything. We showed the man what had been in wrappers in his warehouse, the two kayaks, and explained how everything he could see in front of him would load into them. It did not look possible, but I had confidence. He wished us a good journey, "even better than you expected and free of mishap." He seemed to care.

I was alone once again with Kristin in the tent, stuffing dry-bags with food, still wondering how everything could be organized by morning, when we heard yet another car approaching. I looked at Kristin, momentarily blinding her with my headlamp, but read "Who now?" in her expression. The car stopped with the lights shining full on the tent. I heard doors click open while the engine continued to run. I crawled out to see Sara's round face smiling at me. She introduced her boyfriend Larry. "We were concerned about you leaving without firearms," Larry said, "so we would like to lend you two guns." We stepped over to the car where he produced for Kristin a small game rifle that we could use for hunting. It took apart and packed up into its plastic stock. Apparently it would float. As we huddled beside the back door of the car, its engine still running and its lights still on, it felt very covert. "Now for you," Larry said, "a high-powered rifle." This should protect us from polar bears. If we couldn't scare away an attacking bear with warning shots, our last resort would be to shoot it. He handed me a heavy plastic bag of ammunition that felt cold in my hand. Sara, standing with Kristin, was reassuring her. "If you have to shoot a bear, you can do it. You can be brave." I looked at Sara. She had a look of calm confidence in Kristin, as she looked her straight in the eyes. I could see Kristin taking her words to heart. If she had to point a gun at a polar bear she would remember those words and do it. But it seemed so unlikely we would see a bear, the thought of having to shoot one was far from my mind. I made a note to return with every round unused. We stowed the guns in the tent while we showed Larry the kayaks and answered his questions about our trip. They wished us well and drove away, leaving us in darkness and quiet. I felt quite emotional about the tender care these strangers were taking of us.

I recalled my Baffin Island trip. That was the first trip I had ever made into bear country and I was naïve. For a start, I cooked in the entrance to my tent. I had been used to camping in places like Scotland and Iceland, where causing a fire or perhaps attracting ants were the only concerns. But I've camped in bear country enough since to adopt precautions, like slinging a line over the bough of a tree to hang food out of reach of bears, and cooking under a tarp far away to keep food scents from the tent. But we would not see trees, and with them black bear territory, until near the end of the trip; for the rest of the time we would be camping on rock and tundra, where conditions are too harsh for trees to grow. That is why we chose to carry a second tent. It was a single-skin structure of silicone-impregnated rip-stop nylon, green, propped up by a single central pole, and looking a little like a teepee. We called it the "shelter," or "shelter tent," to distinguish it from the "tent," or "sleeping tent," which was yellow. It served as a freestanding tarp into which we could escape from mosquitoes or rain. Since it had no sewn-in groundsheet, we could bundle inside it to change from clothing saturated with salt water and still have a dry, salt-free tent to sleep in at night. We could store our food there. If a bear came searching for food it would clatter the pans and warn us, but not claw into our kayaks looking for food. Brown bears, the bears we might expect to see on tundra, are now extinct in Labrador, but black bears have been moving north of the trees and adopting the habits of the brown bears, becoming more carnivorous. Black bears aside, we might see polar bears. Polar bears hunt around sea ice. In winter they stalk seals along the ice edge and wait for them at breathing holes; when that ice drifts south and melts in July, they swim ashore and slowly migrate north up the coast until the sea freezes again in November.

Our talk about bears and guns faded as we focused on getting everything secure for the night. We zipped our sleeping bags together and scrambled in, piling our clothes under our heads as pillows. Now, with the wonderful close comfort of Kristin's warm body in the cushioning darkness, the sound of mosquitoes whining, mostly outside the tent but very audible from inside, I thought about the trip. We were finally ready. We had but a few hours of darkness in which to rest. Already I could hear Kristin's breathing, soft in sleep. She had been tired. But how wonderful it felt curled together like this, secure in the total comfort of an enveloping downy cloud. I love feeling her breath against my shoulder. There is something basic and reassuring about retreating into the cramped space of a cave-like tent to sleep. I was not awake for long.

CHAPTER 3

Ungava Bay

In the morning sun the Koksoak River stretched before us like a lake. The tide had risen, swelling this portion, thirty miles inland from Ungava Bay, to one and a half miles wide. We planned to launch while the water was still high and use the falling tide to help carry us toward the coast. Mosquitoes flew everywhere, making it difficult to stand still long enough to appreciate the scene, so we set to work carrying the empty kayaks to the shore to load them. Now that everything was in a waterproof bag, neither of us had a dry-bag long enough for the rifle. Our longest bag was almost long enough, but with the rifle inside it was too tight to seal. We would have to carry it in one of the rear hatches or the metal would affect the compass on the front; to fit it had to be loaded first, along the center of the hull. Loading a kayak is an art. Each bag has to be slipped into place without leaving any empty space. Long, narrow items fit into the very bow and stern, two places where fatter bags tend to leave empty spaces and short bags get stuck beyond reach. By the time the rear compartment was full there was no sign of the rifle. Everything would have to be unloaded before we would see it again. "I can't believe how generous Larry and Sara were last night," I exclaimed, and not for the first time. "They hadn't even met us before."

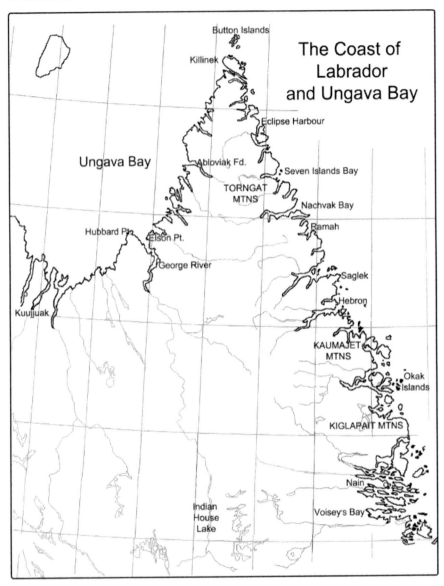

The Coast of Labrador and Ungava Bay

Button Islands
Killinek
Eclipse Harbour
Ungava Bay
Abloviak Fd.
Seven Islands Bay
TORNGAT MTNS
Nachvak Bay
Ramah
Hubbard Pk.
Elson Pt.
George River
Saglek
Hebron
Kuujjuak
KAUMAJET MTNS
Okak Islands
KIGLAPAIT MTNS
Nain
Indian House Lake
Voisey's Bay

We left at 8:30. The heavily laden kayaks slipped through the water and bounced through the tidal rapids as we ran with the ebbing tide. I felt relieved and lighthearted to be paddling at last after all the preparation and travel. I wondered whether the Inuit had felt this same exhilaration when finally the water was open enough to launch a hunting kayak after a winter icebound. The heavy load in my kayak steadied it in a way I had not felt for some time. Neither of us had been in a kayak for several weeks, and then not in one packed for a trip. I watched with satisfaction at how easily Kristin maintained speed beside me. Her load was at least as heavy as my own.

We passed two small service boats pushing a small barge carrying yellow forklift trucks against the tide toward the landing. They must have come from the small red freighter anchored midstream that we passed later. A ramp at the freighter's stern looked as if it would offer an easy loading dock for the barge. Here, where the water was deep must have also been a good place for fishing; two or three freight canoes and small open boats drifted with lines out. Keen to make as much use of the falling tide as possible, we paddled almost constantly, passing two small huts on the shore and skiffs drifting on the current with people fishing. The low cliffs to either side were horizontally banded with lichens, bare rock, and a thin growth on the wet rock where the tide had fallen. We talked little as we paddled side by side hot in the sun in all the warm clothing we thought we needed. When we needed a break we drew our kayaks together with our paddles and delved in our pockets for dried cranberries and mango and beef jerky, and sipped hot water from the flask. I figured it would take us a day or two on the water to become efficient. Loading the kayaks would get easier once we had found the best place for things, and then we would be able to pull out items like tea without thinking. We would also carry more water. I had miscalculated the volume of water we would need for our evening meal, our breakfast, and a day of paddling when we shopped in Kuujjuaq, and of course there was no fresh water where we spent the night. Consequently we were now paying for it in the heat.

The river that had spread to more than a mile wide now was pinched tight ahead of us between high bluffs at the narrows, where the tide reputedly reaches speeds up to 12 knots on a spring tide. I wondered how rough it might get in the gap, but although the water rushed us quickly through, the tide was past its fastest. As the tide lost energy, so did we. We slowed down and drifted. Studying the chart together, we looked ahead to where a misty mirage blurred the view of the cliffs at the mouth of the bay. It was difficult to tell what was real. Minutes later the tide abruptly changed direction. One moment we were drifting slowly north, the next we were being carried swiftly south again. We pushed our kayaks apart and paddled briskly across the current to the low cliff on the eastern shore.

Reluctant to fight the current, we let the rushing water carry us back along the cliff until we could see a place to land. A stream ran down a gash in the hill through bright green vegetation surrounded by bare rock. Where the stream notched the cliff was a rock corner we could climb out onto. We had to be quick. The rising water would soon cover the landing, and we must carry everything to the top of the cliff before that happened. We hurried to unload, but the rocks were soon covered and the kayaks were floating again. We carried the gear up to a ledge and returned for the kayaks. Kristin stepped along the rim between the deep water and a now-flooded pool, carrying one end of the kayak. I lurched from foothold to foothold, carrying the other end, trying not to lose balance or pull Kristin into the water. We made it up the last fifteen feet to the top, straightened our backs, and looked around.

To the north we could see Ungava Bay in a mirage of mist. Above our heads strands of cirrus cloud streaked the blue sky, and at our feet mineral veins in the rock lay frozen into swirled and contorted marbling like the inside of a book cover. I knelt to examine some bright sparkling crystals but saw with horror a fur of flies on the back of my hand. The rocks could wait; we should set the tent. I gathered boulders to pin it down while Kristin threaded the poles. We needed no practice. As soon as the yellow-and-gray tent was secure on top of the cliff, we hurried off with our collapsible bucket to collect fresh water. Short marsh plants and mosses clogged the dark tannic pools of the lower streambed so we climbed higher, parting the dense mosquitoes as we hopped from dry spot to dry spot until we reached a small waterfall to catch free-flowing water. Glassy-clear liquid splashed into the transparent bucket. As it filled I glanced across the sparkling rock. Toward the river the rock stepped down in sloping terraces of smooth gray and pink, crisscrossed by seams of pink pegmatite. Here and there cut-off chunks of ancient bedding planes had metamorphosed into gneiss and mica schist. They looked as flamboyant as exploding twists of unraveled rope, which had been trimmed into wedges and surgically inserted into the flesh of the rock. Everything glittered in the sun. A fat vein of metallic emerald green crystals bulged from the surrounding pink rock like a welt. I was captivated.

We had landed about six miles short of Qirniraujaq, the cape that defines the northeasterly extent of the river entrance. We checked the account of the Moravian missionary expedition to find that on 1 September 1811 they had returned downriver to anchor overnight near here, having been assured there was no place farther west in Ungava Bay where a boat as large as theirs could safely approach land. In any case they should not find any inhabitants, as they would be inland hunting caribou by fall. The party, Kohlmeister and Kmoch with four Inuit families, were sailing a forty-five-foot boat, five feet deep by twelve feet wide, with two masts. It had been an open boat, but the missionaries had built a complete deck over it to create three cabins. They towed a small boat behind them, and a third boat accompanied them, an Inuit umiak. The umiak is a native open boat made by stretching skin over a wooden frame. That evening they put ashore at Qirniraujaq. In a brief ceremony they set up an inscribed board and raised the British flag, claiming the "South River" for the king of England. It had taken them two months to reach the Koksoak River but it would take them just one month to sail home. We expected to take one month. They wrote far more about their outward journey than their return trip, so from this point onward we would follow their journal backward to find their best descriptions of the coast. "You know, everything probably looked exactly the same then as it does now." I speculated, "Except for the stuff we've brought with us." Then, as now, the river reversed its phenomenal tidal flow four times a day, rising and falling against these cliffs.

In 1897, when the geologist A. P. Low had visited this river mouth, he reported the ordinary tides rising more than thirty feet here, with exceptional spring tides rising sixty feet above low water. Sixty feet? Recent observations thirty miles northwest from here suggest a range of 54.8 feet at a big spring tide, equal to the biggest tidal range anywhere in the world, debatably bigger than the Bay of Fundy, although authorities declare it a tie. The worldwide average by contrast is between six and ten feet. But what do these figures really mean? Each story of a city building is typically ten feet in height. Imagine low tide at city street level. The smallest high tides here would rise to cover the roof of every three-story building, but under the biggest tides, five-story buildings would submerge completely, and even the sixth story would flood halfway to the ceiling. I looked down at the swirling water rising toward our tent and marveled at how far it had risen in a few minutes. During the middle of the flood tide it could rise more than three vertical inches every minute. That seemed dramatic. In some areas of Ungava Bay the falling tide exposes rocky ridges and boulder-strewn muddy valleys up to five miles from the high tide shore. There is no way we could outpace the rising tide there while carrying our kayaks and gear.

The evening was dry and the rock still held the warmth of the day's sun. We cooked in the open, then zipped ourselves inside the tent with a burning piece of mosquito coil. Before settling to write our journals we spent a few minutes squashing every mosquito we could see. Finally we were alone.

Ungava Bay measures about 140 nautical miles across its entrance to the north, and about 140 miles from that line south to the middle of the bay. We expected to paddle 325 miles around this relatively uncharted coast to reach the tip of Labrador, but we were anxious to see what that shore would be like. When we rounded Cape Qirniraujaq next morning, the sun was burning down on a coastline of low rocks and islands as far as we could see, with elevations higher inland. The tide was dropping. What we saw was like the birth of a new planet. We sat at water level, which gave the impression our own level never changed, so the land appeared to rise. Slopes of bare rock seemed to slither up from the water, in places adorned with seaweed; a yellow-brown wrack that first appeared on the surface, then crept up from the sea, its previously buoyant fronds settling and readjusting clump by clump with little shakes that caught our attention. Rocks stuck rounded heads from the surface, hour by hour shouldering up into long ridges and cliffs, into sloping ledges and huge perched boulders. The open water between the scattered islands became clogged with obstructions, and although my comparison of buildings uncovering to eventually reveal the street below helped us appreciate the scale, in fact we found it almost impossible to grasp either heights or distances with nothing familiar to measure against.

Scurrying across wide expanses of shallow water bordered on all sides by low islands or ledges, we were dismayed to see boulders and mudflats surfacing all around us. Soon the only deep water left was draining through twisting channels gouged into a vast mudflat. Anxious to avoid getting stranded we followed the flow of the current, even though it was not going in the direction we wanted to go. We found ourselves threading between cliffs and islands that had emerged from the sea and now blocked our view of open water. This was a very different kind of paddling from any I had done before. We were sight-reading routes between features merely hinted at on the map.

So few ships visit Ungava Bay that the water has not been sounded for depth anywhere within about ten miles of shore; supply ships use the ribbon of soundings that run across the chart to follow a deep-water route into Kuujjuaq. The few locals who venture beyond Kuujjuaq to hunt and fish use either freight canoes or shallow-draft aluminum skiffs fitted with outboard motors, and either know the channels, or run semi-blind as we were doing, or go farther out into the bay. The chart shows the borders where land meets water at low tide and high tide, but only guesswork can suggest what might happen between those levels. For us to know where land might first appear above water as the tide fell was impossible. It was also tricky to judge how far away islands and rocks were. Anything, even a tree, would have given an indication of scale but there were none. On the mainland there was only tundra. Now the ledges, exposed ten, twenty, thirty feet and more by the falling water, blocked our view not only of the sea but of the mainland too.

"Would you like a shore break?" I asked. Kristin acquiesced. "There's a beach over there." I pointed to what looked like a sandy beach between the many ledges. We turned toward it and paddled, but although I thought we were paddling quickly the beach hardly seemed to get closer. It dawned on me that it was a pebble beach, not sand, and by the time we reached it we could see it was made of rounded boulders each about eight feet across; not an easy place to land after all. We slipped out of our kayaks onto a slab of rock, leaving the kayaks floating, but the kayaks became grounded so quickly by the falling water that we hurried to get back afloat.

A landscape without reference to scale must have challenged the Inuit too. Hunting by kayak, they would have experienced problems similar to ours. My eyes are just thirty-two inches above the water when I sit in my kayak. I could not see over the many low ledges to identify more distant landmarks. The Inuit devised a solution to this problem. Here and there they built the stone cairns they called *inuksuqs*. Translated, *inuksuq* means "looks like a person." Built to resemble people in both shape and height, they offer scale in a landscape that presents few other visual clues, and they often mark places that are good for camping or fishing or something else of note. We did not see many. As evening approached, we searched for somewhere high where we would be secure from the tide. We looked for a place where the foreshore was narrow on the map, indicating a steep rise, so we would not have to carry the kayaks too far. We saw an *inuksuq* on a low hill and found the sloping rock there almost ideal for hauling out. The naked bedrock sloped gently in shallow steps and rolling ridges from the water up to the lichen-encrusted crest on which the *inuksuq* stood. There was fresh water, a wonderful flat slab of pink rock on which to set the tent, and good visibility all around.

A perfect campsite for me would offer easy sheltered landing, shelter for the tents on flat well-drained ground, fresh water, and a good view. Here I would have to add, "surrounded by open ground across which we could easily spot any polar bears." This site was ideal. We set the tent on an island of pink, sparkling rock surrounded by great sweeps of almost-flat rock that stepped and sloped irregularly but easily down to the sea. Close behind this natural castle were pools of fresh water and areas of boulders and pebbles of bright and sparkling stone. In one pool the points of a caribou antler reached above the water, the rest lying ambiguously beneath the surface and blurring the reflection of the antler above.

We cooked in the open, watching the tide rise as the day drew to a close with a red-streaked sky. Then with stunning effect the moon appeared over the crest right beside the *inuksuq* that had led us in, silhouetting the almost human figure. In the semidarkness we hurried up to the top to look out over the scene now lit by moonlight. It was eerily beautiful with no sign whatsoever of any light other than moon, planets and stars. I grabbed Kristin and we hugged, standing there looking out until the chill drove us to the warmth of our tent.

The next night we spotted another inuksuq. We penetrated a labyrinth of narrow channels toward it and were delighted to find a sheltered landing on sloping rock, tucked away from wind and swell. There were tent circles here, rings of stones that had been used for holding tents down. We found fresh water, and caribou bones. It seemed an *inuksuq* was the equivalent in this landscape to a sign on a freeway announcing "Rest Area." Nobody knows how many there are around here, but Amos, at the interpretive center at North West River near Goose Bay, had encouraged us to repair any damaged ones we found, or, if we found a good landing and camp, build our own if there was not one there. He explained, "They are very useful, but they are falling down with the wind and the frost, and there is nobody there to repair them."

Inuksuqs are not shown on the map. In fact, our topographic maps and nautical charts, which had been made from aerial photographs, frequently showed conflicting information. Both showed the lay of the land, but ledges shown boldly on one might appear as a few scattered rocks on the other, and neither consistently showed more ledges exposed than the other. The discrepancies went both ways—sins of omission and commission. An incorrectly drawn detail sometimes caused us to detour for two or three miles, so we came to rely more on our eyes and judgment for choosing routes, using the charts only to identify the major features. No detailed tidal information exists, either; the best we could get was the approximate time of high tide, which we could see anyway. I had preconceived ideas about what to expect; perhaps a strong tidal stream running along the coast with the rising tide, reversing direction with the falling tide. The vast body of water in Hudson Bay drains eastward through Hudson Strait on the ebb, filling again from the east on the flood. Surely the waters in Ungava Bay must be subject to the same pattern? Apparently no, not in that intricate coastal zone. The falling tide drains from the bays and pools until rock ledges appear. The ledges then channel the flow in different directions. We would run with the current for a while only to find it turning ninety degrees, or even reversing, because of channels drying out ahead. If we left too late to make our way to deeper water, we could be trapped in a maze of narrow channels, surrounded by a jumble of boulders resting on mud flats or by wrack-covered rock. Time and again we would cut across open bays on the falling tide, only to see islands rise out of the water to seaward. The tide would draw us toward them, and we would resist the pull by angling across the current. But we would find our route blocked by rock after ledge and hampered by current. Finally we would change course, letting ourselves be swept out beyond the low islands into the vast Ungava Bay. The mainland would now be two miles away, and the islands and ledges climbing ten, twenty, thirty feet above the water would block our distant view of land. At low tide, the currents would become still for a moment, then the shore would seem to suck the water back from the bay into the narrow channels, swelling them into noisy, rattling rivers, and the rocks and ledges would submerge again.

We landed to climb and get a clear view of our surroundings at low tide. The swirling patterns in the rock, bands of red and pink and silvery black, drew my eyes up the slope, and I found it impossible not to break from a walk to run along the lines and race up the rock. Chasing past pools, we saw the water seeping out across the flat expanses as a thin gleaming film. On drier rock thousands of sparkling crystals reflected the sun. This summit was the highest point around, so we had a view in all directions of more rocky ridges and valleys, mud and stones, wrack and reflective pools. I stuck my finger into the water in a crevice and tasted it. Salty. This was a place we could not camp. At high tide all this strange contorted land now visible for miles around us would rest beneath the water.

I enjoy watching the flow of water, figuring out the currents. On our third day we were aiming our kayaks from tip to tip along a row of ledges that spread fingerlike into the sea. The tide was falling. At each gap we angled our bows into the mouth as we paddled to counter the current that would otherwise carry us from shore. Then the tide turned and the rising water began drawing back in through the channels. Crossing one of these channels I was amazed by how quickly the water ran, and in a moment of impulse I cried, "Let's go down here." Without waiting for Kristin's response I turned and led the way into the narrowing channel. As the channel funneled into a canyon between vertical if not high cliffs, the speed of the water increased until we were sucked into a long twisting cut only a few yards wide, far too narrow for us to turn around. The cold air in the shadows smelled faintly of wet seaweed and pinched at my nostrils. The turbulent water now gushing loudly ran into rapids with curling waves and bursting boils, still narrowly confined between rock walls that left so little room for the paddle blades either side of the kayak that it became difficult to steer. From right behind me I heard Kristin squeal, "Yoo-hoo! This is fun!" Then quite abruptly we burst into a broad calm pool reflecting the blue sky. The air felt warm again and we sat drifting, looking around us. Rock walls hemmed us in all around.

We rafted together for a moment, drifting and studying the chart. I voiced my concern that we might be trapped in this little pool until the tide rose high enough to release us again. The chart did not help us at all, but as soon as we started skirting the perimeter of this salty lake we found another entrance and threaded our way via narrow channels to wider ones, then between islands, until we found open water again. Our excursion had taken us a long time and we had scarcely made any real distance. It had been fun, but we resolved to stay outside the ledges in future.

The evening of the following day we cruised quietly along the outer fringe of coastal rocks while more distant rocks pulsed up and down in an eerie blur. On quiet days the icy water chills the air immediately above it, causing a so-called superior mirage effect. Light, refracted down through the dense blanket of cold air, reveals images of objects beyond the horizon and makes closer features loom or stretch tall. The effect is unstable, so towering cliffs collapse and rear up again in a quite disturbing way. I first experienced the phenomenon when alone on Baffin Island and it played with my mind.

Out to sea was the insistent whine of an outboard motor, although we had yet to spot a boat. An iceberg ahead rapidly shrank and vanished, and for a while appeared as a blotch of snow on the shore. Above us trails of bright white cloud spread thinly in ribbons across a vast blue sky. I watched the water parting at my bow, splitting the cloud reflected in the water, bulging and distorting it as the wake ran outward to each side. The spray from my paddle scattered in gleaming drops, falling to the clouds beneath me as reflected droplets rushed up to collide with the falling orbs. The tide seemed to be against us, and we still had miles to go before we could clear the corner of these ledges and point our kayaks toward the real shore. There wasn't any need to talk. Conversation could only state the obvious during these periods when the surroundings seemed to pull our senses outward and our thoughts inward. Our ears picked up the rush of the hulls through the water, the quiet entry and exit of the paddle blades, the hiss of falling water drops. Our eyes struggled with the impossibility of the mirages, the silk of the water surface, the endless stretch of low red ledges, sky above us, sky beneath us. Sometimes a word or two spoken out loud would penetrate softly as if in a dream. The sounds would take time to interpret, the pause becoming tangible before the reply. Sometimes conversation became an intrusion, pulling the mind away from some deep understanding that seemed almost real into spoken words that couldn't begin to convey anything complex. "I can see the boat."

"Where?"

"Over there!" I followed Kristin's gaze. The misty mirage that shadowed the water hid the horizon and made the sea blend seamlessly into the sky. My eyes struggled to focus on anything at all in that blank space. I couldn't see a boat, but I could hear it. Then all of a sudden it was as clearly visible as if a shutter had lifted. I don't know how I missed it.

"I can see it now." I turned my head to Kristin. When I turned back the boat was gone and I felt frustrated, beginning once more to search for a speck moving somewhere out there.

I refer to this location as "The place where the ledges run out from land like four long fingers." Kristin knows precisely where I mean. The marine chart shows a quarter-moon curve of ledge three miles long, south to north, and three miles from shore at its northern point. The topographic map indicates four pronounced rocky points separated by three bays that dry into mud and boulders. The two disagree about how many small islands remain at high water. The reality was, on the topographic map we could see the points of rock extending into Ungava Bay and measure our progress approximately along the shore in three twenty-minute sections. Had we arrived at a high tide, we could have paddled between the islands and the mainland for just two or three miles to our destination, instead of the seven or so around the outside at low tide. Yet I prefer not to think of it as energy wasted.

Kohlmeister's account refers to these islands and ledges of rock as Arvavik Island, five miles in circumference, covered in the bones of whales the Inuit had caught using their kayaks. He describes many small, low islands with deep pools between them. Whales straying into these pools at high tide could be trapped as the tide dropped, allowing the Inuit to harpoon them. My map calls this place the Arvalik Islands, plural. The reef certainly forms a large island at low tide, extending easily to eight miles circumference, while at high water the chart shows it covered except for a few small islands.

We saw no sign of whales, nor bones, but during the 1880s the Hudson's Bay Company at Kuujjuaq (then Fort Chimo) recorded an annual catch of 85 to 90 belugas. In July each year the Inuit around Fort Chimo assisted in driving whales into a pound in the Koksoak River where they would become stranded as the tide fell. The beluga favored the shallow river mouths where the water would warm in spring, so with the big tidal range, penning and stranding the whales was probably a straightforward way to hunt them. The whales were a reliable resource, seen in the estuaries as we had seen them on the Saguenay during our drive. If the whales had been taken only for subsistence they might be more plentiful nowadays, but the Hudson's Bay Company post at Fort Chimo was fishing for profit. Although 160 were recorded taken in 1889, the fishery failed in 1904. There were no whales to be found. The belugas did survive in Ungava Bay, although they no longer habituated the river mouths where they were most vulnerable. An economic survey in the 1960s reported an annual harvest of fifty to seventy-six belugas in the whole of Ungava Bay, but the numbers continued to fall. By 1988 they were so few that the Ungava Bay beluga was classified as an endangered species. Perhaps fewer than a hundred individuals survive, sad compared to the 1800s when more than that number were taken every year. We were unlikely to see any along this coast. Of course, belugas were not the only whales to suffer that fate. The eastern arctic bowhead whale, likely the food source that attracted the Thule people east across the Arctic in the first place, was also almost wiped out by hunting. These slow-swimming and otherwise long-lived whales were all too easy to catch from commercial whaling vessels.

We reached the corner in the ledge and could make out the hills of the mainland two miles away. The water here was rough, with breaking crests leaping erratically. Tide! The tide was racing us along, but carrying us away from the ledge. I wanted to follow the ledge to land so we could stop for the night, so we turned across the current again. While our kayaks twisted and bucked, water pounding out from each heavy impact as the bows lunged into the troughs, a boat tore past us, headed for land. It was probably too distant for the occupants to see us. We paddled across the fast water to reach a calmer sea closer to the ledge and turned toward the distant hills again. The tide was undoubtedly against us, but we had no option but to keep going if we were to reach a place to camp before dark.

Ten minutes later, two more boats in convoy went racing past, but someone evidently spotted us because one of the boats turned abruptly and opened its throttle straight toward us; the other followed. I felt apprehensive at seeing the boats approaching so fast, but at the last moment the driver dropped speed and drifted to us. On board was a group of men dressed in bright waterproofs. They'd been out fishing for arctic char. Peering over the gunwale of this twenty-foot Princecraft aluminum skiff, I admired their large gleaming fish. Yes, they were on their way back to camp, but they had spotted something yellow on the water and thought the first boat must have capsized, so they'd hurried over to the rescue. It was our kayaks! I laughed. I guess they could not expect to see anything else yellow around here. Where were they from? Mostly Montreal. They had come out to a fishing camp to experience the wilderness, to fish for salmon, sea trout and arctic char, and to get away for an unusual holiday—the vacation of a lifetime. It was the char they were catching today that seemed to excite them most. A smoke house at the lodge would smoke the fish for them to take home. There are two subgroups of char, a landlocked freshwater char and a saltwater char that migrates into the rivers to spawn like its relative the salmon. The saltwater fish only occurs in northern waters; the freshwater fish occurs in lakes, sometimes landlocked since the last ice age quite far south. Freshwater char is often considered the best fly-fishing game fish to be found in fresh water. Of course, out here in Ungava Bay, it was the surface-swimming saltwater variety they caught, and apparently twenty-pound fish are not uncommon.

"Where are you heading tonight?" asked the man at the wheel. "Oh, I've been looking at the map and it looks as if we could find somewhere to camp around this headland, maybe here…" I pointed to a stub of a point jutting from the shore. On the map it appeared the foreshore would be narrower, so landing could be easier. I was growing accustomed to the clues that suggested a good kayak landing. "Huh! That's where our camp is. It's not marked on the map, but it's right about there. You'll probably see us when you get closer. And on the other side of the point there's a house where an Inuit family is staying. Yes, you should find somewhere you can camp. Be sure to stop in when you get there." One of the anglers took out his camera, and we posed for a picture. Then the two boats idled away from us and eased up onto the plane again. Everyone waved, and they roared off into the haze. We were alone again, with the odor of exhaust fumes and fish oil. Looking toward the ledge it was evident we'd been drifting backward while we'd talked. It was time for us to press on.

Closer to our destination we thought we could see the fishing camp. For some time it appeared as a row of tower blocks, or maybe tall oil containers, silver, reflecting the sun. Occasionally the towers would shrink until they almost vanished. Then it was difficult to make out the specks that might be buildings. Mirages are weird. Frustrated by the pulsing shapes I turned my head to line up a point on the ledge to my right with a distant rock that stood behind it, only to grunt with aggravation when the rock vanished. If you can't line up objects it's difficult to gauge progress, and if the shore keeps changing size and other landmarks come and go it's impossible to tell how far away anything is. We were clearly paddling against the tide, but we had no way of telling how fast it was flowing. I kept paddling hard, aware that Kristin was tired and anxious to be ashore. Neither of us wanted to draw out these last hours of the day on the water. Finally we closed on land, crept into a channel between islands, and emerged by a pale sandy shore. The aluminum boats we had seen earlier floated at the water's edge, and up the steep sandy beach I could see five silvery corrugated metal half-cylinders snug in a sea of blue-green marram grass. This must be the fishing camp.

Although we had seen a lot of mosquitoes at Kuujjuaq and the Koksoak River, they hadn't seemed as bad at our camp sites on the ledges. But here around the fish camp there were enough to drive anyone crazy. Eli, the camp manager, met us on the shore and invited us to stay for the night. He also offered us the luxury of a shower and a meal. We needed no further encouragement to escape from the flies. A man who introduced himself as Terry brought an all-terrain four-wheeler with a trailer down to the kayaks to haul our gear, and together we heaved the kayaks farther up the beach against the rise of the tide. A large sled dog prowled around the kayaks, sniffing at the food packets and our kayaking gear, so we sealed the hatches and cockpits before leaving the beach.

The staff cabin was the building at the far end of the row. We were led into the main dormitory where a suffocating array of green mosquito coils burned just inside the door. Steaming boots and socks drying on lines surrounded a big woodstove and several men sprawled across their bunks watching a TV by the door. We heard them grunt greetings as we passed. The bunks lined the walls and the brightly colored waterproofs that were not hung from hooks were draped across empty bunks. Kristin made a tiny gesture to me to notice a large bottle of small, bright pink pills. She had recognized them as the same brand of antihistamine tablets we carried to reduce itching from bites. Our guide led us on, pointing out a cubicle that held a toilet and a shower. In the far corner of the main dormitory, just past the shower, was a small sectioned-off area that I suspect had been vacated to give us a place to sleep in privacy. A bunk the size of a double bed almost filled the space, while rifles and fishing rods stood against the wall. Boots and oilskins lay scattered everywhere. "Come next door to eat as soon as you're ready." Almost choking from the mosquito coils, we squeezed into the shower to rinse off the salt. It was a refreshing luxury, but afterwards we hung our wet kayaking clothes outside instead of by the stove. The smell of fresh air seemed preferable to the smoke. Then we opened the door to the next cabin in the row and stepped into the dining room.

Inukshuk Lodge, as this fishing camp was named, appeared on neither our nautical chart nor our topographic map. Whether that's by design or default I don't know, but the lodge serves mostly French-Canadian fishing enthusiasts from Montreal, and was operated this summer by an English-speaking staff from the Quebec-Newfoundland border by Belle Isle Strait. At the end of the fishing season here most of the staff move on for a spell at the caribou hunting camp before returning home to a winter of snowmobiling. The company that owns the lodge runs other camps for snowmobiling, lake fishing, and caribou and bear hunting, tempting city-dwellers with the glamour and novelty of the wilderness. Judging by the enthusiasm of the clients we met, a stay in the wilderness at one of these camps *could be* the experience of a lifetime, as they said, an unforgettable vacation, well worth waiting for. We felt honored to sit down with Eli and his staff to a meal of pork chops, with a bottle of fine French red wine.

Later we talked with Georgine, in the kitchen, about life at the Lodge, and our conversation turned to the arctic char the group had been catching. It's an oily fish, containing omega-3 fatty acids that are thought to help prevent heart disease. Highly nutritious and abundant, it has been an Inuit staple, but in common with other oily fish, the flesh sours too quickly when frozen using standard methods, so it has not been popular as a commercial fish. When frozen into a block of ice it keeps better, but then it's heavy and bulky. Perhaps a better solution is what they do with their fish here, which is to smoke them. Smoked char tastes wonderful. It is probably my favorite smoked fish, and I clearly remember the first time I tried it, twenty-three years ago. I described to Georgine how I had sampled fish that had been caught by Labrador Inuit and smoked by a Newfoundlander, Ross Travers. He had laid a smoldering fire in a box set in an earth bank and ran the smoke up a long stovepipe into an old refrigerator in which he hung each batch of fish. Experimenting with a different type of wood for each batch, he hoped to identify the one that imparted the best flavor. Labeling each fish with details of its smoke treatment, he waited until the fisherman returned from Labrador to sample them. I happened to be there that day in Saint John's, recovering from the crossing of Hudson Strait, when Ross eagerly unwrapped all the fish and draped them in a row along the counter top. The tight pink flesh had been smoked golden. As he explained in detail how he had prepared each one, we began to sample. Soon Ross was gesticulating with delight and enthusiasm on the flavors, fish in his mouth, fish in his fingers, and fish on the floor as he strode around the room, all six feet three inches of him a bundle of exuberance. I can't recall which smoke created the best flavor, and I don't know if the project continued, but smoked char had worked its magic on me and I was hooked. I could empathize with the excitement at the fishing camp.

Inuit also eat char raw. At Iqaluit in 1981 I was treated to raw char, sliced deftly from a whole fish by a pretty native woman, Naudla, wielding a small, half-moon-shaped knife with a T-shaped handle, an *ulu*. She worked swiftly through the meat with the *ulu* using a pendulum motion of the wrist. The flesh fell away in neat, thin slices, leaving the long, clean, silvery fish skin intact. In the past such skins were cured and sewn together to make waterproof coats for kayakers. The cold, translucent red flesh tasted firm and buttery.

While we talked, the remaining fishermen stood up a few at time and drifted from the dining room toward their cabins, calling, "Bon nuit!" Soon we were the only ones left. When we stood to leave, Georgine suggested we take the half-empty bottle of wine and our glasses with us to a small square cabin used as a meeting room. There we watched the sun sink red into the bay, studied our charts at a table, and wrote in our journals.

Our sleep was fitful that night in the soft bed. The heat from the stove compounded the throat-gripping fug of mosquito coils. It was stifling. We had become accustomed to cool air in the tent and firm ground beneath us. I longed for a blast of that cold fresh air. By morning I was claustrophobic and anxious to get up. We tried not to get in the way as anglers and staff ate breakfast and prepared for their day, but everyone was curious about our journey and full of questions. Our schedule was dictated by the tide, so as the water rose closer to our kayaks, we quickly reloaded what little we had taken out for the night and slipped quietly afloat. Our goal today was to reach the mouth of the George River. Armed with our first weather forecast, we anticipated twenty-knot offshore winds. In view of that we planned to hug the shore to avoid the full force of the wind.

CHAPTER 4

Polar bears

We easily rounded that first small promontory, hugging the cliff until we could see a house on the other side with a boat moored offshore. This was the home of Johnny May, the Inuk we'd met at the fish camp. It was his bearlike dog that so casually peed on my jacket where it lay drying in the morning at the fishing camp even as I snatched it up from the ground. Johnny's house was in an enviable spot, overlooking a bay, with a view both inland and out to sea. The place, with its launch site, the little house on the open grassy slope atop the low, dark cliff, reminded me very much of Scotland. Perhaps it was the combination of the dark cliff, the green slope, and the whitecapped sea. It looked different from the coast we had been passing. Johnny was one of the very few people who live on the coast away from the main settlements of Kuujjuaq and Kangiqsualujjuaq, (George River) but he and his wife like this site on Black Point. Beside the house, a line of washing was blowing almost horizontally in the wind, and the sheets flapped so vigorously I was surprised I couldn't hear them snap and crack.

We set our kayaks at an angle to the wind and began to sidestep across the bay. We did not expect squall winds until we reached the

Labrador coast, where the wind gets funneled through the mountain passes and blasts down the fjords. Small boats there have been blown out to sea by the offshore winds, sometimes taking days to get back to land again. Here in Ungava Bay, the lower-lying topography was unlikely to cause such violent winds, yet I weighed the potential for being blown away from shore. To be safe, instead of taking a direct line across the wind to the next prominent point, we pushed into the bay directly against the wind. We earned a rest break in the lee of the first rocky outcrop, then pushed out again toward a series of sheltered points around the back of the bay. In the beginning it went easily, with us ferry-gliding across the wind from point to point, but between shelter points were broad stretches of shallow water blown into short, steely whitecaps. The shallow water extended surprisingly far from shore, and our route became more congested with boulders as the tide receded. Each time we avoided an obstacle we were blown farther from shore and had to regain the lost ground. As we crabbed along the coast, we began to see low hills beyond the shore, a welcome change from the flat land we had been passing. Beneath our kayaks the water was receding, boulders stuck their heads up, and our paddles occasionally scraped bottom.

It is difficult to feel good about paddling in water a foot deep. Not only is it impossible to get a full, deep stroke with the paddle, but the bottom-drag experienced in shallow water causes the hull to squat, which reduces forward speed drastically no matter how hard you paddle. It's like pedaling a bicycle with the brakes on. Over my shoulder, out to sea along the skyline, was the familiar line of reefs. They would ultimately form an arm around the bay, with us in it, while the water drained out through the small channels across the flats. I didn't want us to be trapped as the tide fell, but I preferred to remain inside the reefs and close to shore in this wind. We paddled on, and soon the seaward outcrops grew into taller islands that slowly joined together as the gaps between them shrank. Beneath our kayaks the water had become so shallow that without holding ourselves against the bottom we could not stop ourselves from being blown from shore. It was time to find an exit into Ungava Bay before we ran out of water completely. This was the easy part! We simply turned our backs to the wind and let the wind and tide push us out—the wind whipping spray from the tumbling crests around us—until we were beyond the line of outer reefs, when we could turn once more to face the wind. The distant view that opened up revealed little to obstruct us, but we had to paddle hard to keep close to the rock. If we stopped for even a moment the wind pushed us from shore.

Between us and our target for the day, the mouth of the George River, a series of ledges ran far out into Ungava Bay to envelope a scattering of small islands. We crept along the outer edge of the ledges, tucked in close for shelter. Through gaps between ledges, we could see shallow water in the bays behind and vast mud flats clogged with boulders. From time to time we could turn to have the wind at our backs for a few blissful minutes as we crossed to the next ledge, then, around it we would gain against the wind until the curve of land permitted another downwind stretch. With the wind offshore the sea was never rough, but always choppy. The wind has to blow across a greater expanse of water before it can blow a chop into a swell, a longer formation with bigger waves. Heading into this short chop the kayaks pitched and slammed, throwing handfuls of water out for the wind to cast into our faces. As rapidly as the wind dried our skin, the spray wet it again, until a damp white crust of salt gathered to sting our eyes and chafe our skin. Awkward and wet as this was, it was preferable to an onshore wind, which would have sent swells breaking in all directions across the myriad rocks and reefs. So we continued to make progress, hugging the shore for shelter. It seemed the appropriate tactic.

The George River defines the boundary between what the *Arctic Pilot* calls the head of Ungava Bay and its northeastern shore. The river entrance opens to the north; separating us from that entrance lay a broad low cape, rising a few miles inland to a thousand feet. Paddling north, we skirted the offshore ledges along the western side of the cape for about ten miles. Sooner or later we would clear the farthest point of rock and be able to turn almost due east, and later roughly south, into the river mouth.

Those directions refer to true north, or map north, a pinpoint at the top of the world. Our compasses point to magnetic north, a force field in Arctic Canada; we allow for the difference. When we turn east toward the George River, the pencil line on our chart will point to 90 degrees off the north-south grid, but our compasses will read 125, or close to it.

Most of the time we only use the compass to back up what our eyes tell us about the major coastal features marked on the map. Even in this part of the world, where the visual features often do not match easily with the mapped features, we have sufficient clues to work with: knowing how long we have paddled and our approximate speed and direction. Of course we could have carried a GPS to pinpoint our position, if we had also been prepared to carry enough batteries to last five weeks. I am not a fan of electronic gadgets around salt water. I prefer seat-of-the-pants navigation using a map, a compass and observation. Even if we became misplaced for a time we would surely be able to pinpoint our position on the map by identifying land features as we went along. It is possible to not know where you are without being lost.

Near Hubbard Point we were sent more than two miles offshore as a falling tide uncovered tidal ledges, and we were looking for a way around the corner. When finally we could turn east, we could see yet another long spur of ledges extending northward to block our path off Cape Naujaat. At high tide we could have floated over these ledges and avoided the five-mile detour. More aggravating than the detour was the tidal stream that now ran strongly against us. Fighting both current and wind we paddled around the point of ledges, threading between shoals and isolated exposed rocks, sprinting across shallows, and constantly glancing sideways to make sure we were still making progress. We were only gradually gaining ground despite working our hardest. We toiled on close to shore, the wind whipping salt spray in our faces. Then Kristin called out, "Nigel! What are those white shapes up there on the rock?" I tried to look, squinting into the wind, but my eyes kept blurring with the salt and it was difficult to focus.

A broad pink vein of quartz rock ran up the lumpy gray rock to the top where an odd-shaped block of white quartz jutted out. White quartz. Or maybe I was looking at driftwood logs. I couldn't be certain. My eyes watered from looking into the wind. "Logs, or quartz, I can't really tell," I called back. Wrong. Whatever it was, it stood up. I was looking at a pair of polar bears, who were looking back at us. I was shocked. I had overlooked them so easily, even when I was looking right at them. I felt excited, yet apprehensive, and we stopped to see what they would do. They ambled down the steep rock toward us, long necks extended, checking us out; then they turned and paused, heads lifted slightly.

Kristin rafted her kayak against mine, and we watched them turn in unison and run back up the rock. At the top they paused, then bounded over the summit and vanished. "Polar bears!" Kristin exclaimed softly, expressing both delight and awe. "That's exactly how I wanted to see bears: from a safe distance while we're out on the water." I was thinking ahead. Where were the bears now? Waiting for us behind the rock? So despite the current and wind we headed farther from shore before rounding the rock. In the distance a flurry of gulls rose into the air, swirling in a cloud like a dust devil. The bears were ambling past that spot. They must have run quickly to get that far so soon.

I felt reassured by the distance now between us and by the impression that our kayaks had scared them away, but the bears were headed in the same direction we were. We would need to be watchful especially when we found a place to camp. It dawned on me that if polar bears could cover such a distance in that short time, they could approach us that quickly. That made me uneasy. We pulled out farther from shore. We could not risk staying close to the rocks to get shelter. We pressed on against the full force of wind and current, keeping what we thought was a safe distance from shore, watchful for signs of bears, onshore or in the water.

CHAPTER 5

Hubbard Expedition, 1903

In the late 1970s I was browsing a used bookstore at Hay-on-Wye. The village of Hay-on-Wye is one of those sleepy places on the flat river valley where the meandering River Wye runs quietly through water meadows and beneath bridges, the summer river flies snatched from above by iridescent swallows and from beneath by silver-flashing salmon. Hay-on-Wye rests in rural England, close to the Welsh border. It is a place one expects to see ducklings in procession at the side of the winding road and cottage spinsters trimming hybrid roses, or dealing firmly with the aphids. Hay-on-Wye, however, is the site of probably the biggest collection of used bookstores in Britain. My eyes snagged on the gold lettering on the spine of a red-bound book, *A Woman's Way through Unknown Labrador*. I drew it out, and as I read, the unfolding story of an early twentieth century canoeing adventure began to inspire and haunt me.

Here was a young American woman tracing a route from the Labrador coast, tracking inland through the wilderness of northeastern Quebec toward Ungava Bay, an impetuous woman dressed in a skirt and sweater. She slept in her tent at night on an air mattress, warmed by a hot-water bottle beneath wool blankets, her head resting on a "little feather pillow." Her route was the one her late husband had died attempting to follow. I was sucked into her story. She fared better than her husband. He had struggled through rain and cold with two companions, so desperate with starvation they had cut their worn moccasins into strips to eat. He became so weak his companions hurried ahead on the last stretch to summon help. Starved and chilled, and with the snows of approaching winter settling around his tent, Leonidas Hubbard died.

Mina Hubbard described her own expedition in her book, adding the diary of her husband and the narrative of his guide, George Elson, one of the men she enlisted to accompany her. Two expeditions, one tragic, one successful, each heading for the Hudson's Bay Company trading post just fifteen miles upstream from the mouth of the George River that Kristin and I were now approaching. Each party had hoped to reach the post before the annual visit of the company's supply ship, the *Pelican*, so as to have a means of escape before winter. On maps I have finger-traced the thin blue veins and amoeboid lake-blots to follow that inland canoe route from Goose Bay in Labrador to the upper reaches of the George River; a route across a landscape even now devoid of roads.

Between 1892 and 1895, a decade before Hubbard's demise, the seemingly untiring geologist A.P. Low had been exploring the interior of Quebec and Labrador for the Geological Survey of Canada. He published a particularly significant report that identified the potential for hydroelectric power production at Grand Falls on the Hamilton or Grand River. The falls are now known as Churchill Falls, on what is now the Churchill River. As part of the same survey, Low partly explored and mapped Lake Michikamau, a large lake in the interior. He was unable to survey the whole lake, but drew part of his map from descriptions offered by his Indian guides. He marked the approximate position of the lake and the river running from it into Grand Lake. It was perhaps significant that this was the river typically used for passage by the Innu. They were called "Nascopie Indians," hence the name the Nascaupie River, or Nascaupi on later maps. Hubbard's dotted line, speculating the course of the river, was the only river he showed flowing into Grand Lake, near the modern settlements of North West River and Goose Bay. In truth, five rivers flow into Grand Lake. Low did not survey that area, but if he had done so before 1903 the outcome of Hubbard's expedition might have been different. In his report Low noted that at Indian House Lake, on a branch of the George River, "Indians of the region assemble in September to spear the caribou, which then cross the river in immense herds in the course of their annual migration from the high barren grounds behind Nain to the wooded region of the interior, where they pass the winter." The Innu were trying to lay-in enough meat to last the winter. In years when they failed they faced starvation, or at best a bleak survival, depending on their success at fishing through holes in the ice and catching the occasional small animal or bird.

The tantalizing lack of detailed information from Low's account appealed to the New York writer, Leonidas Hubbard. Inspired to find something exciting to present in an article for the *Outing Magazine*, he was drawn to the idea of following the old Indian route from North West River into Grand Lake and upstream to Lake Michikamau. Crossing that lake, he would travel north to the headwaters of the George River. On his way down the George River he hoped to reach Indian House Lake by September to witness the Innu hunting the caribou. From there he would choose between continuing north to Ungava Bay, returning to North West River, or trekking out south to the Saint Lawrence. It should have made a great travel account, with the story of the caribou hunt central within it. I suspect he had not read the accounts of the tough journeys between Ungava Bay and Northwest River by McLean, and before him Erlandson, who trekked across that wilderness with Indian guides several times using different routes between 1834 and 1842, or he might have planned differently.

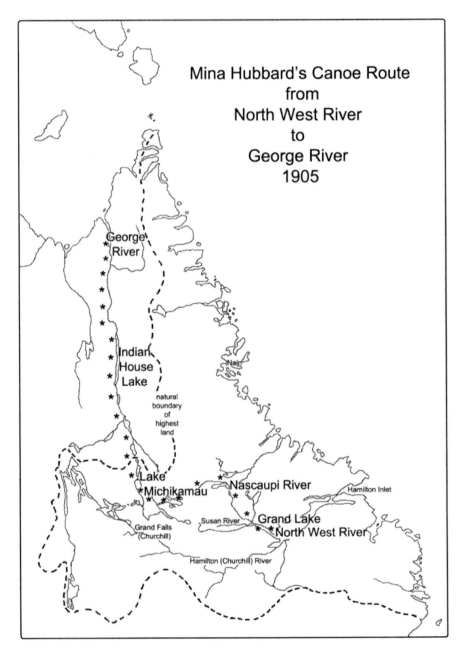

With New York attorney Dillon Wallace, and George Elson, their guide from James Bay in Hudson Bay, the thirty-year-old Hubbard left by canoe from Hamilton Inlet toward Grand Lake on 15 July 1903. With their map, presumably derived from Low's, on which only the North West River is shown flowing into Grand Lake, they turned up what they assumed was that river. In reality they had just started up the Susan River. This was one of the misfortunes that led to Hubbard's death.

The Susan River was not an easy route to follow. In one of the worst hunting seasons on record for the region, and struggling to align the course of the Susan River with the map of the North West River, the party abandoned its goal and tried to retrace its route. During the return Hubbard, exhausted, died of starvation and cold.

The publication of Wallace's highly popular book about the ill-fated expedition, *The Lure of the Labrador Wild*, displeased Hubbard's wife, Mina. Perhaps she was simply irritated at the success of the book, dramatized as it was by her husband's death. Maybe she felt Wallace had described her dead husband less favorably than he ought. She clung to the journals of her husband and his guide, George Elson, discounting alternative accounts that appeared elsewhere as "misleading." In his book Wallace reported the dying Hubbard as saying, "The work must be done, Wallace, and if one of us fails before it is completed, the other must finish it." Mina Hubbard may have been anxious that if Wallace made a second expedition to "finish it," and published a book about it, he would be using her husband's death as a springboard into success, while her husband's version of the story would be left untold. Doubts might be cast on her husband's leadership skills and integrity. When Wallace began to plan a return to Labrador in 1905 to make a second attempt at the trip, Mina Benson Hubbard began secretly to plan her own journey. She enlisted four Indian guides, including George Elson, her husband's guide two years earlier. It must have come as a shock to Wallace to find her expedition traveling on the same ship to Labrador as his. The two parties seemed ready to race against each other into the interior.

On 27 June in 1905, three weeks earlier in the season than her husband had set out, Mina Benson Hubbard's party left in two nineteen-foot-long canvas-covered canoes. After an eventful 576-mile journey they reached the trading post of George River (Kangiqsualujjuaq) on 27 August after forty-three days. From there they made the thirty-mile journey to Ungava Bay in the post yacht, *Lily*.

Wallace began his own trip at Grand Lake on the same day as Mrs. Hubbard, and started up the same river, taking off on what appeared to be an Indian portage route. They became lost somewhere east of Lake Michikamau. By the time they had found and reached the lake on 3 September, possibly one-third of the way to Ungava Bay, Mrs. Hubbard had already completed her journey. Wallace's food supplies were by then so low he sent three of his party back to North West River. Traveling on with Clifford Easton, Wallace reached the George River trading post late on 16 October. The supply ship *Pelican*, which normally visited the post once a year, was late that year; by the time it left George River (Kangiqsualujjuaq) on 22 October it could have carried both Wallace and Hubbard homeward, but Wallace decided to stay longer. His stated reason was to travel to Fort Chimo by *umiak* with an Inuit party. There he would remain through the winter until he could leave by dog sled to cross the mountains of Labrador, and from there south. One could infer that his plan offered him the means to make amends for losing his way and taking seven weeks longer to reach George River (Kangiqsualujjuaq) than Mrs. Hubbard. It might have been embarrassing to meet the press with her when the *Pelican* returned home, and to answer their questions. Under the circumstances he barely survived the journey to Fort Chimo. When the ice closed in, the boat party became marooned on land. Stranded for days on end in a hut, with little more food than a ten-inch square of caribou hide, Wallace and Easton sat it out while the Inuit continued overland and brought back a rescue team.

When Wallace published *The Long Labrador Trail* about his expedition in 1907, he made no mention of Mina Hubbard's expedition whatsoever. Mina Hubbard in turn offered *A Woman's*

Way Through Unknown Labrador to the public in 1908, in which she described her journey through Labrador, adding the diary of her late husband and a narrative by George Elson. Nowhere does she mention Wallace's expedition of 1905. Folded inside the back cover is a new map, showing the route she took, the land she surveyed, and the correct course of the river. Inset is a map from 1905 with its erroneously positioned rivers.

In 2003, four canoeists retraced Hubbard's 1903 expedition route to reach the brass memorial plaque mounted at the place he died. They returned north to follow the route from the Smallwood Reservoir to George River (Kangiqsualujjuaq), making what was possibly the first canoe trek from North West River to there since 1905, certainly the first by an outsider. Part of the landscape is very different nowadays. Lake Michikamau, held sacred by the Innu, has been swallowed by the sprawling Smallwood reservoir that now covers 2,225.8 square miles of territory. Nobody thought it appropriate to consult or inform the Innu. Lands that technically still belong to them today including traditional burial places were flooded without warning. Water from the reservoir drives the Churchill Falls hydroelectric power plant, bypassing what used to be the Grand Falls. The power plant is a great source of pride elsewhere in Canada with its declared generating capacity of almost five and a half million kilowatts of "cleanly produced" electricity. Electricity from this underground facility, the largest in the world, powers the huge iron mines and mining towns of Labrador City and Wabush, with its massive electrical surplus sold across the border to Quebec.

When A.P. Low tramped through the region conducting his geological surveys and mapping the area for the first time, he overlooked or misplaced whole rivers in the forested interior. Sometimes he penciled in lake shorelines he had not time to fully survey to show them approximately on otherwise unmapped territory. I cannot imagine tackling the task of mapping those huge tracts of forested land, lakes, muskeg and river for the first time, and on foot. With such an immense task it is remarkable how much was even fairly accurate. It wasn't until the 1930s, with the help of aircraft, that surveying became easier and more precise. Even today's maps are not always accurate or complete. The charts Kristin and I were using for Ungava Bay were the most up to date available for 2004, yet they still carry the advice, "Much of the information on this chart is of a reconnaissance nature and mariners are warned to exercise caution when navigating in these waters." That said, modern-day discrepancies are miniscule when set against a map that shows the approximate route of a river wandering fifty miles from its actual course, as Hubbard's did.

Hubbard had picked a linear route already traveled by natives, a natural course, like a crack that runs up a cliff face. It was what I consider a good route, in this case defined by natural access and egress points, following a line of least resistance and offering in reward, had he found the way, a natural sense of completion. Since Hubbard's death many adventurers have taken canoes and kayaks to Labrador with less dire consequences, and some have returned for more. Wilderness canoeist George Luste began one of his many notable journeys at Nain in Labrador in 1988. Paddling north to Nachvak Fjord, his group crossed the Torngat Mountains via the Palmer River valley and descended the Korok River to Ungava Bay, rounding the coast to finish at Kangiqsualujjuaq. In 1995, he set out from Kuujjuaq with three other canoeists, including his daughter Tija. Despite one team member suffering a back injury and being evacuated by plane with his paddling partner, George and Tija reached Nain after thirty-five days of paddling. These two of Luste's trips effectively circle the northern Labrador Peninsula, poetically joining two achievements, each an outstanding canoe journey. There are plenty of well-rounded routes waiting to be found on the map of Labrador. One might begin with Mina Hubbard's route from Goose Bay to George River, returning to Goose Bay by sea around Labrador. I have pored over the maps, chasing ideas along blue lines. I hope that maps forever inspire the dreams of mankind, but also hope that they never become so accurate as to preclude the possibility of adventure.

Hubbard Point remained hidden behind the tidal ledges when

we passed it on our way toward the mouth of the George River. On the other side of the broad river mouth, and also hidden from us, lay Elson Point, named after the guide who had accompanied first Leonidas Hubbard, then Mina Hubbard. Seeing these two names on the chart, one to the east, the other to the west, reminded me once again how so often behind a place-name there is a tale.

A few miles into the estuary we at last felt the pull of the rising tide dragging us upriver toward distinctive domelike hills. We cruised close beneath the dark cliff of an island vibrant with the echoing cries and frenetic activity of sea birds. We passed mudflats at the mouth of a tide-drained bay and selected a landing at the edge of a buff-yellow sand beach. I ran up to the headland to check for polar bears and to verify we could find pools of fresh water. We carried our gear and kayaks up the long beach to a fringe of knee-high marram grass and purple willowherb. Tracks of wolf and caribou crisscrossed the top of the beach. The dark green ground-hugging crowberry that covered the valley in a thin layer above the lichens was buried in dirty snow above the beach. The snow ramped up to a low hill of dark rock, likely pink granite, for that was the color revealed along the top of the far shore. Lower down the rock was covered in silt and wrack; higher it would be covered with a tight growth of lichens. When we studied the lichens close up, the tiny growths were variously dark green, brown, or black, studded with or bordering pale gray-green or blue-gray. Despite the array of colors up close, at a distance the wet lichen-coated rock was invariably dark gray.

Once our tents were pitched, with stakes thrust into the sand beneath the stiff crowberry and the stakes held down with boulders, we strolled up the slope to find a shallow lake that was marked on the map. Bakeapples, or cloudberries, extended their heavy stalks above the surrounding vegetation at the base of a low cliff, but they had not yet begun fruiting. A peregrine falcon voiced a shrill protest at our presence. We found the lake and strolled around the edge. In the damp sand we followed the huge paw prints of wolf and the deep hoof prints of caribou. Here also were the webbed fans from the feet of geese. Beyond the pool the land rolled empty into the distance.

Kristin said she appreciated how the vastness and the emptiness, held together by the richness of minutiae, defined the tundra. Up until now each place we had found to camp had been out on exposed rock ledges, where our view was of the sea and the sky and our focus was on the rise and fall of tide. Here was a view of the land: low hills where caribou grazed and where bird nests were simply linings tucked into hollows in the ground. Lemmings and mice left their tiny vermicelli droppings and their snaking passages beneath the lichens. Crispy fragments of goose eggshell lay in or near the sodden dead grass of deserted nests on the ground. Here was a caribou skull, almost polished white but showing the first salt-and-pepper growth of lichen. The crinkled seams between the bones were crumbling open. In time the skull would collapse inward into a puzzle of pieces that once formed the eye sockets and nasal passages and held the antlers high. When it disintegrates, the blanket of spongy lichens, mosses and berry plants will engulf it, sucking in the new source of nutrients. Kristin and I stood there beside it, our feet denting the wet mosses. Perhaps moved by this demonstration of fragility and mortality, Kristin remarked, "When Hubbard's party ran out of food, they ended up eating their shoes, didn't they? If we run out of food do we have to eat our neoprene boots?"

CHAPTER 6

Moravian Missionaries

Mist billowed up the beach as the tide rose, flooding from Ungava Bay into the George River and scenting the air with a tang of the sea. Beads of water ran down the inside of our shelter, where we cradled our hot mugs between our palms and read to each other from the Moravian journal. According to Kohlmeister, the Moravians landed at the mouth of this river, somewhere close to here, in the summer of 1811. The missionaries had hoped to find Inuit here but did not. Before leaving they erected cairns on two hills at the entrance to the bay and set up a signboard declaring the river the George River in the name of King George the Third of England. When McLean established a Hudson's Bay company post farther upstream in about 1939, he sometimes referred to it as the East River. The Inuit families who accompanied the Moravians from Okak more than a century ago knew it as the Kangertlualuksoak.

Place names are part of the legacy of the Moravian missionaries, who brought change to the Inuit way of life in Labrador and Ungava Bay. Before their arrival, trading encounters between outsiders and local people sometimes spilled into violence. Under the influence of the missionaries, trading became more civilized and controlled, and Inuit families adopted Christian values to varying degrees. As the mission posts became accepted as gathering places for families, the missionaries offered formal education and medical aid.

Moravian involvement in Labrador began at the suggestion of a German mariner, Johann Christian Erhardt. He had spent travel time with missionaries while returning from the West Indies and then joined the Moravian church. He later sailed on the Moravian vessel, the *Irene*, between Europe and North America, helping to settle missionaries in the New World. Toward the mid 1700s Erhardt spent some months living among natives on Greenland. Moravians had already started converting that population to Christianity. Convinced that Greenlanders and the inhabitants of Labrador were of the same race, Erhardt contacted the bishop to suggest a combined trading and missionary voyage to Labrador to establish a base there. It would have to be somewhere new, where they would not conflict with trading posts already established, such as the Hudson's Bay Company. The timing was right. In 1749 an act of parliament validated the Moravians as an "Ancient Protestant Episcopal Church." This recognition opened the way for them to extend their influence throughout the British colonies as well as in Labrador.

Erhard suggested a group of missionaries should build a house in Labrador, overwinter there, and then decide whether it would be a suitable place for a larger Moravian settlement. Taking up his suggestion, church officials proposed linking new missions with the Hudson's Bay Company posts, but their talks with the Hudson's Bay Company made no progress. Three years later, however, a group of Moravian businessmen in England approached Erhardt to propose a joint missionary and trading journey to Labrador. Erhardt was keen to go. The church granted permission for an exploratory mission so long as the trading remained separate from the mission work. Erhardt was enlisted as the trade agent, while four missionaries were chosen to stay at the outpost.

Setting sail in the *Hope,* they landed in Labrador in the summer of 1752, at a place north of Hamilton Inlet that Erhardt named Nisbet Harbor. During the first few days ashore they explored the area and then chose a site for their mission. They laid a foundation stone and called the settlement Hopedale. (This, incidentally, is not where the village of Hopedale is located today.) Using materials they had brought from England and what they could find locally, they built a log house twenty-two feet long by sixteen feet wide. They dug a garden and began planting vegetables.

Erhardt traded with Inuit who were camped nearby, obtaining whalebone, sealskins and oil, but he was frustrated to find that even if the people were of the same race as those in Greenland, as he had imagined, these Inuit could not understand his Greenland language. Despite this difficulty, his trading success gave him optimism that he would also be able to trade elsewhere. So in September the *Hope* sailed north in search of opportunities. Erhardt and six of the crew left in the ship's boat to follow some Inuit behind an island to trade and never returned. Without another small boat, the remaining crew was unable to follow to find out what had happened. Fearing the worst, the ship returned without them to Nisbet Harbor and headed home to England.

A search party was mounted the following year when the ship returned. It found the remains of one of the lost men close to where they had gone missing. There was no sign of Erhardt. All that remained of Hopedale was the burned-out shell of the building with charred human remains, thought to be Inuit who had inadvertently ignited gunpowder left there in storage. More than 20 years later, an exploratory party looking for a suitable site for a southern settlement in 1775 found what was left, but the ruins then lay untouched until rediscovered in 2000, and excavated in 2001. They are located in what is known as Ford's Bight in the southernmost bay, at the present-day town of Makkovik.

The inauspicious start did not deter the Moravians. In 1771 they established a permanent settlement at Nain, where they had secured 100,000 acres of land. Nain became the spiritual and administrative center for the Moravians as they expanded their influence up and down the coast. It remained the primary center until 1959, when the headquarters moved to Goose Bay. The historic eighteenth-

and nineteenth-century buildings at Nain no longer remain, and a recent fire destroyed most of the Moravian records, which had been meticulously handwritten in German.

From the main base at Nain, a group of missionaries moved north in 1776 to settle at Okak; in the early 1800s a site even farther north, at Hebron, was chosen for another mission. The 1811 journey by Kohlmeister and Kmoch did not produce missions farther north; the British Government objected, saying they would interfere with the privileges of the Hudson's Bay Company. A site was chosen at Nachvak but the building was moved to Ramah, and this became a base from 1871 to 1908. In the early twentieth century a missionary was posted to Killinek. That man, Samuel Milliken Stewart, had a hard time there, so in the winter of 1904-1905 he journeyed west and south to the Hudson's Bay Company post at Fort Chimo (Kuujjuaq), barely surviving the journey. The factor, or agent, there offered Stewart the use of two small buildings, one as a cabin and the other as a chapel. Stewart was there when Wallace and Easton arrived in 1905, after being rescued from their trek along the Ungava coast following their canoe trip to George River (Kangiqsualujjuaq). In *The Long Labrador Trail* Wallace described finding Stewart in his little cabin, cooking a pot of high-smelling seal meat for his dogs and frying a pan of dough cakes for himself. Wallace professed to have enjoyed Stewart's stories and his sunny temperament while he waited until New Years to leave by dog sled for the Labrador coast.

I ticked off the places on the map where we might see something remaining from the years of Moravian influence: Killinek, Ramah, Hebron, Okak, and Nain, all in Labrador. The Hudson's Bay Company dominated trade in Ungava, primarily from Fort Chimo (Kuujjuaq), but also, for short periods, the unsustainable post on the George River. Yet because of the high cost of maintaining these far-flung outposts, the company paid less for furs and oils than the missionaries in Labrador. The Ungava Bay Inuit, preferring the missionaries' terms, traveled to Labrador to trade, a two-year round trip by *umiak*.

CHAPTER 7

Inuit camp

Morning rain hammered against the tent with insistence while, still dry inside, Kristin unzipped our sleeping bags and stuffed them into their dry-bags. I slipped out through the sodden entrance carrying my rifle and kneeling mat and, head-down, made a dash for the green shelter. "What luxury to have this extra tent for cooking," I thought as I zipped up the front, leaving a few inches at the top open for ventilation. I fired up the Primus stove and loaded the espresso maker with the fine-ground French blend coffee we'd brought from Seattle. The outer rim of the tiny pot was supported precariously by the three stove supports as I balanced it over the heat. I perched our little stainless steel drinking cup beneath the copper tube, ready to catch the hot liquid. While I waited, I pumped water from our bucket through the filter and into the small red kettle, ready to place over the heat as soon as the coffee was ready. The rain now drummed more lightly on the tent. Periodically a burst of wind shook the tent and showered condensation over me. This morning our tent had a sweet, slightly musty scent reminiscent of flowers and mushrooms and sweet-grass, but probably from the lichens and tiny berry bushes underneath. There was a warning cry—"Nigel! I'm coming in!"—

and the zipper ran open. Stepping between the scattered utensils and bags, Kristin crouched forward and eased around to kneel on her pad. She huddled beside me for warmth while I closed the zipper behind her.

Now the day felt more alive. I lifted a tiny ceramic cup of espresso into her wet hand, we had our perfunctory moment of eye contact that said, "Thanks!" and "You're welcome!" before we began to prepare breakfast together. Kneeling comfortably shoulder to shoulder, with our eyes indicating where our arms could not reach, we focused more on tasks than conversation. It seemed likely we would have to pack up in the rain today. But first we would run up the hill again to find the caribou skull and the antlers, to photograph them in the rain. We pulled on waterproofs and ducked outside. As I emerged, it took me a moment to adjust to the shift of color from the green shade beneath the nylon to the mauve-gray cloudy sky and the panorama around us.

The land rose in a series of high banks and narrow plains through which a stream had cut a wandering V-shaped gash about ten feet deep. Small bushes grew in the shelter of this notch, and here and there the brilliant color of a flower contrasted with the pale yellow-green of lichen. The dying wind allowed hordes of mosquitoes to follow us and to settle on our clothing and our hands and faces. Peering into the viewfinder of my camera I was distracted by the sight of mosquitoes covering my nose, but to brush them away was futile; others would alight. If I wanted to photograph I would have to ignore their bites. I took a few of the caribou skull, then hurried up to join Kristin at the next flat area. Here, pieces of plywood and painted wood, stove parts, and other debris were scattered across the tundra, remains from a summer campsite or perhaps a small cabin. Caribou antlers and bones were scattered everywhere too, remnants of meals. Fingerlike points curled outward and upward from the palm-like slabs of antler in the grass, reaching as if to grasp—dead hands that gleamed slick olive green in the rain with the filmy growth of molds and mosses.

My eyes scanned the distance for polar bears. At the far end of the beach, dirty white slopes of snow rested against the grassy bank. In the bay, white mist drifted among boulders that rested plump and dark on the mud flats. Pale green spikes of marram grass bristled above the high tide mark, shot through in places with the deep pink of willowherb flowers. Rain was falling and mosquitoes dodged and hovered. I scanned once more, trying to see through and between the patches of mist that drifted from the water across the beach and up the grass. I could not see any polar bears, so we ran back down the slopes, chasing each other to the tents, and packed. The tide was flooding so we carried the kayaks halfway down the beach, making a guess at how far the water might rise while we loaded them. Our guess was not far wrong. By the time we were ready the water had risen to within a few feet of where they sat heavily on the sand, so we indulged in the luxury of relaxing for a few minutes, watching the mist and the splashes of rain on the water. Then we began to compare the little pebbles we each found in the sand. Soon the rising water floated the kayaks and it was time to leave.

It was about five miles across the mouth of the George River at that point. Because the flood tide is reported to attain eight knots, we crossed before high tide so we might be swept inland slightly through the first part of the crossing and back out again as the tide began to fall. I love the simplicity of this kind of planning. Here, where the tidal information is as sparse as the charts are vague, making crossings and figuring out compass bearings becomes as artful as riding a wave. There's no real science to it, just educated guesswork, followed by a period of heightened awareness, when almost every new observation adds a factor worth considering. As we paddled we drifted upstream sideways for a time, then were carried downstream, and then the stream was directly against us. Could this be an eddy created by the outgoing tide? We pushed forward between islands, dodging the reefs that jutted up above the water, and soon crossed the next bay, and then the mouth of the Korok River.

Mist rolled in and out, pulsing, in a strange, almost organic way. One moment we could see ahead and could adjust our compass reading according to the drift of the tide. Then that view dissolved and only the wave breaking over the reef beside us was visible. A solitary bald rock protruding from the water confirmed that we were making progress as we pulled past it. We kept the shore to our right, aware that there should be islands on our left if the mist opened sufficiently for us to see them. The shore was a jumble of boulders, and between the shore and us we could see more boulders sticking out of the water, their shining tops smooth and seal-like. Under our hulls were bulging ledges of gray and green rock scribed with white quartz serpents and marbled surfaces; looking down, the refraction and movement of the water made the patterns move and shudder across the rock as if alive. Between these meaty ledges that could be whales ran deeper water, green and indistinct. The mist cleared for a moment to reveal rounded green hills close behind the shore, which shrank again into the grainy mist.

Our route was through a channel between an island and a point, but the channel made a right-angle turn from east to north. Three of my topographic maps met right here, the channel crossing the corners of all three, so I relied on my nautical chart instead of struggling with four maps on my deck at once. I used both land and sea charts because each offered different details. Unfortunately this turned out to be the wrong time to rely on the sea chart. Noting that it showed a clear channel between island and mainland unencumbered by shallows, I led us straight ahead, pushing into the tide that now ran powerfully against us. Rain splashed down, bouncing droplets into the air and creating blurry swirls as fresh water pooled on top of the salt water. The fog closed in around us until our view was confined to boulders sticking up out of rain-spattered water. The boulders just beneath the surface were more of a hazard than those we could see, as every now and then one of us would ride up with a screech of gel-coat against rock, which sounding like fingernails across a chalkboard raised the hairs on the back of my neck. We slowed down to reduce the impact of any collisions, but it was difficult to tell the depth of the water over the rocks we approached because of the blurry surface and the refraction. We made progress against the current but the water grew shallower, until we caught mud with our blades while avoiding the boulders. We had almost run out of water. We crept along from eddy to eddy, boulder to boulder, in water little more than five inches deep.

"Is that a tent?" I exclaimed. Scarcely visible through the mist were two white tents pitched on the rock at the top of the muddy slope. We continued, paddling and peering up the slope. Kristin said "There are people." I had not seen the slight figures looking down at us from the top. As we paddled they made their way down to reach the water's edge before we did, two boys and a man in his thirties. We scooted ourselves toward them, gripping against the mud with the edges of our paddle blades until we slid to a standstill.

There were a few minutes of shyness between us, mutual curiosity but uncertainty about the protocol. "The tide is still falling," the man said, sweeping his hand in an arc above the water. By his reckoning we would be stuck there for a few hours. "Come up to the tent for tea." We lifted the kayaks a few yards from the water, then trudged up the slope. The slick, buff-colored skin of the silt punctured beneath each footstep, revealing black mud underneath. Boulders protruded everywhere through it. Near the top of the slope rested a long, grey freight canoe painted teal green above the waterline. A large outboard motor clung to the transom. An elderly man, his tanned face creased and wrinkled, stood leaning against the canoe gazing into it. Water streamed past his rubber boots and filled his footprints. Inside the boat lay carcasses of ducks, loons, and a seal. His party, he explained, had been out hunting from George River (Kangiqsualujjuaq) and had motored around the corner to find the tent here. It was raining, and the boys were cold and wet, so they had set up their tent beside the first one to wait for better weather.

Higher up the shore was a second boat and two tall tents. Sewn in heavy white canvas, each tent stood like a low cylinder with short walls and a conical roof sloping upward to a point supported by a central pole. I have heard that sled dogs like to lift their legs to mark the outside corners of tents, which makes the inside corners damp and smelly, which is sufficient reason to adopt a circular floor and eliminate the corners. We lifted the entrance flap of the closest tent and stooped to go inside. It was warm and steamy. An elderly man with a full-moon smiling face framed in almost white short-cut hair, sat on a plastic cooler with his back against the wall of the tent. He wore a thick blue-check quilted shirt and navy pants stuck into knee-length rubber boots. An old woman in a blue jacket lay on the floor, with a colorful scarf pinning her hair. She lay on a pile of jackets, tending a fire in a metal firebox.

The man said something in Inuktitut and motioned to us to come in and sit down. I followed Kristin to crouch on a plywood board on the ground at the back of the tent. The two boys, in their early teens and wearing baseball caps, and a young girl piled in behind us so we shuffled around to make room. Everyone settled down onto the ground, grinning. We introduced ourselves. The old man spoke. His name was David; his wife was Suzie. The boys were sons of the man who had just squeezed in at the entrance. He was with *his* father, the man who had been standing beside his boat. David and Suzie were camping with their granddaughter. The little girl smiled.

The man by the door translated. Suzie had cancer. She was ill. She couldn't walk any more, but she liked camping here, so her husband had brought her out to camp for a few days. Now they had more or less run out of food, so they would go back tonight when the tide had lifted enough to launch their boat. The other party would help them launch and would also leave at high tide. They asked if we wanted to camp there. We said no, that it wasn't easy for us to unload and carry our stuff up muddy shores. We'd much rather land on rock, so we waited for the tide.

Suzie poured water into a large kettle and set it hissing on the stove. She coughed for a while, awkwardly and apparently with pain. When she stopped I smiled at her and her eyes warmed. I looked around at our new surroundings. A rusty stovepipe ran up from the firebox through a hole in the roof, the cloth shielded from the heat by a metal plate sewn to the canvas. I pointed to this neat heat barrier and made comment, and the old woman indicated with a smile that she had sewn it herself.

David had once been a seal hunter, hunting in summer from his kayak. His father had built his first kayak for him out of wood and sealskin when he was young. He had built several more for him over the years, four in all. That was on the east coast, at Nutak I think he said, in Labrador. He was proud of his skills, but now, he said, he was too stiff. He couldn't bend enough to squeeze into a kayak. The translator laughed and poked fun, saying "Too much television! Too much food!" and he patted the air in front of his stomach, suggesting a paunch.

David smiled and continued, "But we had to move away, some of us to Nain in Labrador, some of us to Ungava Bay, to Kangiqsualujjuaq and Kuujjuaq. Our families were split up, and the government told us we were to stay apart. We were forbidden from crossing to see our families. They didn't want people to keep moving from Quebec to Labrador and back. They wanted people to stay in one place. They wanted to know where people were. I came to Kangiqsualujjuaq with my uncle. My sister went to Nain, but we cross now to see them."

The girl was fascinated by Kristin's camera in its waterproof case. Kristin took her photograph and showed her the image, but with limited battery power for the five-week trip she was reluctant to take a lot of pictures. She distracted the girl by switching on the little red emergency light she carried clipped to the shoulder of her float-vest. The old man continued, "But things change. Always there is something good. If things are bad, then you can say, things will get better, and they do." Optimism beamed from his blue eyes. He leaned his broad head forward and smiled. His tanned face, dark beneath almost white hair, radiated confidence. I glanced to my left to see the row of faces turned to watch him, waiting for his next words, but he just smiled, gazing as if into some inner thought.

The kettle was now boiling strongly; his wife struggled onto her side to lift it from the heat. Her deft fingers plucked off the lid and thrust in tea bags. She motioned to her granddaughter, who passed her several empty enamel cups, stained with rings of tannin, and she lined them up.

David continued, explaining how people crossed the mountains from Ungava Bay into Labrador in winter. When he was 10 years old or so, he first saw a white man. "He was the best survivalist. When he first arrived the people didn't know how he would eat, but he ate raw meat off a split log like they did." David lifted a piece of wood from the floor to illustrate how they would use a newly split slab of wood as a plate. Then he handed it to Suzie who slid the kettle aside and fed the wood to the fire. "Yes," he repeated, "that white man ate meat like us, using a split log, cutting pieces of blubber like we did, even eating stinky fish in winter. He was a survivalist."

Suzie lifted the heavy kettle and poured tea, passing the mugs first to Kristin, who was nearest. As Kristin reached to receive them, Suzie noticed the dressings on Kristin's hands and indicated that she wanted to see. She held Kristin's hands in her own and stroked them tenderly, talking quietly to herself. David said Kristin's hands would become tougher as she paddled. "First you get blisters, then your hands will be tough. You'll see." I hoped he would be right. As a ceramicist, Kristin's hands were constantly being abraded by clay, to the point that when she worked long hours her fingerprints wore completely flat. She didn't have a thick protective layer of hide to begin with, and her hands had blistered almost as soon as we began full paddling days.

David lifted the tent flap to look outside. One of the boys scrambled out, and moments later we heard the sound of an axe chopping wood. "We bring the wood!" our translator explained. "The wood for the fire we get in winter with the snowmobiles. There are no trees here. We go inland," he said, pointing. "We also bring the plywood." He pointed to the boards we knelt on. David let the tent flap close and swatted at a mosquito, prompting Kristin to ask how they had managed with mosquitoes in the past. The translator pointed to a burning green coil near the door with a smile. Kristin said, "But you haven't always had coils. What did you do before?" David reached down and pulled a handful of leafy twigs from the ground. "We burned this." I tried to make out what it was. It looked like the aromatic leaves of crowberry. He continued, "But when we traveled, sometimes the flies were very bad. We couldn't sleep. We would keep going until there was some wind, and then we would all lie down on the ground and sleep. Without a breeze it was impossible to sleep with the mosquitoes. You can't sleep when there are too many flies. Sometimes we would keep going for days with no sleep. There is enough light in the summer to keep going all night."

David peered out from the tent again. He explained, "The tide, sometimes you wait for it to come. You are impatient. You say, 'Come on tide! Hurry up! I can't wait all day! Won't you come faster!' but it doesn't come. It comes, but very slowly. Then it starts to come, and you think, 'Good, now at last!' But it comes too fast. Then you say 'Tide! Can't you come slower?' " We smiled. This visit was precious. Although I had wanted to get through the channel earlier, our enforced wait brought us an unexpected and wonderful experience, so I understood his story. But I had missed his point entirely.

Suzie began gathering items from around her, pouring flour into a bowl, and mixing a ball of dough. She struggled with a wide cast iron frying pan, moving the kettle to reveal the fire through a hole underneath. The fire was low. One of the boys left again to chop wood, coming back with an armful of short, split chunks. Suzie fed some onto the fire and sat the pan on top with a piece of white lard, which gradually melted until the tent was clouded with eye-stinging smoke. Then she spread her soft dough into it to form a pancake that rose slowly into a deep bannock. Flipped, it revealed a golden brown underside. The bready smell made my stomach ache. I was hungry, and eagerly accepted the piece she broke for me. Our translator began to ask about food. "Do you like duck?" "Yes," I replied. "Do you know what to do with a duck, how to cook it?" Again I said yes. I've prepared animals and cooked them often enough before. In Iceland it was ducks and puffins, fulmars and gulls. He disappeared and came back with the gift of a duck. "You sure you know what to do with it?" he checked again. "Yes! This will be wonderful! And yes, I do know how to prepare it." The duck lay on the ground in front of me, and the boy on my left and the granddaughter idly played with it, making the head peck at the ground, and look around. They fingered the feathers and legs, as at ease with this dead creature as they would have been with a stuffed toy.

David opened the door again and peered out. "I can hear it now. It won't be long." He spoke of the tide. "Soon! There is a place just around the corner where you can land in a kayak. You can camp there. It's a good place." To Kristin he added, "You will have a good journey. The current will be strong but you can make it."

We continued talking, but a few moments later David spoke again. Translated he said, "It's time for you to go." I began thanking Suzie, saying goodbye, and then shuffled around to get out of the tent. Outside I shook hands with each person, saying, "Thank you." But David interrupted. He pointed. "It's time for you to go!" I looked. The water had reached to within a few yards of the kayaks. I turned to thank the uncle for the duck. "Nigel!" Kristin shrieked. "The kayaks! We've got to go!"

I turned again to look; it didn't sound like her, and we were not *that* rushed for time. But Kristin had already gone. She was hurtling down the muddy slope with the jerky movement of someone not quite in control of her feet. Tripping on a rock, she flew headlong into the mud, then scrambled to her feet and ran on. Then I saw the kayaks. They were almost floating! A flood of water cascaded downhill from above the rocky dam to the north to meet the tide that had been rising from the south. The levels were so different that the current roared audibly as it rushed downhill. Kristin fell again, then regained her feet. I hurried down the mud clasping the duck in one hand. There was no way I could reach the kayaks. They were now drifting from shore and the current was carrying them downstream. With a final burst of speed Kristin ran right into the water and grabbed first one, then the other. The water was up to her thighs. She waded back to shore shaking her head. I held the kayaks while she pulled off each boot in turn to pour out the water. Her feet must have been frozen.

We stowed our cockpit covers and climbed into our seats. Gliding from shore we pointed our kayaks against the current and paddled hard. Now each boulder that stood in the current offered us an eddy to ease our way. We sprinted from one eddy to the next, pausing for a moment then darting up to the next large stone, pushing upstream as if against a river. Up on the hill stood our friends, their figures half-obscured by the gathering darkness. They waved, and we waved back. A mile, maybe two, of hard paddling against the stream and there was the corner at the end of the island that David had described. I slipped from my cockpit and lifted the bow of my kayak onto the rock to hold it against the tide while I helped Kristin. We hurried to unload the gear and carried it high up the rock to where some rough circles of stones lay. People had camped here before, and these stones had held down their tents. There is something poetic about using the stones others have gathered for the same purpose. Who knows who was first to collect them, or how many times they have been spread into a new circle on the slab of rock to hold yet another tent? Who knows who would use them next after us, or when that might be?

The rain had filled shallow pools that reflected the last of the light as we struggled to erect the tents and get organized before darkness enveloped us. Working by flashlight, we caught the gleams and sparkles as the crystals in the rocks reflected our lights. I lit candles to help dry the inside of the sleeping tent while we prepared a meal in the shelter. We had made it through the channel that my nautical chart showed as deep water. I took out the three topographic maps and matched them together. "Look at this!" The topographic map showed the channel filled with mud and boulders. If I had seen that earlier we would have gone around the outside of the island. And we would have missed the meeting with the Inuit people. As Kristin put it, "Good fortune smiled on us."

CHAPTER 8

East and North along Ungava Bay

We awoke to a still, damp morning. The lichens and liverworts, now dark and swollen with water, sat plump on the rocks like squashed goose droppings. Fat cushions of green moss clung to crevices. Rounded boulders bigger than our tent rested as if scattered across the ledges. Mist shrouded the islands, blurring the distant edge of water. The tide had gone. The rock on which we were camped sloped down in steps to a yellow-brown fringe of wrack. Beyond, a vast bay of mud lay studded with smooth boulders, each skirted with seaweed and surrounded by a pool of water. Patches of mist drifted above the mud, and here and there the gray sky was reflected in the glassy pools. We draped our wet gear over the tall blocks of granite so it could drip a little drier. There was scarcely a sound, except for the distant clamor of rushing water that eventually faded and disappeared. We could have walked the mile of mud to the misty hill on the next island.

Water began to inundate the mudflats, gathering momentum until we could hear it rushing. It fingered through the lower channels in the mud toward us, rumbling and rattling between the boulders and stones until only the tops of the bigger ones showed. Now it was rising fast, and it seemed to carry the mist away with it. In a short time the boulders and flats were covered in a satin sheet of water that dully reflected the low dark islands to the west and north. It crept up the bedrock slopes, filling the notches and crevices and lapping against the ramps until it reached our kayaks. We eased the kayaks onto the water and slipped into our seats. Now there was hardly a sound. We could hear every little splash and gurgle, and we could hear the quiet rattle of falling water in the distance as if amplified across the bay. The low islands and hills beyond arched gently like the backs of dolphins to form a darker horizon above the dark, lusterless, blue-gray sea. Clumps of soft fog reached down toward the water, adding form to the low cladding of cloud. The rain that beaded lightly on our yellow decks also dampened the islands, making the rock glisten like sweaty skin. We threaded silently through the channels between islands.

Around high water we crossed Keglo Bay, keeping inside a line of shoals that reach across the mouth. The tide stream helped us. Offshore of the rocks, tendrils of white mist floated above the water. Looking inland, east beyond the bay, hills and islands layered one behind the other, each distant layer of color more subdued and faded than the one in front of it. There was plenty of time to gaze across the water; at this distance the scene changed slowly. An island would pass gradually in front of a mountain, confirming our progress, but it was easier to gauge our progress by watching the rocks and shoals close by.

Beyond Keglo Bay we cut between ledges with plenty of water to float us; farther north, navigation became more complex. The five miles ahead was shown on the map as a string of islands that join at low tide to form a massive ledge running four miles out from shore. It was difficult to see which gaps we would be able to float through and which would be blocked by the time we reached them. Pools of water two miles long would become isolated when the falling water exposed the rock surrounding them. It was truly a maze, through which we could not see, but to circle the perimeter would double the distance, from five miles to ten, so we took our chances and headed into it. It made me anxious, because to run aground would slow us considerably more than to make the detour. We emerged near Cape Kattaktok on the northern point of the peninsula. Relieved, we turned east into the chilly wind and rain.

The geology here did not offer an easy landing. Extensive beaches of mud and boulders, streaked with seaweed, ran to steep slopes with haphazardly arranged sharp-edged steps and inclined blocks. Scouting for a possible camping place I climbed the slick rock, but there was no place flat enough to anchor a tent between the water that pooled in every gash. Paddling onward we encountered dark islands of rusty-black rock that looked like iron ore, with mineral stains of livid orange and blue-green streaking the landscape. The low cloud and rain brought evening prematurely. With the newly turned tide running against us, we were prepared to consider any landing that looked practical. But whichever side of a point we looked from, the rock rose awkwardly. We skirted muddy flats and checked out rocky points, dismissing them because they were too low and would not offer access to ground high enough to camp.

I took a chance on a steep slope composed of chunky steps draped in seaweed, and stepped ashore. Here the rock was treacherously slippery, so we would have to be extremely cautious if we decided to carry everything up here. I climbed until I was beyond the weed, finding the rock above irregularly layered and sharp-edged, each ledge tilting outward and upward to create a crevasse a foot or two wide that dropped into shadow. Scrambling up the slope in rain and in the gloom of failing light, I found a small flat area of sharp rock chippings beside a protruding keel of rock. This would be enough for a tent. Water? Yes, there were pools of it. Bears? None that I could see. I retraced my route down the rocks and devised a strategy with Kristin. Because there was nowhere secure to rest our kayaks while we unloaded them, Kristin pulled the gear from each hatch into our large bags for me to carry up. As she did so, she floated the boats up a few feet at a time to keep pace with the rising tide. It was slow and laborious, but we got everything to the top, both of us wet and chilled. We prepared the duck by the water by flashlight, changed hurriedly into warm dry clothes, and retreated to the shelter tent. By the light of candles and headlamps, we boiled the duck in a sauce concocted from dried cranberry and mango and served it with hash browns. It was succulent and flavorful, and there was more in the pot for another meal. Then, while we were still warm and full, we retreated to our sleeping bag. I wrote in my journal "Tough little day. Glad to get to sleeping bag. We were cold."

We chose to remain the following day at this spot. A cold rain was blowing in from the north, and the prospect of a day paddling straight into it didn't appeal to either of us. We folded the groundsheet in half in the shelter tent and knelt on our foam pads with our backs resisting the push of the wind against the tent fabric. Our simple kitchen consisted of a few small slabs of stone for our hot pans to rest on, everything we needed to prepare hot drinks to one side, and all the food to the other. I made a stream of hot drinks: espresso and tea. The tea was prepared using an insulated stainless steel mug as a teapot, rattling in a few hard rabbit-dropping balls of jasmine tea that Kristin's brother Brad had brought us from China, and pouring on boiling water. Slowly the tight balls of tea unfolded into long slender leaves. Each time we poured tea out through the notched lid of the mug into our little ceramic tumblers, we topped up the mug with boiling water. It was comforting to cradle the warm cups between our palms to sip the liquid. We sliced the remaining meat from the duck and ate it with the mango and cranberry sauce, and then boiled the bones to make stock for a soup we poured onto couscous.

Outside the tent the wind blew, and the tide rose until it almost enveloped the islands, leaving only slivers of rock lying above the vast water. It was engrossing to observe the tide cycle from above. With scarcely a pause, the tide began to drop away again, draining past in long curving rapids between the islands. Gradually the falling waterline exposed more rock, layer by layer, to reveal canyons that deepened, and dark cliffs and steps. Finally broad ledges with pale brown seaweed shouldered up from the water, and slick slopes of fine mud and wrack joined each island to the next. Loons hurtled past crying in the wind.

Hardly a single mosquito was to be seen all day. Comfortable in our shelter, we used a magnifying glass to examine the mosses, lichens and small plants inside the tent, viewing a rich, dense world of tiny growth on the stones and looking closely at the crystals in the rock. The crispy pink granite outcrops were exfoliating to leave a fragile crust of sharp edges that crumbled when touched, the pieces tinkling down among the other sharp shards. Clinging to the shards were tiny pancakes of crisp black lichen, miniature tumbleweed balls of pastel gray lichen, and tongue-shaped fragments of bright yellow. The harsh winter frosts had been making their mark through centuries, gradually breaking down the ridges of rock like the one that offered shelter for our tents and creating flat areas of fragments. The broken pieces were sharp. In the night not only had our groundsheet been slit open beneath us, but our sleeping mattresses had been punctured, dropping us onto the sharp stones.

Although the wind still blew from the north next morning, the weather was clearer, the colors more vibrant, and the rocks glittered in the light. We took our time getting ready, for day by day the high tide was getting later. We burned our little bag of garbage on a small fire of twigs. We folded back the tops of our neoprene boots to encourage the insides to dry and spread our wet kayaking clothing and pinned it down with rocks in the breeze to dry. While the gear struggled and fluttered like trapped birds, we huddled down together in a rock hollow and surveyed the tide rising across the ledges. Our island shrank as the many waterways merged to form one wide expanse of water, studded here and there with the rounded summit of an island. Predictably it was much easier to launch with the tide full than it had been to land with the tide lower. We spun our kayaks into the fast current and skirted the shore of the island, gazing up at the gloomy dark rock.

Paddling northeast we crossed a series of channels that ran between low fingers of land jutting northwest. Each time we hit land we turned northwest and followed the shore until we reached the end of that island or peninsula, then resumed our northeast course across the next gap. Chunks of bright ice floated on the dark blue sea. The air felt cold and fresh. Kristin observed that the sea smelled different from the Pacific Ocean. Approaching the end of one point of land we came to a narrow opening into it. By the time we were partway across we could see out to the other side. Here was a possible shortcut between an island, at this state of the tide, and the mainland. We entered the gap and discovered that, although the channel narrowed and ran right through, there was a second exit to the left. The wind funneled through this second channel making the water choppy. I suggested landing on the sheltered side of the second island. I needed a pee break. A shallow inlet just wide enough for a kayak ran to a dead end in complete calm. It was a perfect harbor. I drifted in and stepped out onto low rock. Kristin floated in behind me but, warm in her kayak, decided to stay afloat. My kayak was effectively corralled so I left it floating.

I strolled a few yards up the smooth rock that rose in sensuous sweeping terraces toward a rounded summit. I looked out across the rock and water. The sky was bright, with a few wisps of cloud. Little wavelets pushed through the channel between the islands. Kristin sat relaxing in her kayak. To the east lay the entrance to Abloviak Fjord. Today was 6 August 2004. On 6 August 1811 the missionaries on their way from Okak Island passed seaward of this spot heading the opposite direction. One of their Inuit guides had pointed out in the distance the "lair of Torngarsoak." Kohlmeister wrote of a "wide and deep cavern shaped like the gable end of a house, situated at the top of a precipice, in a black mountain, of very horrid and dark appearance." This, he explained, was the place the Inuit believe to be the dwelling place of Torngak, the evil spirit. He described the scenery as extremely wild and terrible, with the prospect of the rocks and islands at low water offering the country "a most singularly gloomy character." The cavern was called "the dragon's dwelling." Kohlmeister questioned whether their Inuit guide Uttakiyok might be persuaded to go into the cavern even if offered the opportunity, given his beliefs. He carried a raven's claw at his breast and fixed the inflated stomach of a seal to a tent pole at one side of his boat as protection against evil while passing this point of danger.

Torngat, or Torngait, means a place of the spirits, so the Torngat Mountains are a place of the spirits. This name is derived from the controlling spirit Torngarsoak, the Great Spirit, who takes the form of a huge polar bear and controls the sea and all the sea creatures. His wife Suporuksoak, the Great Wind, has power over the land and its animals. Giant caribou are said to defend their cave in the mountains.

Well, it was time to go. Time to get back in the boat.

Click. I snapped the second shoulder strap buckle into place and reached down for my anorak and float-vest. I froze before my fingers got there. My calm shattered like glass. An ivory-white clump of fur rose from the skyline sixty feet away. The shaggy mass pitched up further into view to reveal the broad, gleaming back of a large animal, and my gut sank. One more lurch and I could see the whole polar bear, head low, striding purposefully toward me, its long fur folding and swaying around its body like an overcoat with each long rolling step. I snatched my gear from the rock and turned away, trying to appear unhurried, trying not to appear as fleeing prey. Kristin sat with her back to me in her kayak in the narrow finger of water I'd chosen for a sheltered landing. "Okay, Kristin! Start backing out now! Back onto deep water! Let's get going!" Something in my voice made her look around to see me walking with the bear now only thirty feet behind. Jolted into action she tried to push off, but her kayak was aground. She pushed again. By now I was slipping into my kayak, but Kristin was blocking my escape. "Come on, Kristin! Let's get out of here!"

"I'm stuck!" she said. I got out of my kayak and crouched beside it. The huge bear lurched to a stop at Kristin's kayak. She was truly stranded by the falling tide. "Nigel, should I get out of my boat?" I wasn't sure. The bear was close enough to swipe her with its great paw whatever she chose to do. I popped the lid off my day-hatch and grabbed my flare gun. The bear stood motionless, staring at her. If I could fire a flare I might distract it, but did I have time? I plucked a cartridge from the storage rack. However long it took, I needed to focus and get it done right the first time, no fumbling. I broke open the gun, pushed the red cartridge home and snapped the barrel closed. Kristin was looking up at the bear's head. I cocked the firing mechanism and aimed. If the bear attacked I should try to hit it in the face, or in the mouth, but that should be my last resort. I had to scare the bear away, not enrage it, so I aimed at the rock beyond the bear and fired. "Whoof!" The flare launched with an explosion disappointingly soft and ineffectual, but the bright flash whizzing past its head startled the bear, and it bounded sideways and ran thirty feet in a few paces. It stopped and turned, paused, then walked straight back to us. Kristin had slid out of her kayak and was standing beside it in the shallow water in front of me. We had neither time to escape nor any place to go. I opened the gun, pulled out the spent case, and inserted another. The bear stuck its long neck forward and sniffed the bag on Kristin's rear deck. Freeze-dried food, vacuum-bagged. The bear raised its heavy head and stared right at her. There was such a majestic calm assuredness about this bear. It would do whatever it wanted to do. What would it be like to be eaten alive by a bear, torn apart? Perhaps a swift death, but I had heard polar bears don't bother to kill first and eat afterwards, they simply begin eating. What if the bear started to eat Kristin first? I moved up behind her.

Kristin was staring straight at the bear. "Bear!" she said, "Be gone!" Her voice held the same firm edge she used for commanding her dog. She repeated her demand, slowly and clearly. "Bear, be gone!" I snapped shut the flare gun and cocked it ready to fire. "Bear, be gone!" She had already voiced expectation; she shifted emphasis. "BEAR! Be GONE!"

I squeezed the trigger. This time the flare ricocheted off the rock beside the bear's right forefoot. The huge animal shuffled sideways, put its head down and sniffed the rock, then raised its head to Kristin again. I was disappointed in these flares. I really had hoped for more effect. I pried out the spent case, dropped it and reloaded. I felt completely helpless. I aimed past Kristin, and from about eight feet away my third flare flew past its head. This time the bear didn't even shift its gaze. I flipped the gun open and reloaded. This would be my last shot, used only if attacked and then aimed directly at the bear. Again she insisted; "BEAR! BE GONE!"

A polar bear can pounce twenty feet from standing, and this one was less than ten feet from us. "Bear! Be gone!" The bear looked at me, looked back at her, half-turned, and shuffled its huge feet. It moved a few paces up the rock away from us. Kristin didn't hesitate. She dragged her kayak backward till it floated and with a single fluid movement was in the cockpit reversing toward open water. The bear turned. I followed Kristin as quickly as I could. Hauling my kayak across the rocks to the water, I almost tumbled into the cockpit. I stuffed my float-vest and spray skirt into my lap and began to reverse. The bear, now staring straight at me, came striding down the rock. In a few fluid steps it reached the water's edge, but I had reversed far enough to clear the rocks, and now alongside Kristin I was powering forward toward the opening between the island and shore. Steady, strong strokes. No splash, no wasted energy, just the most effective strokes I could make. Curbing my adrenalin-induced energy, I paddled exactly the same pace as Kristin, keeping our kayaks close together and side by side, hoping they would appear as one large unit. The bear ambled over the rocks at the water's edge, matching our pace with ease. Even the steep, cliff-like steps in the rock didn't slow it down. There was something elegant and graceful about the way it loped along, gathering momentum like a ball rolling down a hill. It was hurrying to head us off.

Then it paused, distracted. We had reached the mouth of the channel, where it began to open like a funnel. We pulled farther from shore, at last gaining distance from it. Feeling safer for the moment, I pulled out my camera to take a far-off shot, but even as I paused the bear stepped down to the water, sniffed the surface, then walked boldly headlong into the sea. I could see the white wake, the head pushing along the surface, then even that vanished. Polar bears are superb swimmers, able to hold their breath for two minutes at a time under water and by many accounts able to swim at up to six knots. If this bear wanted to catch us it was certainly capable of doing so. The thought of a polar bear erupting from the water beside us was too vivid. We hurried away and didn't relax our pace for more than an hour.

Islands stud the bay at the mouth of Abloviak Fjord. Pieces of floating ice now drew our attention. Could they be polar bears? When we reached the far shore we discussed every uncertain feature in the distance. Could that be a bear? Perhaps it's a waterfall. Is that pale shape a block of stone? How big do you think it is, how far?

The polar bear, classified a marine mammal as its name, *ursus maritimus* or sea bear, suggests, is also the largest carnivore on land. The males, eight to ten feet long and weighing 750 to 1,500 pounds, are bigger than the females. By comparison, the original Austin Mini Cooper had a curbside weight of 1,314 pounds and a length of ten feet. The largest polar bear recorded measured twelve feet long and weighed 2,209 pounds. The bear's normal daily cycle has it being most active in the first third of the day and least active in the final third.

Polar bears hunt for about 25 percent of the time during spring, 40 percent during summer. Their average walking speed is 3.4 miles per hour but they can run for short distances at 25 miles per hour. They can swim at 6.2 miles per hour and have been tracked swimming for more than 50 miles without stopping; they have been seen more than 50 miles from land. Their sense of sight and hearing are probably similar to ours, but their sense of smell is extraordinary. It has been reported they can smell a seal more than 20 miles away. Compared to other bears, the polar bear is more willing to consider humans as prey, so anyone attacked is usually killed unless the bear is killed first. Females with cubs are more likely to attack because they have themselves and their cubs to feed, and young independent bears are also more likely to attack because they are more often hungry. Attacks on people do not happen often, so fatalities are rare. In all of Canada there are only seven recorded cases of people being killed by polar bears in the last thirty years, although many more bears have been killed "in self-defense." The Inuit say a polar bear can read a person's mind and hear his thoughts, so one should never think ill of a bear because it may hear and become angry.

Late that day we saw a huge white rock on the skyline that looked so much like a bear we nearly passed an excellent camping site. When we figured out it was probably limestone, we pulled ashore and strode up the curving pages of rock from ledge to ledge to discover the flat top of the broad island littered with tent circles and piles of blue mussel shells. Farther along was a prominent *inuksuq* and pools of fresh water. The openness of the landscape made me less apprehensive about bears, so although it meant a long carry we hurried to establish our camp. Wild serpentine pink patterns swirled across the white rock slabs, looking like mother-of-pearl until we looked more closely to discover they were bands of pink garnet. It was almost dark by the time we had set the tents in the shelter of a step of rock. Collecting water later in the chill wind, we were rewarded by the sight of a curtain of green light playing across the sky, while a deep yellow moon rose to silhouette a distant hill. This was our first sight of the northern lights on this trip, and it was a spectacle that thrilled both of us. The lights' glow increased in intensity, then burst sporadically into waving curtains that appeared to consist of fine, vertical, flickering threads of green fire. Yet the fire of nature did nothing to warm us. Even hugging failed to dispel the chill of the night. The wind rattled the tent fabric, and I felt cold even after we had retreated to the sleeping bag. There, holding each other, we talked over the scene on the little island with the polar bear, repeating our questions, "What if?" over and over until finally we slept. Next morning I was slow to emerge to greet the sun and the breeze.

I felt relaxed in our morning tasks. Journeys have routines, like spreading our damp clothing and pinning it with rocks to stop it blowing away, turning down the legs of our knee-length neoprene boots to let the fleece liners air out, and burning our garbage before setting the stove in a sheltered corner to cook. The routines are simpler than those of city life. We took time to write in our journals and to explore the tent circles and pools. We found toadstools, and we found scraps of wood with such deep layers of paint peeling from them we imagined they were more likely from a boat than a house.

All morning we scanned around us for signs of polar bears. The shock of the bear appearing so suddenly, so close to us, yesterday made us now imagine all the places a bear might be lying, perhaps asleep, perhaps watchful. I found myself planning what I would do if a bear appeared over there, or from behind that rock, and I restricted my movements accordingly, so I would be close to Kristin if one did approach. Yet despite the unease it was pleasant to spend an efficient morning with no more fixed schedule than to go for a paddle on a sunny day.

When we resumed paddling, we found a light following breeze made our day perfect. The jumbled rocks on shore appeared to rise to flat-topped sections of raised beach. We rounded a point and cut across toward the next line of land, aiming for a low hill about a quarter of a mile away with an *inuksuq* on the top, content with our easy paddle rhythm, our kayaks skipping along side by side. Kristin was leaning forward to scrutinize her map so I watched her. It is easy to wander off course while studying the chart, but if I paid attention I could follow her to avoid collision. When she looked up again she said, "Nigel, you see that marker straight ahead on the hill? It looks like a beacon. Can you see it on your chart?" I looked but saw nothing marked. "No. But if it's an *inuksuq* it won't be shown anyway."

"But that looks more like a navigation beacon than an *inuksuq* doesn't it? Aren't *inuksuqs* about the size of a person? This is bigger and it looks as if it's been painted."

I looked more closely. It was a very symmetrical, almost conical, structure, and I agreed it did look more official than a simple stone *inuksuq*. It looked just like the painted stone transit markers I've often seen on the British coast. "Hang on, I'll check my topo' map." I stopped paddling and slipped the map out so I could see it. "Point Le Droit," I read. "No, there's nothing shown on that either." There was about a mile and a half of coast between the *inuksuq* and the most prominent point along this whole stretch of coast. If we were going to find a beacon, it would surely be on the point. We paddled in silence for a few minutes. "Nigel! The beacon's standing up!" I looked up. The regular, conical shape had gone. In its place was a polar bear, huge. It stared across at us, and then started running down the hill toward us. We changed direction immediately and paddled hard from shore.

The bear ran much more quickly than we could paddle and was soon at the water's edge. It seemed much more purposeful than the bear we saw yesterday. We aimed across its line of sight, still angling offshore but making progress toward the headland. Paddling close together side by side I hoped we would look too big to tackle, but the bear followed along the shore, watching us. Gradually we pulled farther from shore, although we still needed to round the point. Sometimes the bear vanished behind rocks and we would watch for it, eventually spotting it watching us from farther along the coast, huge and motionless. Kristin said, "It's more scary than the one yesterday." "That was so sudden we just had to react. This one's really stalking us and it's spooky. Nigel, I don't like it."

We paddled swiftly for another twenty minutes, when, just before we reached the end of the point, the bear launched into the water and we could see the white head pushing out from shore toward us. Then it vanished. It is unsettling to know a bear is following you. It is more unsettling when you can no longer see it. We paddled hard, looking behind us frequently, speeding along with the tide on open water.

Later that day, we were about to pass through a gap in a reef between two islands when we saw what may have been another bear. It might have been something else, but we chose not go closer. Instead we turned to make a wide detour around the other side of the island. Scattered chunks of ice kept us alert, but our next sighting was a pale shape on a high reef. This one might have been an ivory colored boulder, but it was about the right size for a bear. Kristin asked at this point how much I really wanted to go to the Button Islands. Something was worrying her. "If all the bears are moving north at this time of year, there will be even more there than anywhere else, won't there?" She had a point. "No, we don't need to go looking for bears," I said. "We can cut through McLelan

Strait. I've been to the Buttons before." I had my own concerns about our progress. I had expected to cover the Ungava coast more quickly than this. We might not have time to detour around the Button Islands anyway.

We kept our distance from land until evening, then rafted our kayaks together while Kristin scanned the coast through her binoculars before we paddled closer. The landing place we found was on a rock that rose so steeply we were challenged to hoist our kayaks even after we had emptied them. Kristin again scrutinize the landscape with binoculars, checking out every ambiguous pale object; when she was satisfied, we picked our tent site right at the top, in a small, flat, gravelly oasis surrounded by low ramparts of bedrock. There was just enough room for our tents.

Over the edge we could see straight to the bottom of what looked like a small lake. Fish breaking the surface sent concentric ripples across the surface. Where we had landed our kayaks the channel was constricted, and we could see water streaming out into the bay as the tide fell. The low sun sent a glow of orange and gold across the surrounding islands and shelves, sending into relief the endless pattern of hill-like ledges of bare rock and calm pools.

Kristin examined all the lichens that coated the rocks. Some were black, others were speckled with discs of blue-gray and pale gray.

These seemed to be the color and texture of the rock until she looked more closely and found that everything was studded with translucent pink crystals: white rock studded with pink, dark rock studded with pink and gleaming with mica. A deposit of sharp gravel had drifts of pink garnets we could pick up by the handful.

The sun dimmed to deep ruby red and bloated into the horizon. In the half-light we heard geese honking, and the strange call of loons. We cooked out in the open, watching the changing light, seeing the half-moon rise above the rock into a still-glowing sky. We reminisced about our day as we ate. In the tent I pulled out the little whisky flask our friend Russell had given us, and we each had a sip to commemorate passing another bear. As we lay together in our sleeping bag recalling our previous, closer, encounter, we agreed we had been lucky. I was so glad that Kristin had kept her head and faced up to the bear. We had the rifles with us now, as they always were when we were on land for the night, one to either side. Tomorrow I would figure out a way to carry the rifle in my cockpit. I would have to be careful not to swamp the cockpit, but from now on the rifle was going to be a closer companion.

The next day we paddled offshore beyond the outer reefs, content with a long view of rounded small hills shading away layer behind layer, in ever-fainter shades of blue-gray, to distant mountains dappled with snow. Even way out here rocks poked up through the surface, so we had to take care. Everything was ambiguous. We were uncertain what we were looking at when we approached floating ice, wary in case a polar bear was among the floating chunks. We viewed a substantial white shape in the distance that took us a long time to reach. The object was a small iceberg, mushroom-shaped, grounded on the tip of a shoal. The cap was a flattened dome, smooth and white; the rim was undercut all around, sculpted like a limestone formation in a cave or the gills of a mushroom. But these gills glowed intense blue-green as if lit from within. Little trickles ran down the fluted surface and dripped into the sea. Beneath us the bright ice bulging out under our hulls glowed green. We could hear the quiet grinding of ice against rock and the tinkling drip of water, and feel the temperature chilling as we drew close. Above the sculpted ice the clouds had been building all morning, bubbling out and blistering. By evening we were paddling in cold rain.

CHAPTER **9**

Killinek and Polar Air Routes

The tide picked up speed as we approached Forbes Sound. The weather glowered with overcast skies, light rain, and poor visibility, and it was cold. Out of the mist appeared seabirds. These were not the ducks and loons and geese we'd seen so many of in Ungava Bay, these were the sea birds I was used to seeing in the North Atlantic around Iceland and Scotland and Norway. Fulmars slid by, a wingtip to the water, negotiating the gray waves without a shift of their dark-eyed gaze as they circled close, scrutinizing us. There were skuas, too, six in the first group, then a crowd of fourteen more, all winging in the direction of Hudson Strait. Heavy gannets flew past, their white plumage brilliant against the dark sky. The birds brightened my mood, helping me to ignore the cold, and making each paddle stroke lighter and easier. Judging by the riffles and then the rapids we were coming to, the tide was helping us plenty. Seals surfaced, one puffing repeatedly and loudly, oblivious to our being so close. Its two sucking nostrils puckered and wrinkled as they closed before the seal slowly arched forward and dived.

We crossed Forbes Sound toward Jackson Island, barely able to see the dark mountains at the back of the sound. McLelan Strait, the extension of Forbes Sound, fingers right through the Torngat Mountains from here on the west side in Quebec to emerge in Labrador on the east coast. Despite help from the tide and the distraction of trying to see the mountains, it seemed to take a long time to cross the sound. When we reached Jackson Island we were ready for a break. I spotted reefs that might offer shelter from the swell, and we aimed to pass behind them, accelerating into the gap with a powerful river of tide pulling us along. We turned from the current to spin into an eddy in the shelter of the reef.

Sheltered now from the full force of the swell, we were not sheltered from the chill rain. My fingers were almost useless with the cold, and I found it difficult to open my zippers and fasteners. I succeeded in unwrapping a chocolate bar, bit off a hard chunk, and looked around. What a noisy place. The tide was roaring past between the reef and the island, waves breaking everywhere, and the swell thundered ponderously on the outer side of the reef. The sounds seemed magnified and focused by the dark cliff of Jackson Island a few yards away. A dozen or more seals darted through the water in the tide race, bounding up through the surface as if super-energized by the frenzied waves. The cliffs, the heavy rounded shape of the hills, and the coastal features all looked familiar to me. So, too, did the shrouds of mist and persistent cold rain. The form of the land was very different from that we had been passing: steeper, darker, heavier; I recognized those characteristics from 1981 and felt excited.

We would soon intersect with my earlier route close to the northwest corner of Jackson Island, and for a short distance we would follow the same course I had paddled on my last day here in 1981. After that, we would continue what I began. For the last eight days of that trip I had relied on driftwood fires for cooking, having lost my stove at Lacy Island. The stove is likely rusting apart on the seabed; it sank during my night crash-landing on the rocks. But about where Kristin and I would join my earlier route is the spot where someone else's lost equipment rests on the bottom. Somewhere down there beneath the dark surface lies the corroding wreckage of a Sikorsky

S-38B seaplane that sank in 1929.

It gave me pause to consider how absorbing a personal challenge can be, and what it is that makes people start over after failure. I felt emotional at reaching this place after so many years, the place from which I could begin another attempt to see Labrador, in a kayak of my own design. Igor Sikorsky, fleeing from the Russian civil war, left his old life behind and began to work again using what he had learned of aircraft design in Russia to build aircraft in the United States. He is better known for the huge amphibious clipper planes and the helicopters he produced later in his career, but the S-38 lying on the seabed here was one of his early successes.

I tried to imagine myself in the 1920s caught up in the whirlwind of enthusiasm surrounding the development of airplane flight. The only experience I have to compare with it is the buzz of excitement and camaraderie, rivalry and secrecy, surrounding sea-kayaking projects in the 1970s. Milestone kayaking trips were being attempted, yet there were not many sea kayakers, and it was possible to know many of them personally and to know of many of the others. Much of the equipment for those kayak trips was adapted from other sports, and the kayaks themselves were often designed in garages and jury-rigged at home, not built in commercial workshops. In the 1920s airplanes were hand-framed in wood and usually skinned with cloth, allowing plenty of leeway for experimentation and modification. It was easy for us to sit here off northern Labrador, where the cloud-clogged landscapes revealed nothing man-made, and imagine the scene seventy years earlier.

At a time when Inuit here in Labrador still stretched sealskins over wooden frames to make hunting kayaks, Igor Sikorsky, working on Long Island, New York, stretched aluminum alloy skins over wooden frames to make the hulls of his new seaplanes, vehicles perhaps capable of carrying passengers to Europe and back. By 1929 the question was not whether airplanes could do that, for Alcock and Brown had already made the first nonstop flight across the Atlantic in June 1919 carrying with them a bag of mail. No, the questions were, "Who will be first?" and "When?" and "By what route?"

The crossing by Alcock and Brown from Newfoundland to Ireland took less than seventeen hours and finished ignominiously in a bog. But theirs was a far more direct route than that taken by three U.S. Navy Curtiss flying boats that had left Newfoundland a month earlier. Naval vessels positioned along the route for safety were able to assist the two planes that did not finish their journey. The third landed at the Azores after a fifteen-hour crossing, then stopped for a few days before crossing to Lisbon, Portugal. After a few days there the plane flew on to Plymouth, England. It was a large plane, 45 feet long with a wingspan of 126 feet, certainly big enough to carry a payload.

There were plenty of other adventurers meeting challenges and perhaps seeking glory. The Norwegian explorer, Roald Amundsen, who had already reached the South Pole overland, tried and failed to fly across the North Pole from Alaska to Spitzbergen in 1923. He made a second attempt in 1925 but was forced to land 120 miles short. In 1926 he finally flew over the pole in the dirigible *Norge*, piloted by the Italian, Nobile, flying east to west this time and making the first crossing of the Arctic Ocean by air from Spitzbergen to Alaska. The only round trip across the Atlantic by air had been done by the British in 1919 in an R-34 dirigible.

It was in this challenge-rich time of exploratory flights—in one-of-a-kind aircraft, among publicly feted successes and spectacular and often fatal failures—that Parker Dresser Cramer became visible. He figured the best way to fly transatlantic would be north, following a great-circle route from the United States over Labrador, Greenland, Iceland, and the Faroe Islands to Europe. This would take him well north of the polar front, where the polar air mass interacts with the tropical air mass to spawn the weather systems that march across the Atlantic from west to east. It would also break the journey into sections of no more than 500 miles each, offering the possibility of refueling on route. Refueling would be crucial to Cramer's vision of a two-way air route that could carry mail and passengers across the Atlantic, for the weight of fuel needed for a nonstop flight would preclude carrying passengers.

The world map we saw in grammar school uses a Mercator projection, which displays north-south distances accurately but greatly stretches the east-west distances to fit the paper. The North Pole is shown as the line along the top of the map, equaling the circumference at the equator, and the vertical lines of longitude are depicted as parallel, not converging as they are in life. Such a projection creates the illusion that the shortest distance from London to Seattle would cross over the island of Newfoundland. But if we look at a globe, we can see that the shortest route passes over Arctic Canada.

Cramer made his first attempt in 1928, leaving Rockford, Illinois, with Bert J. R. Hassell in a Stinson monoplane. Their attempt to fly to Sweden ended when they missed their target on Greenland, ran out of fuel, and made a forced landing. They hiked out across the icecap and reappeared two weeks later at a University of Michigan Meteorological Expedition base in Greenland, after being presumed dead. They received considerable notice for the adventure. Undeterred, in April 1929 Cramer flew a Cessna monoplane from Nome, Alaska, over Siberia to return to Nome and continue to New York. Still harboring his dream of a northern great-circle flight, Cramer needed a backer, and he approached the owner of the *Chicago Tribune*, Colonel Robert R. McCormick.

McCormick was a flying enthusiast. He owned airplanes and he had survived several crashes. He was the man who founded the town and the pulp mills at Baie Comeau, where we had turned inland from the Saint Lawrence River on our drive across the continent. He used one of his airplanes, a Sikorsky S-38 amphibian, to reach the Canadian lakes where he had vacation lodges and paper pulp mills. McCormick was intrigued by Cramer's proposition, particularly because of its potential for a payload. He understood what Cramer meant when he declared the Sikorsky S-38 the only seagoing plane capable of making the route possible, because he flew one. If Cramer wanted to be able to carry passengers across the north Atlantic, the S-38 was already equipped to carry eight or nine passengers with baggage in addition to the crew of two, a load of up to 3,930 pounds. It also had a range of more than 500 miles without refueling. McCormick was excited by the idea. This could be a perfect exclusive story for his newspaper that would guarantee increased sales.

For this great-circle route attempt, he did not offer the plane he owned. Instead he ordered a new one, the first of an upgrade model, the S-38B. With a standard fuel capacity of 180 to 270 gallons, the S-38B offered a range of 750 miles at a cruising speed of 110 miles per hour. McCormick had it modified by removing the cabin accommodations to make room for three 100-gallon fuel tanks, in that way doubling its useful range. He named his new purchase the *Untin Bowler*. The name was inspired by a remark from a London hatter who had made him a cork derby to wear while riding to hounds. The hatter told him he needed "a 'untin' bowler so if you fall off yer 'orse you won't 'urt yer 'ead."

The Sikorsky S38 was a strange-looking contraption. Designed as a seaplane, the wood-frame fuselage was shaped like a boat, but covered with a skin of Duralumin, an aluminum alloy that is resistant to corrosion from salt water yet light in weight. The cockpit and cabin were a single enclosed chamber, divided by an interior bulkhead with windows. Technically a sesquiplane rather than a true biplane, having one-and-a-half wings rather than two, the short lower wings were fitted with pontoons to keep the wings above water and offer stability. Struts and wires held the upper wing high above the cabin, and also held the framework that extended rearward from the upper wing to support the tail and rudder.

Two Pratt & Whitney 450-horsepower Wasp engines, suspended beneath the upper wing, powered the plane with two-bladed propellers. Wheels in addition to the pontoons permitted the plane to operate from land as well as water. The craft was quite large. It measured 40 feet 3 inches in length, with the span of the upper wings reaching 71 feet 8 inches, almost twice the span of the floatplanes the Canadian government had used for the first explorations of Ungava Bay. The smaller and lighter floatplanes could be pulled ashore, a distinct advantage over larger seaplanes, but they could not carry the desired load.

On 28 June 1929, with Robert H. Gast as pilot and Cramer as copilot, navigator, and radioman, the aircraft took off from the water at Flushing Bay, New York, and headed for Albany. Two days later the plane reached Chicago amid considerable publicity. Cramer had negotiated the use of the aircraft in return for exclusive news rights for McCormick and the *Chicago Tribune* newspaper. They would carry the Tribune's aviation editor, Robert W. Wood, with them.

In preparation for launching from the fresh water of Lake Michigan they filled their regular fuel tanks but left their extra tanks empty. They planned to fill all the tanks at James Bay on the way north, where the salt water would make the plane more buoyant and better able to take off with the extra fuel load. Wood, before leaving, described for the newspaper the arctic equipment in the cabin and the full mailbag they hoped to deliver to Europe.

They left on 3 July. The planned route would cross the wilderness of northern Quebec to Remi Lake, Rupert House, and Port Burwell, then Greenland, Iceland, Norway and Berlin. Their safety depended on their being able to see landmarks. When they encountered bad weather they landed and waited. One such delay was at the Hudson's Bay Company post at the mouth of the Great Whale River, 600 miles short of Port Burwell, in weather that was a foggy and chilly 32 degrees Fahrenheit. Finally, with a forecast of overcast skies, Gast took to the air again on 7 July.

After four hours flying the S-38B crossed over Ungava Bay and followed the eastern shore until again it hit bad weather. Backtracking toward Kuujjuaq, the crew then decided the weather wasn't too bad, so they landed on the water near an island in a channel protected from the bigger ice. According to Robert Wood, three Inuit who were out hunting seals on the northern shore of the bay sighted the *Bowler* riding at anchor and scrambled through the ice in their kayaks, defying all laws of equilibrium. The three brown men with walrus mustaches stood thunderstruck before the big kayak with wings.

Cramer tried out a few Inuit words to find the direction and distance to Port Burwell. He wrote out a message to the Northwest Mounted Police there, reporting their position as forty miles south of Port Burwell, and saying that the plane and crew were safe but were waiting for the fog to clear. He added they might be marooned for several days, so if possible they should look for them by motorboat. He asked the Inuit to deliver the note to Port Burwell; it took them three weeks to get there with the message.

The fog lifted on the ninth and the plane was able to fly north, with the tops of the Torngat Mountains visible to the east. Northern Labrador was enveloped in fog. Unable to find Port Burwell because they could not see it, they selected a place to land. When the morning sun and a northwest wind had cleared the fog, they flew north until they saw the three buildings that made up the Port Burwell settlement. They landed nearby in Amittoq Inlet at 7:10 a.m. on 9 July 1929. The water was scattered with ice.

Amittoq Inlet is a long narrow channel that cuts deeply into Killinek Island. Thirty-foot tides drain and fill it, making a current like a river. Shifting ice, rain, and poor visibility now trapped the plane. Enlisting the Port Burwell community, the crew organized the Inuit to carry fuel from the harbor on the south side of the hill to the inlet on the north side. Each carried on his back ten gallons at a time—sixty pounds—and the refueling took all day. Despite the heavy labor, Wood wrote that the factor of the Hudson's Bay Company Post would give them each a portion of tobacco for their trouble "and they will be well satisfied." Maybe that was what he thought his readers in the United States expected to hear, but the pay was not that mean: a receipt in Cramer's notes said the factor collected $200 in wages for the Inuit.

Drifting ice and the threat of grounding on the rocks as the tide fell complicated their task, and there was always the chance the plane could be swept away by the outgoing tide. Two tons of fuel had been loaded by the Inuit, and all the tanks were full. At midnight Gast taxied the airplane into the current and moored it. The crew prepared to fend off any ice that floated near and waited for good weather.

On 11 July, ice shoved the aircraft onto the rocks and punctured it three feet above the waterline. While six Inuit sat on the wings and tail pushing away floating ice, Gast and Cramer mended the hole. The tide fell and the airplane was left stranded on the rocks. Early the next morning, a piece of ice "as big as a house" floated into it and crumpled part of the rudder. Once again the pilots made repairs, but each time the tide fell and dropped it on the rocks the plane was battered more. Eventually the wind pushed the ice out into Ungava Bay, freeing the plane to taxi around into Fox Harbor, nearby.

With the plane moored to a stable platform of ice at the head of the harbor, a few hundred yards from the abandoned Moravian church, the crew returned to the machine shop where the broken pontoon fittings were being repaired. The barometer dropped and the wind rose. Soon came the message that the winds had cracked the ice, and by the time they reached the shore the plane had already drifted into midstream and was heading for open water, where the ice finished her off. It tore holes in the hull, water poured in, and the *Bowler* sank. Gast, Cramer, and Wood eventually found their way home on a ship that stopped at Port Burwell. Their attempt to fly to Europe was foiled by northern Labrador's tides, fog, and ice.

Cramer persisted. For his third attempt at a great-circle flight, in August 1931, he followed a slightly different route. He had Oliver Paquette as copilot. They crossed Canada, Baffin Island, Greenland, and Iceland to the Shetland Islands, passing over the Arctic Circle on the way. After refueling on Shetland, and on the last leg of the journey, Cramer radioed that they could see Norway. They never made it. A Dutch fishing boat picked up Cramer's briefcase from the North Sea not far from the coast of Norway. Five months later the wreckage of his airplane was found drifting hundreds of miles away. Cramer had pushed the boundaries of what was possible.

Today aircraft crossing from Europe to North America's West Coast commonly fly north over Scotland and Iceland, cross Greenland, and pass over the coast of Baffin Island or northern Labrador, or above Hudson Strait. They do not need to refuel. Labrador is now merely a landmark, often obscured by fog and cloud.

And here we were, in modern times, Kristin and I in kayaks near Port Burwell, contemplating a landing. Port Burwell lies to the eastern end of a channel between Killinek Island and Jackson Island. A boulder beach joins the two at low tide, creating two bays, back to back, but the size of the boulders makes it an unfriendly landing for heavily laden kayaks. Instead we headed toward the little ruined church that sits on the hillside to the west, beneath which is a gentle beach. The rain that spattered and rebounded from the dark water fell from heavy cloud that barely cleared the steep dark cliffs. I looked around the narrow channel and felt shut in a box.

I drifted to a standstill in the shallows and slipped my feet down into the clear water onto gravel and mud. Kristin grounded beside me. We lifted the kayaks one at a time onto the beach. We were both in a whirl of emotion, Kristin because she knew how much it meant to me to return to this spot, and me for the memories it brought back. For all that, it seemed a sad place.

Years before, the settlement at Port Burwell had been a successful community. The trading post manager, who was also responsible for handing out federal welfare, reported there was almost no occasion when he needed to do so. The community supported itself entirely by hunting and fishing, and it was a great place for it. With areas nearby where the sea never froze over completely because of the powerful tidal streams, the hunting season for seal and walrus was long and reliable. Seals migrated through McLelan Strait so there was opportunity to hunt them while they passed, and fishing everywhere was excellent. Caribou were seldom seen this far north but the hunters did not have to travel far to find them. The meat was eaten and the furs were sold to purchase new necessities such as guns and ammunition, boats, fuel and vehicles.

Although little was needed from outside except medical help and a means to trade, the government's plan to centralize the population eventually overruled the wishes of the people. The forty-seven residents were notified by radio in February 1978 that the federal government was sending planes to fly everyone out. Port

Burwell, or Killinek as it was called historically, was to be closed down. Since that date northern Labrador has been uninhabited. That does not mean nobody ever visits. When I reached Port Burwell on my journey in 1981 the buildings were still in good condition. Three French-speaking Canadians had taken over one of the buildings as a base for the summer while they monitored the weather in Hudson Strait. They seemed very comfortable.

By now we had reached the top of the beach and I could see that the buildings, which looked almost complete from the water, were actually decayed and holed and showing signs of collapse. The roadway running between the buildings toward the banded red and white antennas on the hill was muddy and churned up. We trudged in our wet clothes past deep puddles to the first buildings. In the open front of a hangar we could see a bulldozer with tracks, no doubt the cause of the churned mud.

We stepped up into a building where turquoise paint still clung to rotted wood. The smell of decay was almost overpowering, dispelling any idea I might have harbored about pitching the tent inside. Rain had pooled on the vinyl-covered floor. Half-expecting to fall through the sodden wood steps on our way out we used just the edges and retraced our path down the hill. To one side lay the rubbish dump, a tangle of rusty metal that cascaded from the ruined church to the steep rock slope and dropped to the sea. Along with the carcasses of tracked vehicles were rusted bedsprings. I don't know how much of this dump was created when the people moved out and had to abandon everything they couldn't carry. Told to take only their most portable belongings, the Port Burwell people were split into five groups to be relocated into five different communities, none of which was expecting them. They were dropped off without housing or any way to make a living, and far from their hunting territory. There have been no follow up programs or funding initiatives to help these people in their new situation.

Killinek is one of those areas possibly populated for thousands of years. Kohlmeister and Kmoch knew of a community there prior to their 1811 journey, because they had spent time with Killinek families who had traveled south to Okak to trade. Commander Gordon is credited with discovering the harbor of Port Burwell in 1884. He named it after Mr. H.W. Burwell of London, Ontario, the man he left in charge of the observation station they built there that year, part of the government expedition to study ice conditions and their effect on navigation in Hudson Strait. This was the observation station they called Number One. Two Inuit families were living about six miles away. The study group spent one winter recording weather and ice conditions before being picked up again.

Knowledge of Hudson Strait conditions might have been useful. Beginning in the 1860s, Newfoundland cod fishermen began to exploit the grounds off Labrador, and by the late 1800s it was estimated that 30,000 fishermen in 1,000 to 1,200 vessels arrived on the Labrador coast every year between June and October. During August and September a fleet of schooners fished the northern coast from Cape Mugford to the entrance to Hudson Strait. Job Brothers of Saint Johns, Newfoundland, opened a trading post at Port Burwell in 1898. They constructed four buildings, using one as a store.

One summer, the enigmatic Sir Wilfred Grenfell, known as the "Labrador Doctor" for his years of medical work up and down the coast each summer, took a representative of the Moravian brethren north to Killinek Island in the ship *Strathcona*. Grenfell was looking for McLelan Strait and sailed through it. The Moravian representative was looking for a mission site, and he selected one that year at Port Burwell. When the Job Brothers sold them their trading station in 1904, the Moravians gained a potential source of income.

Samuel Milliken Stewart, the missionary who moved there in 1904, is the man who escaped east that winter to Fort Chimo, and by chance met the New Yorker, Dillon Wallace, after his canoe trip. The Killinek mission effort was not dashed; a large new building constructed during the next few years was operational until 1928. A Doctor Hutton, who spent some years living in Labrador in the early twentieth century, visited Killinek in September 1908. He described arriving on the mission supply ship *Harmony* through the "awkward" currents of Gray Strait. It took two men to steady the wheel as the ship "danced and throbbed, and the water was all broken by little whirlpools on which the sea-birds feared to settle." From the hill behind the settlement an Inuit guide pointed out the Tutjat, or Button Islands, to the north. Tutjat means Stepping Stones, the name offering credence for Hutton to an old Inuit story. Long ago, Inuit people from Labrador went north beyond Killinek—the name means "the end" or "the limit" —crossed Gray Strait, and traveled through the Button Islands. From the farthest Button Island, Lacy, which rises to more than a thousand feet, it was sometimes possible to see what we call Resolution Island in the distance. The party crossed in their kayaks and found people there whose words they could understand, who were different from themselves only because they had lived apart for so long. From then on the islands were called Tutjat, Stepping Stones, and Resolution Island was called Tutjarluk, the Big Stepping Stone, from which one can cross to the Lower Savage Islands to reach Baffin Island.

By 1925 the Hudson's Bay Company had taken over all the Moravian trading posts in Labrador, and three years later the Killinek mission was abandoned. The following year, 1929, the *Untin Bowler* pilot, Robert Gast, stranded after the sinking of the Sikorsky flying boat, rehung the old bell at the abandoned Moravian church and rang it. All the Inuit in the area gathered, expecting a sermon, but none was forthcoming. By 1950 even the Hudson's Bay trading post had closed. Until the people were flown out from Port Burwell (Killinek) in 1978, trade continued under Newfoundland government control through the North Labrador Trading Operations.

Evening was approaching, and I was anxious to camp away from this area, in a place where the surroundings were more pristine. We launched and returned along the north side of the channel, creeping through a narrow cut in the cliff to Amittoq Inlet. Looking east, we could see one or two places we could land, but eliminated the first few before crossing to a tiny gut with a beach. I scrambled up the boulders of a waterfall to discover flat grass at the top. Clumps of purple-flowering willowherb shuddered in the breeze. With potential for a view if the weather improved, plus fresh water and flat ground for the tent, this seemed as good a place as any to stay, so we unloaded and carried everything up. Uncertain how high the waves would reach if the wind blew hard, we also carried the kayaks up.

In the chill of evening we moved rapidly to get everything organized, anticipating warmth and coziness. I fired up the stove and reheated the warm water from the flask to make hot chocolate. That revived us for long enough to change and cook, but even then I felt cold. I pulled on all my layers of clothing—thick socks, hat, extra jacket—and huddled in the sleeping bag, and still I felt cold. It was that gnawing cold, when the temperature may be above freezing but the humidity is high. It is the weather for which this area is notorious. I had brought from my kayak the little flask of whisky, and I poured two tiny measures into thimble-sized ceramic tumblers. I proposed a toast to safe journeys and a second to the well-being of all the people who were forced against their wishes to leave this place. The day was 9 August. In 1981 I had hiked on 5 September to this side of Amittoq Inlet from my landing place on the northern coast of Killinek Island while waiting for gales to subside. I felt moved. The map showed us at the northern tip of Labrador, beyond the northeastern tip of mainland North America. From here we would turn south. Turning the map upside down I could see the perspective of the coast spreading south. So many memories and emotions flooded through me I simply said, "I can't believe I'm here again." From the map I guessed we were directly across the inlet from where the *Untin Bowler* had been tethered for refueling. The *Bowler* had finished its trip here in northern Labrador, and so had I last time. But this time? This time, with Kristin, I was better situated for a second attempt. We were in good shape.

Next morning, wind and fog presented themselves together, typical summer weather for the entrance to Hudson Strait. In most places in this world, wind blows mist away, so it's rare to find the two at the same time, but not here. Bundled in warm clothing and waterproofs, we wandered around the immediate vicinity peering down the cliff to the noisy sea. We clambered down the waterfall to the beach to look at the rocks, and collected driftwood sticks, which we set under an overhang to dry, ready for a small fire. Finally we crawled into the shelter tent and relaxed with hot chocolate. But there was far too much to look at to spend our day inside.

I was out looking at flowers when I heard Kristin's stage whisper, "Nigel! Are you there?" There was such urgency in her whisper that I found her quickly. "There's a polar bear," she announced brusquely. "It's back a bit from our tents. I didn't know where you were." With rifles on our shoulders we skirted the hill until we could see the bear. It was a quarter of a mile away and apparently just walking past. It dawdled, sniffing to one side, then to the other, taking a few paces, then dawdling and sniffing again. Maybe it was finding berries? We climbed to get a better view. Kristin made sure we didn't break the skyline, but the bear seemed oblivious to our presence. Perhaps the wind was working in our favor. The large white shape dissolved into the mist.

Toward evening the weather cleared to reveal a blue horizon. Icebergs far from shore appeared crisp and close. Sun reflected from the water to drench the headland in golden light. The low light from the sun combined with the reflected light from the water made the lichens and grasses glow as if lit from within. It was like stepping up from a basement to discover full sunshine on a summer day, dazzling and uplifting. Now expecting to be able to leave in the morning, we carried our kayaks down to the beach and propped them sideways on the steep bank of pebbles above the reach of the tide, wedging them in place with pieces of driftwood. On my deck was the chart showing McLelan Strait. I slipped it out from under the bungees to study it.

I wanted to visit Port Burwell once more, to look inside the church. But the falling tide that could speed us through McLelan Strait was due to begin far too early for us to use if we stopped there. So we would take our time at Port Burwell tomorrow and then aim for an ancient Inuit village site at the western end of the strait for the night. We could spend the afternoon exploring, find a good place to camp, and be perfectly placed to catch the tide the following morning. The northern shore of Forbes Sound, between Port Burwell and the entrance to McLelan Strait, is indented enough to offer eddies in which we could avoid paddling against the west-going tide. Those eddies would allow us to creep right into the mouth of McLelan Strait as far as the shore opposite the village site. From there it is less than two hundred yards to cross the strait, a distance we could easily ferry-glide if the current ran against us by adjusting our angle into the current, constantly compensating to make a straight-line crossing. We had a good plan. I did not see any way it could come unstuck. I just felt content.

I crouched low on a slab of golden rock. With the sun low on the horizon, the water droplets clinging between the stiff leaves and stem of the short roseroot plants gleamed like tiny glass globes on miniature Christmas trees. Roseroot. This small succulent with its plump purple-tinged leaves triggered a memory. I had crouched like this to paint a picture of such a roseroot plant just a few miles north from here on the Button Islands in 1981, my numb fingers struggling to control the paintbrush. Roseroot! That was the day after I had crossed Hudson Strait.

CHAPTER 10

Crossing Hudson Strait

Sitting on Resolution Island in the summer of 1981, I had faced a dilemma, and my options were straightforward: Either I would continue south across Hudson Strait to northern Labrador and onward to Nain, or I would continue around Resolution Island and return north to Iqaluit, Baffin Island. The series of delays that had begun at the London airport with a bomb alert had stretched into two weeks. Now I was two weeks behind schedule.

Leaving Iqaluit on 19 August I had picked my way along the

southern shore of Frobisher Bay, negotiating the fiercely tidal channels between the islands that spread across that long inlet, to finally reach Resolution Island on 27 August. Everything I had learned about the weather, from research and from talking with the locals at Iqaluit, made me expect strong winds and stormy weather by late August or early September. My twenty-four hours of summer daylight were shrinking toward the equinox on 21 September. Forty miles of open water lay between where I stood and northern Labrador, where the second leg of my coastal journey would begin. The tides that rush through that strait reach seven knots in places and cause tidal rapids that extend fifteen miles south from Resolution Island. On the far side of the strait were the Button Islands, a target four miles wide. I would have to make the crossing in a single day, and I needed one calm day of weather to make it the nonevent I planned. Then I could proceed down the Labrador coast I so wanted to see.

Resolution Island, named in 1612 by Thomas Button after his ship *Resolution*, is a low rugged island of bare-looking rock. During my transit down its western coast it presented an oppressive appearance, worsened by a dark overcast day, rain, and poor visibility. I had landed at dusk and, in the absence of any suitable fresh water, broke ice from a stranded berg and melted it to prepare my meal. I felt ambivalent about crossing Hudson Strait the following day. True, there was little wind, but it was cold, and the fog was so dense I could not see the sea from my tent. I took out my small box of watercolor paints to paint wild flowers. I opened my notebook, and poured some water into an empty film canister. Painting forces me to relax: to focus closely on the proportions, the subtle shading of color, on details I've never noticed before, I scarcely have conscious thought for anything else. Surrounded by cold fog I knelt on the ground with my tiny brush in hand and retreated into myself. Time ceased to have any importance. All that mattered was that gradual application of paint onto the page. When I stopped, I felt calm.

The magnitude of the approaching crossing had been causing me some anxiety ever since I had begun planning the trip. Now I could go no farther without deciding either to turn back or to make the crossing. I had paddled two hundred fifty miles from Iqaluit, on Baffin Island; my destination, Nain, was almost four hundred miles farther to the south. There was nobody to share my final decision, no way to obtain a weather forecast, nobody to double-check my navigation strategy, and of course, in those days, no GPS receiver to indicate my position on the water once I started out. It would be like launching onto a moving sidewalk that would speed up to seven knots in one direction, slow, then reverse direction, and speed up again in the other direction as I crossed it from one side to the other. Beyond the turbulent strait were the Button Islands. I turned the page in my little book and began painting the red foliage of woolly lousewort, its roots embedded in an almost white blanket of lichen. That kept my mind occupied for a time. Then I melted ice and made myself a hot drink before settling to paint the papery cream-colored petals of a mountain avens. Fog plumped up the black lichens that encrusted the rock around me.

My strategy for the crossing was sound enough, considering there was no detailed tidal information to help me. I had drawn a straight line on my chart between Resolution Island and the Button Islands to represent the path straight across as if there were no tide at all. If I aimed at an angle to the tide, to ferry-glide along that line, it would add enormously to the distance I would have to paddle. It would also be impossible to guess the strength of the tide hour by hour and figure out a succession of compass bearings to compensate. If, however, I balanced the expected push in one direction as the tide rose against the pull in the opposite direction when it fell later in the day, then in theory I would need only to paddle the distance signified by my drawn line. I would allow myself to be carried first west, then back east again onto my target. It was not unreasonable to expect to be swept sideways as much as fifteen miles during the six hours of rising tide and to be brought back the same distance through the ebb. That strategy presupposes the tide in the northern half of Hudson Strait on the flood is equal but opposite to the ebb in the southern half. That is unlikely, and there could be a big difference.

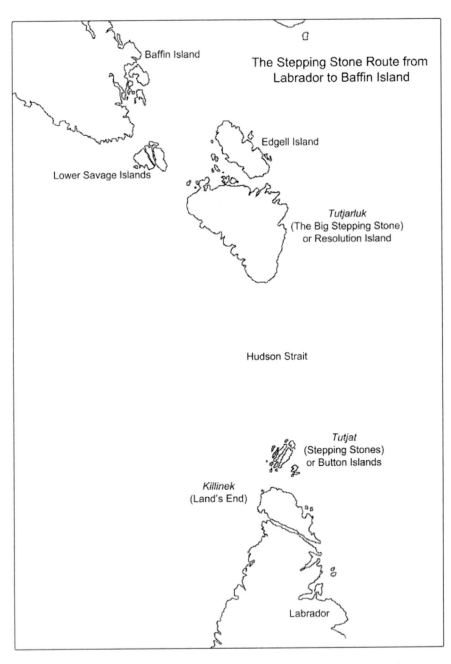

The Admiralty's *Sailing Directions* describes an area of strong overfalls and tide rips that extend eighteen miles southeast and fifteen miles south from Resolution Island. I could avoid paddling through this area by allowing the flood tide to sweep me west during the first hours of my crossing. If I aimed east of the Button Islands, instead of at them, any difference in the flow in either direction would result in my arriving at some undefined place east of the islands—farther or closer depending on the actual strength of the tide. In either case, by now turning west I would sooner or later hit the islands. To achieve that I planned to paddle the last section with the help of the rising tide, and that dictated my departure time from Resolution Island. Without this strategy I would risk missing the islands altogether in poor visibility, and if I did miss them how would I know whether to turn east or west?

Poor visibility was certainly possible. The entrance to Hudson Strait rates as one of the foggiest places in the world, with fog reported on one day in two between June and September. So I deliberated, watched the fog, painted wild flowers, and melted ice for hot drinks.

Next morning, after I had sat in the tent by candlelight and monitored three consecutive hours of steady pressure on my barometer, I decided to make the crossing. It was raining hard and the fog was dense when I launched. Within minutes I was out of sight of land and found myself on a rougher sea than I expected, with lumpy and irregular waves. Encircled by fog, I watched the sea buck and jump restlessly as I tried to keep a steady compass course. I paddled hard. Now that I was committed to the crossing there would be no turning back and no holding back.

A wind began to blow from the west and gradually increased in strength. What began gently soon kicked up marching waves. As the wind increased further, the crests of the waves began tumbling until my small visible area of sea became streaked with whitecaps. Periodically a breaker would wash across my kayak, drenching me. The fog persisted, the wind continued to increase, the waves got bigger, but there was nothing to do but keep on paddling. Hour by hour I kept up my pace, now bracing into breakers powerful enough to carry my kayak sideways. Cold water gushed down my neck and up my sleeves, despite my closing the neck as firmly as I could. Water pooled in the arms of my jacket, sloshing around my elbows until either I braced against a breaking wave, when all the chill water poured down past my armpit into my wetsuit, or I opened the wrist of my jacket to spill the water out. But as soon as my sleeve was drained another wave would fill it again. Occasionally I saw a skua flying low. Sometimes a seal reared its head from the water. Once the huge head of a walrus emerged beside me like the stump of a tree. I was unhappy. My hands were so cold my fingers could hardly grasp the food in my jacket pocket. The cheese, and the chocolate with fruit and nuts, I clung to as the waves crashed, and I bit off chunks when my kayak balanced for a moment, but the honey I carried had set so hard with the cold I could not force it from the tube.

In time the sky brightened, and once or twice the sun appeared as a pale moonlike disc, only to vanish again. After five hours of hard paddling the visibility had improved to maybe half a mile. A whole range of possible outcomes had been marching like demons through my mind regarding the wind. One thought was that I would be blown east so far that to paddle against the wind at the end of the day would be too much for me. What if the wind funneled in squalls around the high ground at Cape Chidley and the Button Islands, and I became too tired to fight my way to shore? What if the wind continued to increase? How strong could it get? After all, September here is notorious for gales. In the end I succumbed to my intuition and decided to change course to narrow my planned margin of error. But by how many degrees should I change? I pushed on through the waves while I pondered this question. There was no easy answer. What effect would a change of ten degrees have? Would I still end up east of the islands? What if I changed by 20 degrees? In the end I made a small adjustment.

After seven hours of paddling out of sight of land I was talking to myself. I began to wish I had waited for a calm day with clear weather with no fog. Part of me wanted to panic, but a voice inside told me to be calm. I knew I should not expect to see land yet in this visibility. Half an hour later the fog parted to reveal a shadow in the distance, and I was overjoyed. My excitement turned to dismay when I pointed my bow at it and noted the direction from my compass. Surely I could not be that far to the east? As I bounded across the waves my mind reeled with the calculation of how far the flood tide might have carried me and how long it might be before the end of the ebb. When I looked again the shadow had changed shape. I was seeing fog banks, not islands. I yearned to see land.

I had been paddling more than eight hours out of sight of land when the dark shapes of rounded headlands and low hills appeared, and this time they did not change shape. Around me the waves continued to tumble from my right side, and the mist still drifted, but now in dense banks with open spaces. I was inexpressibly happy to be in sight of my goal. Paddling on a bearing of 230 degrees I was heading straight for the islands and still traveling fast. I expected to arrive in another two hours according to my estimated speed, but I was prepared for this to be three hours. I was on the home stretch, and relieved to realize that. I looked at my hands. The skin had absorbed a lot of water and looked wrinkled and white. With the constant immersion my right hand was almost completely numb, but I still had feeling in my left. I hurried on.

I don't know how long I paddled before I realized I was making little progress. I was used to open crossings. When approaching land at kayaking speed the view does not change much until you get quite close, but this was different. Instead of being washed toward the islands with the rising tide I seemed to be held off by it. The clouds were slowly breaking up, and although there were still patches of fog, it looked as though the sun would soon shine.

The waves built in size and steepness as the tide began to pick up speed and run more strongly against the wind. The breaks cracked like gunfire and the foam tumbled heavily for some distance before reforming, leaving a stain of lacy white froth behind on the surface. First I tried to dodge the breaks, sprinting ahead or holding back a moment in anticipation. Then as the sea roughened up more and there were breakers everywhere it became futile to try. I had so little opportunity to get out of the way I was frequently buried in a slide of white water that forced itself down my neck and up my sleeves. The sun emerged beneath the cloud and then, all too soon, began to sink over the horizon. As I was forced farther past the islands by the tide, darkness fell. The beacon on Goodwin Island, flashing every six seconds, shone ever more clearly, but for long periods it vanished, hidden by the waves.

Slowly I began to gain on the island, scared beyond my grimmest imagination. As the last light from the sun oozed from the sky, to be replaced by a dense cover of stars, I fought to stay upright, skidding across walls of water that reared up at me from the dark. The percussive explosion of each new wave that broke close to me drowned out the background roar of falling water. The sudden appearance of white broken water glowing in the dark was all I could see of the waves. I could not tell if a wave was about to break except by the way it lifted my stern abruptly, throwing my bow into the trough. Then my paddling accelerated me into a surf ride, until either the falling crest engulfed me and threw my kayak sideways into a broach, or I stalled out, the starry sky showing at my bow for a moment as my stern dropped to meet the next approaching wall. I kept reminding myself of all the surfing I had done over the years. I kept telling myself that I should be able to work with the waves in the dark, that I had paddled many times in the dark before, that I had enough experience to do this if I kept my head, but the truth was I was close to terrified.

It is hard to tell when I knew I was creeping up toward land again. But the shock of seeing the bright white line of a breaker across my bow rather than coming from behind startled me into panic. As my bow lifted abruptly and the force of the break hit me full in the chest, I realized I could be over a rock or a shoal. In the dark I had no way to tell. I paddled frantically and later found myself riding on smaller waves. The waves were breaking more gently close to me while the deeper thunder of heavier breakers continued at a distance. Perhaps I was clear of the main tide race. Bright sparks of bioluminescence frothed in the water around me and I looked up at a densely star-studded sky. I had made it! I pushed forward quickly toward the flashing beacon, toward land. The dark shape of the cliff loomed against the stars, and I could see I was being carried along rapidly by the tide. Close to the cliff, I looked for the opening that should run between Lacy and Goodwin Islands. I had to enter that channel to reach calm water. There I would find somewhere safe to land.

The current sped me quickly along until I could see the entrance, but I couldn't enter. I was paddling forward with all my might but my kayak was swept across the entrance and farther from the cliff. I realized the tide was running out of the channel much faster than I could paddle. I was being swept back out to sea. Changing tactics I aimed across the channel toward Lacy Island, sprinting hard for it in my desperation not to be distanced again from land. I reached close enough to smell sour dankness and to see the white foam of swells breaking up against its base.

Powerless to reach the shelter of the channel between the islands, I still had to land somewhere. The current swept me along, rushing me east so quickly I was afraid I might be carried from the islands again. I just had to land, but where? The charts and topographic maps were useless to me in the dark without access to a flashlight, and I had studied them well enough to know they lacked enough detail to show me places to land. I already knew the best of the likely places lay between the islands. Tormented, I skirted the shore straining to see any detail in the dark.

These cliffs rise steeply to almost a thousand feet. As I rounded the headland I could see a low spine of land extending from the base. Could this be a beach? I peered at the dark line silhouetted against the sky, but as I came farther around the corner it separated from the cliff. It was a distant island. I reached a shore where I thought I might try to land, but I could not make it out clearly enough to risk paddling closer. Waves were crashing against the shore. I could not get close enough to see what the shore was like while staying beyond the breakers. I paddled farther, finding another slope silhouetted against the sky, this one less steep than the last. I sat offshore trying to sense what sort of shore this was. If only I could see. I felt totally chilled. I had to make shore as soon as possible.

I could hear that tumbling-wave sound, so different from the impact of the waves against the cliff around the corner. I could no longer see the sheets of white rising against the dark that I saw earlier beneath the cliff, where swells were impacting. Surely this must be a beach. I decided to land here and eased closer. Without warning I was lifted and pushed rapidly forward by a wave breaking around me. I steered with my paddle to keep straight then rammed into something solid. The jarring crash threw me forward onto my deck. Then as broken water churned around the kayak my bow bobbed free and the wave swept me forward again. Realizing I was on a ledge of rock, not a beach, I pushed out from my cockpit into waist deep water and grabbed my kayak to run up the shore. But as my feet hit the rock I knew I was in trouble. The rock was slick as ice. I could not gain my feet.

The backwash swept me off balance and dragged me sprawling down over the ledges into the next pile of broken water. I clung to the kayak, not knowing which way was up or which way was down under the dark water. The moment my head broke the surface I gasped for air, but the wave tumbled me over and over up the slippery rock. Frantically trying to stand, I was bowled over by the kayak and dragged back into the sea. I felt angry. I had finally got to touch land but was unable to cross these last few feet. Then my foot caught in a crack in the rock. I clung on, forcing my foot down, willing it to remain stuck while the wave drained. Quickly I crawled up to the next big step in the ledge, dragging my kayak behind me. Desperate to maintain my new-won ground, I clung on tightly to the rock with one hand and my kayak with the other while wave after wave pounded around me. I managed to haul the kayak up over the step onto the next level and kept dragging it until I was out of the reach of the waves. I felt spent. Moving quickly, I pulled off the hatches with numb hands and started unloading. I ate mouthfuls of fruitcake as I pulled out bag after bag of gear. Giddy with cold I pulled on the waterproofs I used on land over the top of my wet clothes, and when I found my sleeping bag I crawled up the rocks to find a spot sheltered from the wind, wriggled into the sleeping bag, and began to shake.

My landing on Lacy Island in the dark was hardly one to be proud of, but I was alive. I discovered the next day that beyond the bruising I had received from the rocks I had also been robbed of feeling in my fingers by frostbite. I had lost a bag from my deck that contained my stove, first aid kit, cutlery, and fishing tackle, items I kept handy for use during the day. I viewed the ledges I had landed on with dismay. I would never have attempted landing there in daylight.

With no choice but to press onward, I carried the kayak and all the gear about a mile along the ledges to a place I could launch, then kayaked south between the Button Islands. Trapped for several days by gales that prevented me from crossing Gray Strait, I marveled at the turbulence and the breakers flying in the wind. When the weather eased it was only briefly, for the wind sprang up almost immediately, catching me mid-channel and then pinning me ashore for another few days. September had arrived with a storm.

I amused myself in the storm by hiking across Killinek Island as far as the Amittoq Inlet and back, but when the wind next began to ease I was on my way again, heading west and south toward Port Burwell and McLelan Strait. My timing was perfect. I passed Amittoq Inlet and rounded the corner between Jackson Island and Killinek Island at the highest point in the tide. From here on through the strait I would have the rushing ebb tide to help me on my way. Near the abandoned village of Port Burwell, I caught sight of a small yellow boat heading for the beach. I sprinted to catch it and pulled ashore just as the men on board were jumping from the bow onto the beach. My kayak grounded not six feet from them, and I scrambled from the cockpit as the last man turned to join the group, but they scrunched away from me up the beach without even a nod of acknowledgement. I stared blankly at their backs as they strode away and wondered whether I had died crossing Hudson Strait after all. Surely they had seen me? Running after them I broke into their conversation with "Excuse me!" They turned. I had not died.

The yellow boat was a service vessel from an oil tanker, *Eastern Shell,* anchored out of sight behind Jackson Island. Three Canadians manning a weather station for the summer had based themselves in one of the buildings vacated in 1978 when the townspeople had been relocated, but they had run low on fuel for their generator. *Eastern Shell*, heading home before the Arctic winter arrived in full force, had stopped to refill their tanks. After two of the three weathermen had dined on board the tanker, the service team returned to disconnect the fuel pipe and bring them back. The tanker crew assumed I was the third weatherman; the weathermen figured I was with the tanker. Nobody had thought to greet me. The tanker had approached land on the full tide and was preparing to leave immediately while the tide was still high. A hurried conversation with the ship's master from the weather station radio secured me a passage south. A second call to Iqaluit informed my friends there that I was alive. *Eastern Shell* carried me away through Gray Strait, then south between the icebergs, and on to Nova Scotia. While my fingers burned with pain I counted my blessings.

It took time to recover from that trip. I regained sensation in my fingertips after about three months, and a few years later the circulation in my fingers returned to something like normal, although ligament damage left the knuckles swollen and painful. But the psychological effects haunted me. I found myself unreasonably afraid whenever I paddled more than a few yards from shore. I was scared whenever I ventured onto the water at night and every time it got windy while I was afloat, however benign the shore. These fears rang like fierce alarms in my head, while another part of my brain reasoned, "These would have been everyday paddling conditions for you before. Your kayaking skills are no worse; you can handle this." But the truth was, I needed to step down to calmer, more secure conditions for a while, and then build up slowly, through progressively rougher conditions, until I regained my former level of confidence. Progress was slow. Three years later I paddled with a friend, Alun Hughes, to Saint Kilda, a small island group thirty-five miles offshore from the Scottish Outer Hebrides. Only after that trip did I figure I had left the ghost of Hudson Strait behind me.

But now I was back. Kristin was with me, and at last we were going to see the Labrador coast.

CHAPTER 11

McLelan Strait

Entering the funnel of Forbes Inlet in bright sunshine, Kristin and I drifted along the shore past rusty-orange outcrops. Beneath our kayaks, long writhing fingers of olive-brown kelp flowed with the current in the deep, clear water. I could see fish far below in the clearings between the kelp. Kristin unraveled a length of fishing line from a stick and trailed a spinner behind her in the water, but the fish didn't bite. As we neared the narrows that define the entrance to McLelan Strait the eddy picked up speed and Kristin hauled her line in. Immediately ahead, the Torngat Mountains towered up behind slabs of rocks that sloped steeply into the water. We had reached the mouth of a gash between the mountains. From it the water now swirled and pushed, surging powerfully toward Ungava Bay. Although the moon was only half, which heralds the period of smaller tides known as neaps, there was a strong current running. After a full moon, the spring tides here could run at ten knots; this was less. I looked across the swirling water to where the mountains ran down to a low green plain. There appeared to be an easy landing place and certainly flat ground on which to camp. Once we had crossed the current we would have no more than a hundred yards to paddle against the tide along the shore before we could land.

I was certain this was the village site described by Dr. Robert Bell in 1877. He described the location as Nunaingok, the "hidden place," situated on an alluvial flat extending between the two branches of the straits. Circular pits indicated to him where sod houses had been, the older ones partly filled with debris from fallen roofs. Some had apparently been occupied within the previous few years. Bell discovered from Inuit camped nearby that this was a comparatively populous village, with a long history of habitation. Inuit had lived in the underground houses for part of each winter. They moved in around November each year, when the mud walls and floor were frozen sufficiently hard, and left around January to spend the rest of the winter in snow houses. McLelan Strait remained open all winter, so it was a good place for seals, which they hunted from their kayaks. They also speared them from stone blinds, built close to the shore at rocky points or ledges.

We rested for a moment, selecting a suitable target across the channel. To monitor our progress we would use transit points, lining up a rock on the far shore with some feature, perhaps a shadow, in the hill beyond and keeping the two in line while we paddled. If the marks drifted apart we would know we were being pushed off course and could make the necessary adjustments. In strong current we would have to angle our bows high into the current to keep the marks in line; in slow current we could point almost straight toward them. I looked forward to landing early today. It would be a treat to set the tents and then spend the full afternoon relaxing on land in bright weather for a change instead of in rain. "Ready? Okay, let's go!" We cut into the fast water and paddled swiftly to ferry-glide across.

Paddling quickly, side by side, we kept our eyes fixed on our chosen transit points. I was so focused that I almost reached the far shore before I noticed a boulder about thirty yards directly ahead that was strangely illuminated by the sun. Light was shining through... thick white fur, creating a glowing edge around the large shape. The bear was crouching head-down and perfectly still, focused entirely on us, and we were ferrying straight to it. "Oh no, there's a bear!"

Almost in a single movement we turned our bows around against the current and sprinted back toward the north shore. The bear must have realized it had been spotted the moment we changed direction. It stood up and walked to the water edge. We were now making headway against the current as well as gaining on the far shore. The bear followed along the shore, matching our progress against the current. Then it paused and stretched its head forward as if to examine the water. It waded in and began swimming. We could see the shape of its head on the surface following us, with a big white lump, the upper part of its back, parting the water behind it.

It took us only a few minutes to regain the north shore. There, agreeing to continue through the strait, we hugged the low cliff where, by using eddies and the slower current near shore, we hoped to pull away from the bear. As I paddled I watched the bear following us. We seemed to be drawing away from it. Kristin, now hyper-alert and concerned about what might be ahead, cautioned, "Nigel, be careful as you go around that corner in case there's another bear."

I thought it so unlikely we'd see two polar bears that close together I almost scoffed, but when we rounded the point, there on the edge of the rock by the water stood another bear, huge. "Okay, Kristin, what would you like to do?" Personally I had no real desire to turn back toward the one following us in the water. Kristin, sounding almost irritated by the bears, said, "Just keep paddling. We're just passing by. We're not here to harm them and they've got no reason to harm us. Just keep paddling." We pulled back into the middle of the channel. As we passed the second bear it turned sideways, showing us just how immense it was, then strolled casually up the rocks and vanished into the higher land beyond, walking away with its rear legs spread wide like a tortoise beneath the immense bulk of its body. Maybe it had seen the swimming bear and was avoiding confrontation. But the sight of it so soon after the first had shaken me. We sprinted on.

Drawing away from the swimming bear behind us, we kept to the center of the channel. It seemed foolhardy to use the slower current close to shore. We could not help noticing the large pale boulder on the northern shore, or what was probably a patch of snow in the rocks on the southern shore. We were seeing suspicious white objects everywhere today, and we did not see any really safe-looking landings as we pushed on in the sun. Ironically, it had long been an ambition of mine to shoot through McLelan Strait on a big spring tide. When I was here in 1981, I was set up to do just that, but made the decision to ask for a ride to Nova Scotia on the *Eastern Shell*. This year, not only had we arrived at a neap tide, but we were pushing through against it.

McLelan Strait was a lure attracting me to northern Labrador in 1981. I enjoy places with strong tides and I cherish remoteness. The combination was irresistible, so I began searching for information of any kind. In those days before the Internet my research began in the public library. The first account I found was by Grenfell. On an early trip north he missed what is now called McLelan Strait. He spotted it later from a hilltop and recognized the channel by "the boiling current' he saw below, whose "vicious whirlpools like miniature maelstroms poured like a dashing torrent from Ungava Bay into the Atlantic." On his next arrival he located the strait and sailed the *Strathcona* into it. He described his experience: "It was, however, with our hearts somewhat near our mouths that we made an attempt to get through this year, for we knew nothing of the depth, except that the Eskimos had told us that large icebergs drove through at times. We could steam nine knots, and we essayed to cover the tide, which we found against us, as we neared the narrowest part, which is scarcely one hundred yards wide. The current carried us bodily astern, however, and glad enough we were to drive stern-foremost into a cove on one side and find thirteen fathoms of water to hold on in till the tide should turn. When at last it did turn, and got under way, it fairly took us in its teeth, and we shot through, an impotent plaything on the heaving bosom of the resistless waters."

The channel, known by the Inuit as *ikkerasak*, which means strait, has carried Grenfell's name ever since. For some time the narrows were known as the Grenfell Tickle. Nowadays the whole strait is known as McLelan Strait, but the eastern end is still shown on the map as Grenfell Sound.

In 1911 John T. Rowland delivered a boat for Grenfell, to be used by the factor of a proposed Hudson's Bay Company post in Ungava Bay. He sailed the thirty-foot-long "hunting cabin launch," with a light yawl rig and a heavy-duty kerosene oil engine, from Newfoundland to Ungava Bay. Their journey along this then largely uncharted coast is described in Rowland's book, *North to Adventure*. Arriving at McLelan Strait he recounts, "As the tide had already begun to rise, we lost no time getting under way and running round to the north side of the low point. Here, sure enough, was another inlet, trending west, in which the velocity of the current would have sufficed to tell us that we were in Grenfell Tickle.

"Advancing up the tickle, we soon noticed the strong current running with us. As we approached the narrow, straight-walled gorge and heard the thunder of waters that issued from it, I think we all experienced a sinking of the diaphragm. It was the only time I ever saw my indomitable friend, shipmate, and engineer, Bob English, look nonplused. Too late to turn back, the current had the *Daryl* in its grip…. Watching the water boil against the black walls of the gorge on either side, I could only think of some superthriller in an amusement park.

"I kept *Daryl* going at full speed, the better to maneuver the seething whirlpools which sometimes spun her half around. One curious effect was that the level of the water in the middle of the tickle appeared to be feet lower than where it frothed against the walls. We rushed down a liquid U-shaped flume – a fortunate circumstance, which perhaps saved *Daryl* from butting her brains out against the smooth rock. The worst spot came about halfway through, where the gorge grew narrow and we had to negotiate a sharp turn. Here the current gained even greater speed and hurled itself in fury against the resisting wall. At this point *Daryl* elected to go stern first, and nothing I could do would stop her. Waves broke over her deck, and it looked as if she planned to carom off the wall. We stopped the motor and hung on. In a few moments the current had swept us through, like a chip of wood that is carried down a brook... We emerged in the west and saw spread out before us the blue, inviting waters of Ungava Bay."

Having read these and other equally tantalizing descriptions about this fast-running tidal passage, I had been excited to experience what it was really like. Instead, Kristin and I, fueled by little more than visions of polar bears all around us, had paddled almost the full fifteen miles right down the middle against the tide. Toward evening the sun dazzled the water like polished copper. The hourglass shape created by the scene ahead with its reflection off the calm sea seemed to pour blue sky from above into the blue water beneath, with the slow movement of water being all that betrayed the passing of time.

Ducks exploded into the air ahead as we creased the water. The wakes from our bows folded the reflections to either side until the warping of the inverted view mesmerized me. When I looked up again one solitary duck remained on the water in front of me. Some birds are more confident than others, and occasionally I could pass quite close without them fleeing. These were mostly occasions when I averted my eyes. Probably it is a direct gaze that reveals the attention of a predator, but I am curious whether there is any underlying communication that goes on between creatures that alerts one to the attention of another, the feeling that you are being watched. At any rate I avoided looking directly at this duck, it did not take off, and as we grew close I began to wonder if it was a bird at all. It didn't really look like driftwood, more like a fishing float maybe. I asked Kristin. "Can you make out what that is ahead? I thought it was a duck but it didn't fly away, and the glare's too bright for me to make it out." We were gliding straight for it now.

"I don't know. Do you get otters up here?"

"No," I replied, "I don't..." Kristin interrupted, "Nigel, it's got ears." Simultaneously, we exclaimed, "It's a bear!" Almost at that instant the bear let out a breath of air that expanded to a huge misty cloud above it. Beneath the cloud I could clearly see the bear's dark nose and eyes, its rounded ears. The wake spread from its head as it swam toward us. We turned at once and sprinted away. I wondered what it was doing there. Perhaps it was enjoying the evening just as we were. Maybe it was waiting for the tide to carry it through the strait or perhaps just taking its time crossing to Killinek Island. I wished I knew more about polar bear behavior.

Having left the bear behind, we paused to study the chart. Kristin drifted beside me smiling, her reflection perfectly mirrored in the calm water, the colors crisp and bright, her yellow anorak, orange float-vest, yellow and white kayak, against a blue that seemed a deeper and more perfect blue than the real sky. The tide had eased to a standstill. I gazed around at mountains and cliffs and turned to look behind. From here McLelan Strait appeared as a long fjord sandwiched between cliffs. This was the entrance that the Moravians in 1811, Grenfell in the late 1800s, and Rowland in 1911 had seen as they approached the excitement of the narrowing strait. The only excitement we had found today was three polar bears.

It was time to look for somewhere to camp for the night. I had read about a narrow entrance in the south shore that opens into a calm lagoon, and the feature showed clearly on my large-scale map. The shore there might offer us a special campsite. At least we would check it out. But the entrance was well disguised. When the Moravian missionaries had entered this lagoon in 1811 they wrote that the inlet was just wide enough to admit a boat. More than one narrow inlet in the vicinity met that description, except for the lagoon. On their return journey they spent the night anchored inside. When we found the lagoon and slipped through the gap, the low sun blazed so brightly from the western entrance I could barely see. I squinted, trying to ensure that all the big boulders really were stone. Unable to see clearly I continued to feel apprehensive until we had pulled all the way through the gap and well away from shore into the broad calm lagoon. We agreed the eastern shore by the entrance looked like a great place to camp, but there were so many places where a polar bear could lie hidden that we felt uncomfortable, so we chose to continue paddling through the strait until we were clear of Grenfell Sound. We also agreed it would feel better to have completed this link to the east coast. Once there we would be ready to begin paddling south.

Banks of mist at sea sent long probing fingers toward shore as the sun sank lower. We spotted an *inuksuq* above a beach and considered landing there. It was a likely camping spot, but its exposure and our desire to round the corner to clear the sound made us push a few yards farther into Clark Harbor. A deep narrow gut just a few yards wide ran between the steep, dark, rock walls of Cape Labrador and Amity Island. The light was fading, but the rock and the deep dark swirling water were revealed in crisp clarity that denied the approaching night. The current pushed us through the narrowest part of the gap, to reveal a small beach on the western shore of Amity Island. I left my kayak and quickly scouted the area for bears, as well as for fresh water and flat camping ground. Satisfied, we hastened to unload. The rocks glittered with crystals as we lay our kayaks on the beach beside a low cliff. I threw a few pieces of driftwood under an overhang where it would stay dry to build a fire later. At the top of the rise, overlooking the channel, was a flat area with circles of boulders deeply embedded in moss. The reflections from our headlamps glittered back from myriad tiny crystals in the rocks, and gleamed from the reflective tape on the anchor loops as we hurried to erect the tents. It was all but dark by the time we had scooped a bucketful of water from a murky pool in the marsh across the island and heated some for a hot drink. The last of the sun gleamed from the water and touched the black mountain range to the south with highlights of deep red. Occasionally the plaintive convoluted call of a loon sounded clearly across the tranquil water. We cooked with the shelter open to the northwest, watching the light of day fade from the sky, to be replaced by an aurora of shivering green curtains, punctuated by the streaks of shooting stars.

CHAPTER **12**

Labrador Fog and German Weather Stations

The next morning began cold, just a few degrees above freezing in the tent, and windy. Although the wind was not strong enough to prevent us from paddling, when we unzipped the tent we saw little. Fog had erased our view, hiding the end of the island, and hiding the shore across Clark Harbor. Occasionally the fog eased enough for us to see perhaps two hundred yards. The prospect of setting off into the fog on a compass bearing in this visibility, with a wind kicking up waves, with only that tidal information we could deduce for ourselves considering the lay of the land, seemed only marginally sensible. We could aim for the next landfall, then hug the shore closely until we could recognize a place where we could leave to make the next crossing, and make the sequence of leaps necessary to cross each of the inlets to the south, but the plan seemed wrong. The idea of hugging shore so closely that we would not be able to avoid a polar bear until we were only a few yards away made our decision for us. We had already come too close to polar bears in excellent visibility; in fog the bears would have an undeniable extra advantage. They have a keen sense of smell, and the wind was blowing onshore. We decided not to push our luck, so we placed bigger rocks around the tent against the wind and settled in for the day.

After breakfast we took time to cook pancakes, and rounds of espresso. We examined rocks from the beach and lichens under the magnifying glass, revealing once more the tiny world of crystals and warty growths. Carrying our rifles we crept through the fog to scoop up more of the dark water from the pools in the marsh, and found Inuit graves, slabs of rock loosely forming caverns in which just a few bones remained. In earlier days these above-ground graves were the burial method of choice, because the permafrost discouraged deep digging. Corpses were laid to rest with objects they used in life, such as wooden utensils, old tent poles, and soapstone lamps. Grave robbers have plundered many of these artifacts. The Moravian missionaries approaching Killinek Island reported running out of firewood and robbing "old Eskimaux graves of the wooden utensils, which it is the superstitious practice of the heathen to lay beside the corpses of their owners.... Wood will not decay by mere exposure to the air in Labrador, but wastes away gradually; and after forty or more years, the wood found at the graves is still fit for use." What has not been taken away and burned has sometimes been removed in the name of science by collectors such as Douglas Leechman, who excavated house and gravesites around Port Burwell and on the Button Islands in the search for archaeological evidence of Inuit migrations. He returned for several summers collecting for the National Museum of Canada in the late 1940s. Most of the graves close to the water were by now open, with only a few scattered bones inside.

The next morning the dense fog persisted but now without any wind. Hoping the fog would lift, we prepared to leave. I spread out the chart and made a list of the distances, the expected paddling times, and the compass bearings for the crossings we would make through the day, leaving any adjustments for tide until we were on the water. Still, there was little visibility when we launched at 8:30, heaving the laden kayaks between large boulders onto the water. Almost immediately we were out of sight of land. With no way of telling what the tide was doing, we paddled for the allotted time then stopped. Turning ninety degrees, we paddled into the murk for a minute or two, and land materialized out of the grainy fog right in front of us. So now we knew there was a current running, and in our favor. Hugging the rock, we paddled to the next identifiable point, then after checking the time, launched into the fog again for the next leg of the journey. Using a compass like this is a matter of trust. It's also a time to focus, to concentrate fully. There was little to see ahead or to either side, except a small patch of water surrounded by fog right down on it. Yet there remained a strong temptation to peer ahead into the fog, or to watch the other kayak. A moment's lapse in concentration is all it takes for the kayak to wander off course, when it can easily swing 180 degrees while giving the impression of keeping a straight line. We took pains to watch the compass all the time; we would incur more than enough error from whatever tide might be running without adding to it. Although we anticipated some tidal movement this close to Hudson Strait, there isn't any documented information about how much, or where, or in which direction. But it is stimulating to *feel* a route down the coast, from island to island, along the cliffs. This seat-of-the-pants navigation sometimes gets overlooked when a plethora of charted information is available.

We paused beside the Hutton Peninsula, peering at the indistinct shore; beyond the hazy outline lay dense fog. Hutton Peninsula was somewhere I wanted to stop to explore, but this was not suitable weather for wandering around on land. I didn't want to meet a polar bear in the fog. Yet, somewhere beyond our sight should be a hill, and a hut containing meteorological instruments, a 150-watt short wave transmitter and antenna mast, and nickel-cadmium dry cell batteries in ten tall, heavy cylinders marked "Canadian Weather Station." Fourteen automatic weather stations of this kind were established in arctic and subarctic locations between North America and northern Norway, translating readings of temperature, humidity, wind speed and direction, and air pressure into Morse code and transmitting the information at three-hour intervals. What is remarkable, and also indicative of the remoteness of the site, is that it was a party from a German submarine who installed this weather station in 1943 during the Second World War. U-boat 537 arrived from Bergen, Norway, on 22 October 1943, surfaced in reduced visibility 300 yards from shore, and launched four rubber boats with all the necessary equipment. A meteorological expert with his assistant and ten seamen set up the station. Once assembled and confirmed to be working, they left the station to operate automatically. The submarine left, and overflying Canadian and British patrols never noticed the tiny hut in the wilderness. The site was not discovered until July 1981, and then only as the result of a retired German engineer's researching records for a book about the German weather service. His queries prompted the Canadian Coast Guard to search for the station. The Germans had left empty American cigarette packs and matchbooks at the site to divert suspicion. A second weather station never arrived. U-boat 867, on its way to Labrador with the equipment, was sunk off Norway on 19 September 1944.

What was so special about Labrador that should prompt perhaps the only armed German landing on mainland North America in the Second World War? The Germans wanted early warning of the weather systems that cross the Atlantic from North America to Europe. Weather information was crucial, not only for naval warfare but also for flying, but apart from reports they got from their navy, particularly their U-boats, the Germans had less information on weather from the west than did the Allied forces. The Allied advantage made the D-Day landings possible, on a day the German defenders thought impossible. But today, Friday, 13 August 2004, bad visibility obscured any sign of the station. We reluctantly turned our kayaks and were swallowed again by the fog.

Throughout the day the visibility cleared. From being able to see only a few kayak lengths in any direction, here and there bits of land appeared, while the fog continued to be thick in other directions. As we crept along the north-facing coast, islands began to appear to our left, and with the tide pushing strongly against us through the gaps we pushed ahead onto open water again. We rounded Black Rock Point and resumed our southerly progress toward Cape

Kakkiviak. The cloud base was below the tops of the cliffs, but every now and then we would pass a gully that ran up the cliff and into the cloud, with edges that hinted of a cliff edge beyond.

At one point, high on the cliff edge, we glimpsed a metallic structure, like a pylon. It drifted mysteriously in and out of sight as the cloud swirled. That was all we could see of Lab1, the most northerly of the North Warning System (NWS) sites in Labrador, part of a string of radar sites across North America that replaced the Distant Early Warning (DEW) line built in the 1950s. The NWS system became operational in 1987-88, although Lab1, one of the short-range sites designed to fill the gaps between long-range sites, was not in place until July 1992. It seemed incongruous here, but no more so than the German weather station. Around the time of the Second World War and just after, a number of covert projects put radar stations in remote places like Cape Chidley, on Killinek Island, and on Resolution Island, to the north of Hudson Strait. Several weather stations were established also. How incomprehensible these installations must have been, and perhaps still are, to the people who roamed these areas to hunt for subsistence.

Around Saglarsuk Bay the mountains gradually appeared, draped in diaphanous cloud. Above the beige sand beach where we landed for a break, a sixty-foot high bank of loose glacial till rose steeply, rimmed along the top in delicate green. The crumbling edge had tumbled down to dirty the banks of snow ramped against the base. I meandered along the water's edge, fleeing each time a small wave washed up, trundling little pebbles. The air was damp and my legs felt stiff and awkward with cold, and my knees ached. It wasn't a day for hanging out on the beach where, despite reasonable visibility, I felt unsettled, as if we were being watched. We lifted the kayaks around, kicked the gritty sand from our boots and launched forward. Chilly water pitched into my face as the kayak lurched through the steeper waves.

Somewhere around Murray Head the tide turned against us, and the sea grew choppy. Kristin had a look of determination on her face as she sent her kayak launching skyward over the crests and crashing down to plow deeply into the troughs a few yards to my side, but I was finding the paddling tedious. As my bow plunged, the water streamed along the deck to divide either side of me as the bow rose again. I found solace that I had designed my kayak wisely, with all the fittings recessed to allow free flow. My memories endured of paddling earlier kayaks fitted with a protruding front hatch and compass that would fling water in my face in conditions such as these. The pitching motion in a heavily laden kayak is quite different from that of an empty kayak. Perhaps it is the speed of the lurch, or the depth of the plunge. The buoyant bow, combined with the cockpit set aft of the midpoint, both reduced plunging and kept me dry to a point and still kept the ends light. We always loaded our heaviest items amidships, yet the bow and stern were packed tightly with gear.

We were working hard but making slow progress. It was an opportunity to turn thoughts inward to escape the frustration, but my thoughts today remained stubbornly outward, measuring our miles against the passing time, reconciled to what seemed as rewarding as running up a down escalator. Eventually the mountains that surrounded Eclipse Harbor became visible, draped in fog; the low cloud began misting us with rain. The current was running against us, pouring through a gap between the cliffs to our right and the Chance Rocks to our left, across which a frenzy of waves was breaking. With the funneling effect speeding the current through the constricted channel, we pushed our hardest to pass Chance Rocks. With just eight miles left to paddle today if we were to reach the narrows at the far end of Eclipse Harbor, this was the time to push hardest. Finally the tide against us eased, and we reached flat water that shimmered with the expanding freckles of tiny raindrops.

We crossed the fjord, Eclipse Harbor, to reconnoiter what looked to be a good place to camp. A steep eroded bank formed the edge of a low plain extending a mile or more inland to the base of the mountains. It was clear we could land and camp anywhere along here as long as we could climb the slope with our kayaks. Now that we had the opportunity to stop early, we considered how few miles remained to reach our target. If the shore here been more enticing I might have stopped, but we held to our plan to camp where the end of the fjord was pinched into a tight channel. There, we would be poised in the morning to launch into French Bight and Eclipse Channel on the other side of North Aulatsivik Island and to follow the southern shore back out to open water.

We paddled offshore, yet the water was fairly shallow. Seals popped their heads up to watch us pass. Looking down, I could see tufts of kelp, boulders, and dense shoals of fish. The fish looked narrow, a foot to eighteen inches long, and they swam stiffly. Kristin let out some fishing line with a weighted lure and towed it behind her but caught nothing. Ahead, irregular pieces of ice floated on the now calm water. One piece close to shore appeared to be drifting. I assumed it was caught in the current from a stream, but when we drew closer I could see it had a wake behind it. It turned its head and I could see a black nose pointing at us, but it kept straight on course across the fjord. Kristin began to ask a question but I put my finger across my lips and said, "Shh!"

"What is it?" she asked. "Polar bear," I mouthed quietly, "but it doesn't seem to be taking much notice of us. It's over there, swimming away—just keep quiet." We sneaked behind Bear Number 9, hugging the shore.

Neither the chart nor the topographic map shows a channel running between Eclipse Harbor and French Bight to the south; both show a land bridge to the island. But during my pre-trip research I had discovered that a channel does exist, and I had written a note on my chart. Unfortunately I had not noted which of the two places on the map that could have been the channel was the correct one. The places shown as narrow isthmuses lay about a mile apart. We had passed a river mouth and had almost reached one possible place for the channel when we came across a big polar bear curled up on the rock. It stood up and turned toward us almost as soon as we spotted it. It was close to the water's edge and close to where we expected to camp for the night. We looped sharply away from shore and retreated. Neither of us felt like squeezing into a narrowing channel with a polar bear at the entrance. Instead we retraced our route, eventually passing the area where we had seen the swimming bear. We saw chunks of floating ice, but could not see the bear. With daylight fading we chose a tiny bay at a stream outlet as a landing place. We camped on the flat alluvium, finishing our tent setup just before complete darkness set in. It was not the most relaxing situation. I sometimes wondered how we managed to fall asleep so easily, but I think we were simply tired. Snug and warm in our sleeping bag we felt secure.

So far we had been rather close to ten bears. But that proved not to be the last bear we saw. The following day we ran close beneath a steep cliff and for some reason I looked up—to see a polar bear sleeping on the cliff fifty feet above us, draped like a dead sheep over a spike of rock. It lifted its head and shifted, but settled again. I do not think it was aware of us. I could not see how it had reached that spot. We were in deep water at the base of an almost vertical cliff. Can polar bears really climb rock like that? Had it climbed up from the water, or down from the summit? It had done one or the other, for it was far beyond the level of the high tide.

We reached the entrance to Ryans Bay that evening and paddled far enough in to find a suitable beach, with a tiny stream. Caribou had braided their tracks across the short vegetation near the shore. The 1931 Grenfell Forbes survey expedition camped in this bay. Inuit who were camped across the fjord paddled over to them. The kayaks they used were typical Labrador kayaks, being long, fairly wide and fairly stable. Nowadays sea kayaks typically measure fifteen to eighteen feet in length with a beam seldom more than twenty-four inches. By contrast the single-seat Labrador kayak measured twenty-two to twenty-seven feet long. It had a fairly flat bottom with hard chines, creases created by stretching the sealskin across the wooden stringers that run from bow to stern. The bow had a considerable rake, which offers a drier ride in heavy seas, and the hull was well rockered along its length, perhaps making it easier to handle in ocean swell. A typical Labrador kayak would sit with the bow drawing more water than the stern, and with the stern barely in the water. This configuration created a fast hull that could be paddled easily against the wind and sea. The kayak would also turn easily to face the wind, a useful feature when hunting. Hunters would approach their game from downwind so no warning scent would be blown from hunter to game.

The cockpit of a Labrador kayak is not sloped down from front to back as much as the lower-profile Greenland kayaks, but the extra depth of the hull meant that the paddler's legs could be more easily threaded into the kayak, and the long foredeck helped keep the cockpit dry. The natives' waterproof kayaking clothing included not only a waterproof jacket but also waterproof pants. In that respect it was similar to our own, and suggests that kayakers then might also have expected some water to enter the cockpit, so their legs needed protection. In other regions, waterproof pants were not considered necessary because the anorak effectively sealed around the cockpit to exclude water. Our spray skirts seal less effectively around our larger cockpit openings. The practice of sealing the cockpit may have declined when paddlers began carrying guns. Easy access to a gun stowed in the cockpit might have taken precedence over complete dryness.

The Labrador kayak used the skins of bearded seal or harp seal stitched over a driftwood frame, although cutting trees for wood was another option. With the nearest trees several hundred miles to the south and with a limited supply of driftwood, builders probably traveled south to the tree line over the winter ice to collect wood for kayak building. The wood could be carried back north by sled, or in the form of a sled, to be used for kayak-building later.

In this environment where violent winds can descend from the mountains and rush through the fjords and out over the sea with little warning, fast kayaks that handled well against the wind like these were a good adaptation. But they were also good load carriers. Our kayaks, lacking the bulk of an internal wooden frame, offer more storage space than a framed kayak of the same outer dimensions. We carried enough to supply our needs for five weeks, but each kayak, tightly packed, carried less than 150 pounds of gear. I was astonished when I read an account by Douglas Leechman in his book, *Eskimo Summer,* published in 1950. Leechman spent a summer on the Button Islands with a kayaker from Port Burwell as his guide and assistant. His guide, Bobby, who was running short of meat for his family, went off in his kayak to hunt. Spotting a polar bear swimming, he shot it, then butchered it on the rocks before returning to camp with the skin in tow. Leechman recounts; "Bobby picked up his boat hook and, reaching inside the kayak, he dragged out a fore quarter, then a hind quarter, then half the back. Now he turned about and started pulling pieces of bear from the aft section of the kayak. The other two quarters appeared, the other half of the back and, in due course, the head, all of which were laid up on the rocks near the skin. The intestines had been discarded, but the rest of the internal organs were all there and made yet another section of the bear to be pulled out of the kayak, which seemed to yield up treasure after treasure as though it were Aladdin's cave, till there must have been several hundred pounds of meat piled up."

If the Labrador kayaks were long, so were the paddles. After studying a variety of archival photographs I came to the conclusion that the paddles, which had narrow unfeathered blades, were nine to eleven feet long. Hawkes, in his book, *The Labrador Eskimo,* in 1916 describes paddles as measuring ten to twelve in length, three to five feet longer than the paddle I use. They were made of hardwood when available, otherwise of spruce, and the ends were capped with bone or ivory for protection against splitting. The weight of such long paddles was often supported by the cockpit coaming during paddling.

In Labrador, whole families used the larger flat-bottomed *umiak,* an open boat constructed from skin over a wooden frame, for travel along the coast. Although elsewhere in the Arctic it was typical for women to propel the *umiaks* using long single-bladed paddles, by the early 1900s in Labrador and Ungava men rowed them using long oars. These *umiaks* were usually about twenty-five feet long, although shorter ones were built. They can carry an immense load of people and supplies. Although some hunting was done from the *umiak,* it was mostly for whale and walrus. Seals were hunted from the kayak. The Inuit that paddled to meet Forbes and his party at Ryan Bay in 1931 were a family of eleven from Killinek, camping in two tents. They had been dropped off by boat with their kayaks to hunt and fish. Popularity of the *umiak* declined with the arrival of wooden motorboats, but the kayak continued in use for some time longer.

We lifted our kayaks right to the top of the beach beside the tents, the flattish pebbles clacking together underfoot. After stuffing our neoprene boots under the deck lines, where they could drain and air-out without filling with rain, we sealed the rest of our damp gear inside the cockpits along with our paddles, which we took apart into their two sections. By now the sun had dropped below the mountains, and the thin clouds glowed like embers against the still-blue sky, turning the calm water of the bay into liquid copper. The illusion of warmth contrasted with the snow-streaked spiky peaks that stood around us in shadow. Kristin, beside me in her orange jacket and black rain pants, her turquoise glass beads bright around her neck, reached out to pull me close. The smile on her face as she gazed at that scene brought one to my own. My eyes skipped from smile to shining bay to glowing clouds and the evening sky.

CHAPTER **13**

Wind

The fifteenth of August drifted in as a wonderfully bright morning, with a light breeze blowing out of the fjord and no fog to be seen. I spotted a few insects: a stream of bees entering and leaving a hole beside a large boulder, a few mosquitoes, and I also found some spiders. We slipped easily out of Ryans Bay, our heads swiveling to absorb the steep mountains dappled with snow. Rounding a steep headland, we could see the six miles of Iron Strand beach reaching toward mountains as far as we could see. Icebergs dotted the sea off the coast, and a spectacularly weathered one diverted us for some time. It looked fairly close. It turned out to be farther offshore than we had imagined, and also larger, and when we drew closer it looked precarious, so we kept to a safe distance, which was just as well. We had no sooner turned our gaze from it than it cracked and shifted its position in the water, the incredibly loud retort jolting me. Just above and below the waterline, light seemed to radiate from the ice in a brilliant, deep, sapphire blue. We turned and headed for the shore, but it took us at least an hour of hard paddling to reach the Iron Strand from there. The Four Peaks, which reach over 4,000 feet in several places, appeared close and magnificent in the clear light. After days of watching fog banks, with occasional glimpses of the high mountains behind, it was wonderful to view the steep crags and snowfields, the gashes of gullies, and the knife-edged ridges.

Iron Strand is an enigma. Although a rust-colored mountain rises steeply behind the short coastal plain, it is not rock from the mountain that colors the shore red. Where we landed much of the shore is composed of wonderfully patterned and textured pastel boulders in a wide range of colors, but with no sign of orange or red. Banks of kelp thrown up by the waves looked rusty orange from a distance. But we saw no iron. Surely the beach was named after the rust-colored mountain? But no, the name is given because the sand is red, not iron red, but red from the bright garnets that have weathered out of the rock and now make up much of the sand.

We reached Seven Islands Bay in calm sunny weather, the skies now clear of clouds except for a few small white clumps static above the mountains. The sea was deep blue and calm, so we headed straight out from shore toward Avigalik (Whale) Island, just two miles away. Avigalik Island is the largest and the most northerly in the chain of islands at the mouth of Kangalaksiorvik Fjord. Seven Islands Bay is guarded from the east by the innumerable rocks and shoals of Hogs Back Reef, which before the 1930s made entry into the bay tricky. The Grenfell-Forbes expedition of 1931 used a cove just inside Kangalaksiorvik Fjord as a base; it offered safe anchorage and a place to beach their two seaplanes. The place now appears on the map as Seaplane Cove. On their first approach to Seven Islands Bay by sea, they ran into dense fog. The two best maps available at the time, Grenfell's map and the Admiralty chart, each showed discrepancies of as much as five miles in the position of the shore. Miller, however, had just developed the negatives of photographs he had taken on a reconnaissance flight, and he quickly penciled an outline map. Using this sketch together with the negatives to identify landfalls, the group felt their way along under motor with the sails down in the ninety-seven-foot fishing schooner, the *Ramah*. Through the fog, past islands and uncharted shoals, they motored to Seaplane Cove, much of the time across what the Admiralty Chart showed as land.

We drew closer to the cliffs of Avigalik Island in the clear, with no sign of fog, and we gazed around at the distant mountains and the islands. Then, waves appeared, running out from the fjord. In a few minutes they developed into a steep swell. Since there was no wind, I assumed without really thinking that the tide was running into the fjord, kicking up waves that would naturally run in the opposite direction. Such a current would be welcome, as it would push us on our way around the west side of Avigalik Island. Acting out of my habit to verify things, I turned my kayak to point directly at the cliffs, across the path of the waves and whatever current might be causing them. Then I lined up a crack on the cliff with a distant bump on the skyline behind it and paddled forward, keeping the two in line as transit points. If a current were running one would have to crab into it to keep the two marks in line, but my bow remained right in line with them, indicating there was no current after all. Now I felt uneasy. If a current had not produced the waves, they must have been raised by an offshore wind. But where was the wind? I looked down the fjord toward the mountains and watched the clouds. There seemed to be no movement in the patches of cloud above the mountains and no sign of wind. I said. "I don't like this," and we paddled harder.

Within ten minutes, cloud began pouring over the mountain toward us, and shortly afterward we could see the surface of the water far into the fjord grow darker. The change in appearance accelerated toward us until we could see the spray and the whitecaps. We could hear the rumble like a speeding freight train, and moments later the wind hit us hard. Now we were fighting to make any progress at all. The gusts twisted the paddles in our hands, and the kayaks chopped through the waves, flinging cold water up into the spray already flying in the wind. Water streamed from my face. I could see two options: to push on against the wind, around the corner, and find a landing on the exposed shore of Avigalik Island—for around the corner should be a beach—or to fight across to Amiktok Island. The second option might offer a more sheltered landing and maybe more sheltered camping, compared to Avigalik Island, which offered a beach wide open to the wind beside a hill that would funnel and accelerate it. If Amiktok didn't work out, we could always run with the wind back to the beach on Avigalik.

Kristin had never seen winds so strong, even on land. Keeping as close beside her as practical, I shouted what I thought were the alternatives. She said let's try to make it to Amiktok—it would be little more than a mile. She appeared to be in control of her kayak and paddle and confident, so we pushed onward, into the wind. The sea had been roused into roiling whitecaps, but as we drew closer to Amiktok Island the island blocked the waves and left a patch of flatter sea. But if the sea were calmer, the wind slammed us with greater ferocity with each new gust. It was a classic demonstration of the venturi effect, the wind being accelerated around, rather than being blocked by, the hills. Spray ripped across the water slamming into us from one side, yet as we braced against it, we could see the grated patterns on the water change as the next gust flew toward us from the other side. There was no time for complacency. Any one of the gusts could whip a paddle from our grasp.

As we drew closer to shore, we could see that what we'd identified as little sheltered beaches now seemed rather smaller and more rocky. We landed on a narrow shore of cobbles below a line of irregular sharp-edged boulders. Many of the boulders were newly fallen from the crumbly cliff above and showed no sign of wear by the sea. As for shelter, even here just a few yards from the cliff the gusts of wind still found us, flicking my paddle into the air from the beach into the water.

We had no idea for how long the wind might blow, so we lifted the kayaks beyond the reach of the tide and climbed the steep V of a stream bed up the low cliff onto the island to look around. It was an attractive place. The stream wound gently down to us through a shallow grassy valley amid sundew and butterwort, blueberries and moss, to tumble past us to the beach. The single pale yellow flower of a mountain avens fluttered like tissue on the ground. We were out of the direct wind but we were caught periodically by gusts. One sudden blast hit so hard we leaned against it shrieking while it supported our weight; our clothes stretched tight around us. Then it dropped abruptly, and the air was still for a moment. In the silence we heard the roar of the next gust. The wind howled down the slope to slam against us once more. Tired from the paddling and disoriented by the caterwauling wind and the inconsistent periods of complete silence, we wandered around erratically. We checked everywhere for a site for our tent. The ground all around us was ideal for camping. We had fresh water and a good view, but the wind had the island covered. If we managed to set the tent, I was convinced the wind would snap the poles in an instant, if the tent did not actually take off. We waited to see if the wind might abate, but with no sign of that happening we clambered back down to the beach to see if we could pitch the shelter tent there, close up against the cliff.

With limited space to work between the high tide line and the cliff, we began to level out a platform of sorts, lifting together to roll aside boulders the size of chairs, then filling the biggest hollows with pebbles. Finally making do with a deeply stepped slope, which was the best we could manage, we threaded driftwood sticks through the tent's anchor points and pinned them down with boulders. Even so the fabric flapped crazily whenever a gust passed above. But at least we were tucked away from the main force of the wind. Out over the water, columns of spray twisted in the air like phantoms dancing away downwind.

The tide was rising so we moved the kayaks higher and tethered them to keep the wind from blowing them out to sea. The tide rose to within inches of our kayaks, leaving us a narrow fringe of unsteady boulders between the water and the cliff. Crouched inside the shelter tent, our bodies draped over boulders too large to shift, we made a level place for the stove and opened the chart between us. Then I saw where the wind was coming from.

While the Torngat Mountains here rose to 3,500 or 4,000 feet, the valley running back from Seven Islands Bay went to a pass barely 500 feet high, before descending along the Abloviak River and Fjord into Ungava Bay. This is precisely where Torngarsoak, the Great Spirit of Inuit legend and his wife, Suporuksoak, the Great Wind, are said to reside. No wonder the Inuit could associate Suporuksoak with this place, where a natural funnel focuses the wind through the mountains to jet out across Seven Islands Bay. Every weather system moving in from the west, on hitting the barrier of the Torngat Mountains, would spill over and between the mountains here, sending squalls racing through the fjords.

When darkness came we unwrapped our sleeping bag and mats, and put pads of clothing against the rocks to cushion the sharpest angles. Now surprisingly comfortable, considering the crazy slope of the rocks, we fell asleep. Kristin was woken at 4 in the morning by the percussive slam of a big gust of wind against the tent, and again at 7. When I raised my head the green tent shoved back at me. With my hat pushed low over my head I peered out through the one eye that was clear and saw Kristin zipping closed the door from the outside. Soon I could hear the clacking of boulders moving beneath her feet and the sound of her pulling kayaking gear from the cockpits and spreading it to dry. I unfolded my legs cautiously from between the knobby boulders and followed. Kristin's smile greeted me. She was proud to have made a good start. The sun was bright, so we took the opportunity to rinse clothes in the stream and spread them out before shouldering the rifles for a hike up the island. At the summit the wind was so strong it was scarcely possible to stand. My eyes streamed with the buffeting blasts that pulled hard at my hair.

Yet the sea down below did not look rough. From here the whitecaps looked tiny. The offshore wind had too little fetch across the water to produce big waves. But back toward Avigalik Island we could see where the gusts rasped at the water, the patterns streaming away like shoals of fish, fingering forward, darting outward.

We turned our attention to the ground, crouching for shelter behind an outcrop of rock. Growing here were many familiar little plants of types I have seen in other places in the north. I think of them as friends, and I am always delighted to see them again. The bright yellow flowers of Tormentil, the ubiquitous *Potentilla erecta*— the roots of this tough wiry-rooted plant were once used for tanning nets in the Western Isles of Scotland. Also brightening the ground were lousewort, lilac asters, mountain avens, and the tight, round, pincushion tufts of moss campion, whose tiny pink flowers reveal such a rich, strong scent if you take the trouble to bring your nose close enough. Here, too, were vetch, the ripe blueberries, and the stringent not-quite-ripe mountain cranberries. Tucked between the clumps of vegetation were dense rock chippings that shimmered with bright minerals. The sun felt warm now that we were protected from the wind, and I stared south toward the chunky bulk of Big White Bearskin Island off Deacon head, six miles away across a wind-chipped sea that reflected like beaten steel. Gusts wailed across the rocks behind me. I felt content to wait, tucked down with Kristin in the sun.

Back at the tent we cooked pancakes, one of those time-indulgent activities that we rarely allowed ourselves. The tent grew so warm we took off our jackets, and without warning mosquitoes were everywhere. The wind had died. We pulled out the chart to figure out where we might go, using what was left of the day. While we studied, a small seaplane flew over Avigalik Island, and passed quite close to where we sat, perhaps on its way to Seaplane Cove. I was curious who was on board, and why they were here. Perhaps someone had flown in to fish.

It did not take us long to pack up. We were both relieved not to have to spend another night on the boulders. We headed out confidently toward Big White Bearskin Island, six miles away across the bay. The mountains were clear; Mount Tetragon, rising to 4,510 feet with banks of snow gleaming in the sun, looked huge and startlingly close. Predictably a wind sprang up in our faces as we approached Big White Bearskin Island, funneling between the cliffs of the island and those of the mainland, both rising abruptly to more than 1,000 feet. With taller peaks inland, even a local breeze would be channeled through that gap.

We paused for a snack beneath the precipitous face of the headland. Where should we stop for the night? Our first opportunity would likely be Evans Bight, a small cut in the western side of the entrance to Trout Trap Fjord, the first fjord we would reach on rounding the head. If we landed there we would have time to set our camp before dark. If it was unsuitable we would still have time to look for somewhere else. We pressed on through choppy water and breakers, with the steep rock wall to our right.

Our bows were launching into the air and plunging back down with each wave. It was as if the kayaks had come to life. The lively action made me feel happy. It is easy to submit to the passion of the sea, to become joyful with its action, serene with its calm. Kristin's urgent shout startled me. "Nigel! There are bears right in front of you!" For a moment all I could see was water. Waves everywhere. Rising on the next wave I saw them, only a couple of kayak lengths ahead. I reversed abruptly to stop, hoping I wouldn't be carried right onto them. The two bears, swimming close together, could not have seen us. One turned its head, peering at us, and the other did the same. Then in one synchronized movement they turned their heads down into the water. The two massive pale backs arched though the surface, fur streaming like ghostly seaweed until their huge rumps broke the water. Then they plunged down leaving me with the startling image of their skinny little tails. We resumed paddling, although in a slightly different direction. I felt shaky, and I scanned the surface behind me for anything that would tell me where the bears had gone. They appeared to be heading toward the shore we had come from. I watched but did not see them leave the water.

At the mouth of Evans Bight a long, flat, eroded iceberg rocked on the swell. From the kayaks it looked like a reclining doll, lying on her back with feet sticking up at one end, the slope of the torso rising to the chest and dropping to a neck with the head lifted to clear the water. We sat and watched as it rocked first head down, then feet down, rising and falling on the swell with a loud clonking noise that might have been the sound of the ice hitting the rock beneath, or might have been big pieces of ice colliding. A flattish platform of ice was awash, and waves breaking across the shallows burst into spray against the slick ice cliffs. We left the noisy rocking doll and investigated the bight around the corner. A low, flat plain ran out from the base of the mountains behind, and culminated in a steep bank of glacial till that dropped to the steep boulder beach. Huge boulders were scattered across the slope near the entrance, apparently having rolled down from the mountain behind, so we paddled farther until we found ground that was flatter and less encumbered. It was still an awkward landing, even though there was little swell in the bight. The rocks were big, and there was just enough of a swell to make it impossible to unload the kayaks at the water's edge.

Clinging to the face of a twenty-foot-high crumbling bank above the beach were wild flowers in as dense a meadow as could survive at that angle. The bank was blue with harebells. We crawled our way up and over the top to find ourselves on the dried rim of a peaty marsh, a fringe supporting blueberry, cranberry and ground-hugging dwarf willow, interspersed with moss and lichen. A few yards inland this sank into a damp surface of marsh grasses, dark pools, and oily orange mud patches. We stopped to examine footprints embedded in the soft mud and identified caribou and arctic fox. Mosquitoes whined around us. Once we had portaged all our gear to the top of the slope it took us only a few minutes to situate the tents with a broad view of the bight and the mountains on the other side. For once the ground was flat and soft enough to use tent stakes. We slid our way back down to the beach to move our kayaks beyond the reach of the rising tide. When night deepened, the sky, already richly covered in dense layers of stars, flickered with the Northern Lights.

Morning came with the glow of sun on mist, and with the warmth of the sun came a flurry of new activity. Grasshoppers whirred in the grass and bumblebees flew ponderously past the harebells on the slope. Out on the water a minke whale surfaced between the bobbing heads of seals. During the night the rocking doll had spawned a field of ice fragments, each about the size of a swimming bear. It is little wonder that bears can hunt seals so effectively when they can disguise themselves as something as small as a head-sized piece of floating ice, or a rock or snow patch on land. I was watchful and wary and must have been more tense that I had realized, because when we had launched and finally reached ice-free water I felt myself relax.

Cape White Handkerchief is a significant landmark turning point along this stretch of coast. We looked behind us to see the islands of Seven Islands Bay. Murphy Head at the southeastern end of Iron Strand, and Cape Territok on North Aulatsivik Island were also visible to the northwest. We left all that behind us when we rounded the cape. Now revealed across the rock-studded sea ahead lay Cape Daly. Poking out from behind it were the peaks of Gulch Cape on the far side of Nachvak Bay. There is magic to rounding a cape, first to lose the scenery of the past few days and then to begin to see the distant landmarks that will become your next targets. It is not like turning the page of a book, where the story continues without a breath; that would be like our daily succession of minor changes. This was more like reaching the end of a chapter and turning to reveal a new subject. Apart from the change in direction and the change in view that the headland signaled, Cape White Handkerchief itself was a worthy turning point. The cliffs rose steeply to more than 1,500 feet in pastel shades of rock, subtly tinted with green, orange, lilac and a light, dusty charcoal gray. Shooting up this huge pale mass ran vertically aligned streaks of black rock, bundled stripes threading their serpentine courses like strands of long black hair across pale skin. These narrow black volcanic intrusions ran vertically a full thousand feet. Precipitous rockslide gullies narrowed down to points from which snow fans spread elegantly down to the foot of the cliff until the sea cut the frozen bases off level. It looked as if sugar was leaking from a hole in the rock, spreading like an hourglass as it fell. Rounding the corner revealed a scene of jagged ridges, mountain peaks layered one behind the other, steep cauldrons with sharp-edged rims.

It was a hot day, with cloud building over the mountains inland, so I was anxious about the possibility of offshore squalls as we crossed Nachvak Fjord. The crossing took us only twenty minutes, but soon after we reached the other side wispy drifts of cloud began swirling around the cliff edge above us, moving fast. It would take us several hours to reach the next reasonable landing place, so rather than take a chance we turned back into Bigelow Bay, which we had just passed. The entrance, just one mile wide, was between cliffs that rose to 1,500 feet on one side and to more than 2,000 feet on the other. The gloomy bight itself, pinched tight between slopes of steep gray scree, extends inward almost two miles. We paddled down the center toward the far end where a gray boulder beach curved across in front of the mountains; it seemed to be topped with grass for some of its length. By the time we reached the beach I felt enclosed, even hemmed in, by the steep elevations surrounding us. Cloud swirled in over our heads, but beneath the kayaks the clear dark water brightened to reveal patches of sand bottom, reflecting light back in vibrant deep turquoise. Scanning the shore for signs of polar bears and seeing none, we chose a narrow landing place between the boulders and ran the kayaks up onto a tiny fan of sand.

The beach comprised a jumble of large round boulders thrown up across the end of the bay. In places the boulders were cemented by sand in which marram grass, a few gray-green succulents and black bilberries had taken hold. It formed a sickle-curved bar that held back a broad freshwater lake. The cliffs behind the lake rose steeply from, and in reflection sloped steeply down into its dark water. Having chosen a flat place to spend the night we carried the gear up to the top of the beach, then hopped from boulder to boulder carrying the kayaks. Even while the rain splattered down on us, the sun burst through the twisting cloud. The beach was littered with driftwood, so we collected a pile of small pieces, breaking them into short lengths. I constructed a tiny fireplace using stone blocks. We burned all our garbage and then sat in front of a driftwood fire with a cup of hot chocolate. Around us the tall gray-green marram grass hid our view of the sea, and rain drizzled down.

Warm and revitalized we jumped from boulder to boulder along the beach, stopping in surprise when we came across tent circles. They were well disguised against the other boulders, but once one circle popped into view, others appeared. It's that strange phenomenon of "getting one's eye in," seeing a pattern in an otherwise chaotic scene, which then reveals other similar patterns. It can be the same when hunting for fossils in a ploughed field, or hunting for orange chanterelle mushrooms in a sea of yellow birch leaves. Once you spot one, you see them everywhere. We peered down into narrow circular caches, identified larger tent rings, and then we saw what seemed to be an armchair made of flattish stones. A slab of stone angled back from the seat as a perfect back support, while to either side flat bars of stone rested as arm supports. When I sat in it and gazed around at the other stones making up the tent ring, I realized there were several chairs We found them all quite comfortable. Choosing favorites, we sat back and relaxed, gazing up at the magnificent mountains with cloud cruising around the rim, listening to the call of loons and the whine of mosquitoes. Then we laughed at the absurdity of our situation. The occasional raindrops falling on the ground seemed to release the earthy scent of the grasses. We were looking up and outward, but the armchairs seemed to have been built into a tent circle. We know boulders are used to hold down the canvas flaps inside Inuit tents, perhaps so the flaps do not get frozen to the ground or snowed under, so maybe these chairs would have looked inward toward the center of a tent like the one we had visited near Kangiqsualujjuaq. Or perhaps they were arranged in an open-air circle for friends or family to socialize around a fire, as a wilderness version of deck furniture.

CHAPTER **14**

Ramah

The morning was quiet and the damp rain sheet clung motionless against the tent. We stuck our heads into the open air to discover our visible world had shrunk to a few yards of pebbles and wet marram grass in the fog. This diminished world sloped slightly down away from us in every direction. I knew that steep cliffs towered up quite close and almost surrounded us, that the ocean lay down the beach to one side, and that these wet slabs of gray stone led in the opposite direction to a lake, but really we might have been anywhere. I relit the fire with dry sticks I had prudently stacked in the shelter overnight and fussed on the beach, watching the thin plume of smoke mingle with the fog. I hoped the stunning view would reappear but it didn't, so we gathered our things and prepared to leave. From the water's edge we could not even see the fringe of grass that defined the top of the beach. We scrutinized the charts. Today, we decided, we would detour into Ramah Bay to find the site of the old village there. I was curious to see why this place has attracted people since prehistoric times. It would surely be worth paddling out of our way. Our discussion held us there, clad in fog. We managed to procrastinate until almost ten o'clock, but the fog showed no sign of easing. We launched and skirted the shore with a visibility that never exceeded about three kayak lengths. Only by the change of alignment of the shore with our compass readings did we know when we had turned the corner and left Evans Bight behind.

Measuring our progress by paddling steadily and keeping track of the time, we also eyed the compass to pinpoint exactly where we were. We kept just in sight of the shore almost all the way to Gulch Cape, six miles away, occasionally losing sight of it and angling in again until it reappeared. At the cape the rocks were almost white, with the same crazy vertical black stripes. The cliff was so eerily semi-veiled by the fog it was difficult to tell whether it was a white cliff with black stripes, or a black cliff with white stripes. The stripes ran upward for only a few yards before they blurred into white cloud, but in places they looked like white waterfalls cascading down a black slope, out of the clouds and into the sea. I enjoyed the visual ambiguity.

Around the cape the map indicated two adjacent bights spreading from a common entrance. Here we should leave the shore and head across. We chose to cross each bight separately to make the day more interesting, although as it happened the sky soon cleared to reveal mountain peaks. Gradually the mountains beyond the second bay began to emerge, streaked with patches of heavier cloud that hung across them and cut them in two horizontally; a low plateau visible beneath the cloud base, and an upper range floating on a stormy sea of cloud. We changed our plans and paddled straight across. Behind us, the cliff with the pale rock and black stripes looked tiny and insignificant against the vast mass of Gulch Cape, its mountains and patches of snow.

The sky continued to change. Cloud bubbled up over the land. We rounded the low finger of black rock called North Head to see into Ramah Bay. We could see the mountains of Bluff Point three miles distant dividing the bay into two. To our right the shore rose from North Head to more than 2,500 feet, leading us into Ramah Bay, while south of Bluff Point was the branch known as Little Ramah Bay. I jumped—a whale had surfaced right beside Kristin, startling us both. It immediately sounded again, but it hadn't left us. This minke kept pace with us, surfacing close to the kayaks every few minutes, and it escorted us all the way into the bay. There was seldom any warning of where or when it might appear, so although I sometimes spotted a dark shape crossing underneath me, it was always a surprise when the whale broke the surface a few feet away.

The mountain now beside us, Lookout Point, looked as if it was made of pale slate or shale, with thin strata tilted toward the water, slender lines running side-by-side like a finely detailed engraving. The cliff bled color: ochre yellow, copper green, lilac, red, rust orange, maroon and black, sulfur yellow, and white, with one quartz-like white band running down to meet the water. Not fully believing the colors we saw, we paddled right up to the lumpy beach beneath the undercut cliff to see more clearly. The strata sloped downward and outward so water oozed from the rock, bringing with it minerals that stained the cliff in broad vertical streaks of color. The damp air smelled musty, and it had a chill, metallic tang. As each wave clattered the hard cobblestones of the beach, the hollow cliff amplified the rattle. We pushed on, losing the bright cliff in the massive bulk of the mountain, which appeared bare of vegetation and spiked with slabs that might fall at any moment. Hugging the cliff with apprehension that murderous slates might come cutting down on us, we rounded the last of it to see a gently curving beach, topped with grass on a low coastal platform. Kristin said it felt strangely comforting to land here. Perhaps it was the transition from open sea to sheltered bay, or the sense that what we were doing, arriving by kayak from the sea, was something people had done for centuries. She said she could imagine hunters returning home with meat to feed their families, anticipating a warm reception ahead. After the rocky shore and cliffs, the sandy beach seemed truly inviting. A waterfall pitched out from the last section of cliff, plunging into a dark pool on the gray sand. The distant view now was of mountain peaks encircling the sheltered end of the fjord. We landed on sand and flat pebbles where the cliff disappeared into a wide meadow of grass. We had reached Ramah.

Ramah was the site of a Moravian mission station from 1871 until 1908. The place was chosen to replace an earlier station at Nachvak to the north. When the Hudson's Bay Company also opened a trading post at Nachvak, the missionaries decided their competitor was inappropriately close and moved their building to Ramah. It is perhaps ironic that the Hudson's Bay Company later operated a fur trade post at Ramah also. An 1876 description of the scene at Ramah reads, "About 200 yards to the rear of the buildings is the burial ground, fifteen yards square, marked by four posts; at each corner is a grave…. To the left of the mission premises is the Eskimo village, consisting of five tents in the summer; adjoining are the four winter huts of sods, now standing empty; and likely to require considerable repairs before they again become inhabitable. Upon the side of the Ship-hill are store-houses of the Eskimos, built of slate, and the powder magazine, to reach which you have to cross by stepping stones over a little stream, which, in the spring, forms a torrent with a fine waterfall. The missionary's pantry or meat-safe, invaluable for preserving their supplies of reindeer flesh in the summer, is a cave, which retains some of the winter snow, but has the drawback that it becomes inaccessible when there is a swell landwards."

In 1905 when Dillon Wallace was returning from his canoe trek and passed south along the coast of Labrador by dogsled, he stopped at the Moravian mission at Ramah for one night. He noted that each family had its own living room and bedroom but shared a kitchen and dining room. In winter during the period when seal hunting was impossible, the Inuit at Ramah stayed in sod houses (igloosoaks) at the mission station, using seal-oil lamps for heating. That year sixty-nine Inuit people lived there. As a winter activity the Inuit prepared oil at a blubber station by cutting up frozen seal blubber into small pieces and beating it with large wooden mallets. The pulp was then kept in galvanized vats until summer, when the sun's heat extracted the oil and it could be poured off and sealed into casks. The missionaries gathered the oil and fur in trade from the Inuit and shipped it to Europe each year, applying the profits toward the upkeep of the station.

By 1931 when Alexander Forbes on his mapping expedition with Grenfell sailed into Ramah Bay in the schooner *Ramah,* the station was abandoned, although the Moravian mission buildings were still standing in 1965. Since then the buildings have vanished. From where we stood the grass showed nothing to indicate their presence, except perhaps the incongruous clump of tall rhubarb that towered above the meadow.

The ground was flat, a dense mat of short grass, wild flowers, and ground-hugging shrubs. Kristin spread out the green shelter and soon had it set up; I pitched the sleeping tent. For once we could easily peg the tents and did not need to find boulders to hold them down, but I gathered a few flat slabs of stone to act as my kitchen countertop in the shelter. One flat, buff-colored slab only half an inch thick was subtly striped in almost the same color as yellow lichens, and lightly dusted with them. Other silky slabs glistened with tiny crystals. With the back of the shelter to the breeze, we looked out toward the broad valley and the peaks that rose from gentle green slopes to bare snow-splattered rocky summits at more than 5,500 feet.

Near to the tents was the graveyard, a square, its perimeter marked with flat stones. Some of the graves had small wooden headboards. The weather had erased the names that would have been painted on them. Not all were posted. Some were outlined with rocks, but others simply rose as low grassy mounds, as if the turf had been lifted for a moment like a blanket while the body was laid beneath. In mission graveyards the Inuit graves typically had a twelve-by-eight-inch board painted with the Christian name and dates of baptism and death of the person laid there. The boards nestled close to the ground, fastened to short stakes. Stone markers, usually slate or marble, were reserved for missionaries and their families. One crisply engraved slate headstone remembered Ernestine Schneider, buried here in 1884. Another marked the passing in 1906 of five-year-old Ernst Wilhelm Filshke. That poor child was perhaps the son of Karl Filshke who married Clara Rinderkneckt and spent the years from 1897 to 1916 with trade and mission work in northern Labrador at Okak, Ramah, and Killinek. It must have been a huge step of faith to sail for a new life on the shores of Labrador, far from familiar comforts.

The plateau on which we camped stretched between the shore and the base of the mountains: Quartzite Mountain, 4,000 feet; Cirque Mountain, 5,500 feet. With Lookout Point behind us obscuring any view of the ocean, the surrounding mountains completed the comforting illusion that the bay was a mountain lake. As we left to explore, a caribou stag with huge antlers was wandering slowly down from the hill. It nibbled at low bushes and lowered its head to graze just a few hundred yards away, watchful of us but not unduly concerned. The tall clump of rhubarb visible from the water grew within a square enclosure defined by a low ridge in the grass. Perhaps this was the location of the garden where the mission buildings once stood. We harvested rhubarb to add to our evening meal. Then wandering across the plain we stopped to examine small neat piles of yellow bricks and the remains of rusted-out cast-iron stoves from the mission buildings.

There were many wild flowers. The intense blue stars of gentians stared up at us, but more common were the softer blue harebells, the mauve willowherb, and the yellow fleawort. The gentians, of which we found only a few, reminded me of my father, a keen gardener who takes tender care of every tiny plant. He drew my attention to Gentiana verna, the spring gentian, and to the particularly vibrant blue they display. Here at Ramah the species we found may have been the annual, alpine gentian, G. nivalis. Everything here seemed richly colored, even the trash. Gathered into a hollow at the edge of the hill was an orange pile of oil drums, rusting into dust and contrasting against the verdant grass. Here and there were caribou antlers, bleached white.

We strolled along the dark gray beach looking at pebbles. Kristin stooped to retrieve a small stone being tumbled down the sand by a receding wave. Translucent as agate, it had been sea-smoothed soft as silk to touch. Proud of her find, she held it up to show me how the light passed through it, revealing a faint band of gray that clouded the almost transparent stone. It was the first piece of chert either of us had found here, although Ramah is renowned for its chert. Tools crafted by the Maritime Archaic Indians 7,500 years ago from Ramah chert have been found as far south as Maine. It is a mysterious and useful stone and a good reason for people to live here long, long ago, but we had no idea exactly where it was to be found. Presumably there were bands of the rock in the mountains somewhere.

There is little known about how populations have changed in 7,500 years, but another wave of people is thought to have moved south into the area about 4,000 years ago: the Palaeoeskimos. Although it seems these people were specialized arctic hunters they made little use of chert, at least to begin with, but the people identified as Groswater (2800 to 1900 years ago) and Middle Dorset (2,000 to 1400 years ago) used it more. Either the stone or the tools, or perhaps both, were traded during that period as far away as the west side of Ungava Bay and south to Newfoundland. The Thule people, ancestors of the Inuit, arrived in northern Labrador 600 to 700 years ago. Although they did use a small amount of chert, their materials of choice were ivory and bone, so most chert tools predate the Thule period.

The top of the beach rose into what I had taken to be sand dunes covered in marram grass. When we drew close I realized that these were the bases of sod houses, now grassed over. We waded through the wet grass, almost waist-high, and entered the houses one by one, turning in each to look back at the view across the fjord, a view the inhabitants would have seen. It was interesting to imagine coming out of one of these winter houses to look at this view, but with ice and snow on the ground. The houses shared walls, four or five feet high, made of sod and stones. We withdrew through the tall grass to the beach, our wet leggings peppered with purple anthers.

Beside a rocky point that separated the bay into two ran a steep stream. When we crossed it to get a higher vantage point of the beach, we found remains of more buildings, this time of stone.

These might have been the stone storehouses of the Inuit mentioned in the description of the place by the Moravian representative Levin Theodore Reichel in 1876. We could easily have explored more, but daylight was beginning to fade so we walked back along the water's edge, the cold waves occasionally washing across our bare feet. Our tent and sleeping bag, our home, was here tonight. Sensing that this location had been home for many people before us, we lay there, warm and cozy, listening to the rhythmic breathing sound of the waves as each break ran along the beach, and to the background rush of the waterfall.

The nineteenth of August dawned sunny, with mist partially veiling the fjord and the mountains, cloaking them with a subtle golden glow. I spotted a few puffball mushrooms in the dewy grass and collected a panful. I sliced them and sautéed them in olive oil and flavored them with black pepper and a few dried bacon bits. Kristin described them as, "Oh, so flavorful, so delicate, just like a soufflé!" We took time to walk along the beach, take in the scenery, and look for more chert pebbles. It was already late morning before we launched onto the calm water and paddled back out of the fjord, out of Ramah Bay, crossing to the Muzzle and around that headland into increasingly choppy seas. Beginning as a welcome undulation that brought to life to the kayaks beneath us, the action rapidly grew more severe. Soon the waves had lumped up to become considerably steeper and we had our faces repeatedly doused as the kayaks punched and pitched. The swell was getting higher. Whitecaps built up rapidly with the now driving headwind and were soon breaking heavily. Swells rebounded from the cliffs to create an erratic pattern of colliding swells with exploding breaks. I asked Kristin if she felt OK about the conditions, and she said she thought so. She was nervous. We paddled as close together as seemed safe while the waves reared up explosively to throw our kayaks aside. It was getting worse. I checked again with Kristin and she reaffirmed her willingness to press on. But the sea just kept getting bigger. I could see that it was almost certainly going to get rougher still when the curve of the cliff ahead exposed us to a longer fetch and more wind. We pushed hard yet made slow progress, until we could clearly see the much bigger rollers ahead and a white sea. In view of how hard we had to paddle, how much rougher it was going to get, and how much farther we would have to paddle to reach a place we might land, Kristin thought it wise to turn back. So we turned and surfed downwind, twisting on the lumpy wave faces and bracing against the crashing crests. We were now flying along. Earlier we had passed a gap in the cliffs that had promised shelter from this sea. We aimed for that and cruised the last yards on calm water to a little boulder beach. Kristin was exhausted.

We beached our kayaks but did not unload them. We would watch the weather and see if we could launch again later. Sheltering from the wind beside a low cliff, I assembled the stove on a ledge and brewed a succession of espressos while Kristin stretched out flat on her back in the sun and fell fast asleep. Around me the dark rock sparkled with tiny crystals and was marbled with veins of white, like streaks of fat through meat. Just a few feet away the corner of the cliff was white, not black, but smutted with spots of sparkling black. A clear stream bounded down over white boulders and lapped across the curvaceous water-smoothed rock below my dangling feet. The boulders displayed concentric rings of strata in the same way carved wooden balls reveal grain. A short distance inland, up the valley, was a marsh almost dried up but for a meandering stream cutting deep into the peat. Beyond the marsh, curving gray slopes of scree rose through a series of terraces punctuated by crags from the valley up to the mountains. I felt content sipping my espresso.

When Kristin woke up we wandered together up the valley, rifles on our shoulders just in case, and to our delight found a large *boletus* mushroom with a stipe almost as broad as its plump cushion cap. After spotting one we suddenly saw *boleti* all over the valley floor and wondered how we had not seen them before. It was as if they had sprung up from the earth in those few moments, although really it had been our poor observation. Now we could afford to be selective, choosing only the best, freshest, firmest fungi and leaving any that were even slightly worm-ridden behind. I think *boleti* and caribou probably go together. Wherever we have seen prodigious signs of caribou we have also found *boleti*, suggesting the caribou do a good job spreading the spores around, or providing the needed growing medium. Maybe caribou and mushrooms also go well together on the plate? The British Admiralty Mariner's Handbook advises mariners shipwrecked in the Arctic to avoid all mushroom-like plants unless they can be positively identified as edible. On the same page it asserts that there are no known poisonous plants north of the tree line. Does this mean that the handbook does not categorize fungi as plants, or that although they may not be poisonous, they might not be edible? I mused out loud as we walked until Kristin asked why it mattered anyway. This mushroom, *Boletus edulis*, is easy to identify and is also one of the tastiest wild mushrooms. It is typically described in mushroom books as "edible, delicious and good." We later sliced and sautéed our specimens, added black pepper freshly ground using Kristin's tiny pepper grinder, and then ate them, exclaiming at their exquisite flavor. We had enough to make a soup, too. We were happy to make use of this tasty addition to our menu. *Boleti* contain more protein than most vegetables, but are not high in calories.

In view of the whitecaps that continued to tumble across the mouth of the bay and explode against the cliff, we began to scan the valley for the best place to camp. It was then I spotted a tent circle. It was a recent one, with the stones sitting on top of the turf. Then I saw another. The boulders of the second were well bedded down into the moss. "This is a much older one," I commented, stopping beside it. "The perfect place to find chert implements." Kristin reached down and plucked a stone from beside my foot. "Like this one?" she asked. In her hand nestled an almost flat fragment of translucent stone, maybe two inches long. Clouded gray in color, it had been worked into a symmetrical elongated triangle with the long edges slightly convex, and with two notches toward the broad end at each side, presumably to help in lashing it to a shaft with sinews. The surface was lightly textured, like the matte finish on frosted glass; typical Ramah chert.

We began looking closely around us. The place looked like any other flattish area, with angular blocks of stone scattered about. But what was seemingly random included deliberately placed stones, too. And there were circles everywhere. Some used mostly irregular stones, but in others some of the blocks were more regular and more carefully placed, with flat surfaces uppermost, and looking quite comfortable. Following the concept of the armchairs we found a few days ago, and imagining people sitting on the stones looking toward the center of the circles, we could identify the depressions made by feet. In and around those depressions the peat was packed with chert flakes. Sharp shards pointed their needle-ends into the air and half-hidden gleaming edges warned of consequences like a pocketful of blades. When we held fragments up to the sky, the light shining through revealed moss-like cores, or faint banding in gray and black, and occasionally a green tinge or reddish-brown smudge. It seemed as if we had stumbled into a deserted tool factory. People must have spent a lot of time here, sitting in their tents flaking away at rocks to fashion hunting tools. Assuming there must be chert outcropping here for there to be so much activity, we then cast around, discovering narrow almost opalescent blue veins in the rock only yards from where I had daydreamed with my espresso, toward the shore.

We became so absorbed in what we had found that we hardly noticed the mosquitoes were getting more attentive, and that we were swatting almost constantly. And although we had watched the tide for most of the afternoon we were now so focused we forgot it was still rising until Kristin noticed the kayaks were almost afloat. We hurried down to find the cockpits half-filled with water from the waves. Reluctantly we abandoned our study and busied ourselves unloading and lifting the kayaks beyond the seaweed lines and selecting a high spot for the tents overlooking the village of circles. As the light bled from the sky we feasted on *boleti* cooked with bacon and rehydrated sweet potato, and toasted the day with tiny servings of single-malt whisky that came originally from the island of Islay in Scotland, an ocean away, yet so close in some ways. I have kayaked a lot in Scotland, and on many occasions I have marveled at the many historic remains on the deserted islands. In fact I have retreated to this same tent there and toasted with a similar "wee dram" of single-malt whisky and basked in a similar sweet sense of satisfaction.

CHAPTER **15**

Leaving the Torngats

Rain! The mountains disappeared, to be replaced by what looked like a low wall supporting a level ceiling of cloud. We changed into our kayaking gear and stepped from boulder to boulder with great care now that the rocks were wet and slick. Even so, it did not take us long to ready the kayaks. Waves tumbled noisily around the corner of an outcrop and rushed over and between the large round boulders. Piles of seaweed thrown up by the shore break offered the materials to ease the launch. Armfuls of the slimy amber fronds got ramped up in front of Kristin's kayak and beneath the hull. When she was ready, with her spray skirt securely fastened, we waited for a suitable lull in the waves. Then as the swash from a wave reached almost its highest point up the beach, I launched her down the slippery ramp in time for her to rush out on the backwash. I followed as soon as I could, and we left the shelter of the bay for the cliffs and the complex swell of the open sea. Big swells broke over shoals, trundled over them, and dissipated with a hiss of bubbles as they reached deep water again. Others bounded toward the cliffs to thunder upward into plumes of spray against the walls of rock. Rebounds rushed back from the cliffs, crisscrossing and leaping across the chaotic pattern of waves. Heavier rebounds collided with oncoming waves to explode outward and upward with a startling clap. Gone was the refreshing blue of protected water; here was a cold gray-green, frothed with dirty white foam that matched the cloud wrapped low around the cliffs.

We pounded out to a mile or more from the cliffs until the crisscrossing of wave patterns became less violent and the air quieter. From that distance we could see the white cliffs clawed by the black vertical stripes of the large crevices running up the center of the mountain, but we were far enough from shore to see more birds: fulmars and gannets, guillemots and painted guillemots, a solitary loon, and one black duck. The fulmars have been a favorite of mine since I first heard of them spreading south to colonize the chalk cliffs of southern England where I grew up. I remember an ornithologist friend of mine describing their stiff-winged flight. Children drawing beach scenes always had their seagulls drawn on their paper skies as the letter m. "But imagine drawing it as a small circle with a straight line through it," Ken said, "That's a fulmar. It holds its wings stiffly, and beats them almost arthritically, but when you see a fulmar glide it's like visual poetry." Fulmars have a gray back, so might be mistaken for a gull at first glance, but its plumage is pearly, not a uniform gray.

Fulmars were newcomers to southern England in the 1960s. Once confined to the Scottish outlier islands such as Saint Kilda, and to places farther north such as the Faroe Islands and Iceland, they found an easy supply of food when fishing boats began to process their catch at sea and throw the offal over the side. Although they cannot dive to catch the sinking morsels, they drop onto the water to snatch the pieces as they fall. They gradually increased their range south, and when their source of food from the boats dried up, they reverted to their more typical plankton diet and stayed in the new areas. Where there are few predators, fulmars nest on open flat ground, tucked in pockets of grass, sometimes in the mouth of a rabbit burrow; in the crowded south of England they find refuge on small ledges on the white chalk cliffs. They lay one white egg each year, which they have high success in raising because they produce an evil-smelling oil that they spit out when provoked. It damages the natural oils on the feathers of other birds. I know the smell, and the tenacity of the oil. Geoff Hunter, my companion in 1977 when I circumnavigated Iceland by kayak, caught a fulmar when our food supply had run out. He was hit on the head with the oil, and because I shared a tent with him I know the scent lingered for days.

Here the fulmars scythed across the water, surfing diagonally along the waves just above the water on the air cushion hidden between the crests, then banking up and around to cross the wind, hurtling from crest to crest with scarcely a wobble in those stiff wings. A patch of dark plumage surrounds each eye, perhaps helping protect against glare, although I see nothing wrong with the idea of a little eye shadow for cosmetic purposes. The shadow accentuated the gaze from the soft brown eyes that scrutinized us as the birds circled once, twice, sometimes three times, in curiosity before resuming their wandering. Perhaps it is this evident curiosity on the part of the fulmar that makes it more endearing to me than other species. Or perhaps it is the display of flying so perfectly executed that it demands my attention and simultaneously inspires and humbles me.

Seals surfaced in a gathering of seven or so, moving fast and packed so close together the group rose and dipped like a single many-headed creature, combing along the surface as if in a rush to get somewhere. At one large headland our eyes were drawn upward by broad vertical stripes of a soft black rock that ran up into the cloud. The softer rock had been worn into a gully, with the color a subtle reddish black on one side, the other side a greenish black. The cliffs continued without break around Itigaiyavik Cape (Cold Feet Cape), offering no opportunity to land. With just an occasional stop while we docked side by side for a bite of Kristin's beef jerky or a candy bar, we pushed on in quite rough conditions until we found shelter behind Kangalasorvik Island at the northern entrance to Saglek Bay. The island and its unnamed rocks almost form a bay, except for narrow channels leaking out at the southern end, so the farther into the bay we paddled the calmer the sea. The chart indicates an anchorage at the southern end, while the topographic map shows a seaplane anchorage, so we expected to find a gentle place to land. But the beaches appeared to be mostly steep ramps of boulders, and most of the possible landing choices did not excite us as places to camp. We pushed on, checking out small beach after small beach. Like an island in the bay sat a large iceberg that glowed in greens and blues and rose in vertical towers like city blocks. We skirted most of the mainland side of the inlet before spotting a place that offered easy camping above the beach. Boulders stuck up from the water for some distance offshore, so we maneuvered and backtracked and tried again until we could find a route to the beach. We were cold; my fingers were stiff. Kristin must have been suffering; her fingers tend to get colder than mine.

Above the beach the ground was fairly flat, and with a little scouting around we found water in shallow peaty pools. Caribou had worn pathways through it, stripping the peaty ground with their hooves to expose the white rock underneath which showed like bone through a wound. Here were shrubs, the tallest we had seen since the start of our trip. In sheltered pockets these dense clouds of stiff growth reached six or eight inches high in places. One huge caribou antler lay bleached at the top of the beach. With our legs free of confinement for the day, we enjoyed striding up the hill, pausing occasionally to gather *boleti* and puffballs. By the time we had climbed high enough to see down into the next little bay, the light was beginning to fade. Down below on that broad pool of water, secure within a narrow entrance, flocks of ducks were gathering in complete shelter. We had walked as far as we dared if we were to return to the tents before dark, but we stood a moment longer to discuss and reflect on exactly where we were.

Here at the north side of Saglek Bay we stood at the southern end of the Torngat Mountains. Almost the entire bulk of Labrador north from here was slated to become the Torngat Mountains National Park of Canada. This was subject to consultation with the Nunatsiavut Government and subject to the settlement of the land claims between the Canadian and Newfoundland governments and the Labrador Inuit Association. The very idea of such consultation was a new development for Canada. It had never happened before. The federal Heritage Minister had completed the planning process for the Torngat Mountains to become a National Park and had already decided where the boundaries should lie without consulting the Inuit. It was only intervention by Inuit in the Federal Court in Montreal that stopped the project until the land claims were settled. The settlement was supposed to compensate the Inuit for being removed from the land. That a federal minister could press ahead so far toward taking land without consulting the people who lived on it is outrageous. Perhaps the government presumed that whatever it could grab before anything was signed would be exempt from consideration. What a great idea a National Park would have been had it come from the Inuit who have known that land for thousands of years. Making their land a park without consulting them seems presumptuous if not insulting.

Turning our backs to the Torngat Mountains and the coast we had paddled so far, we looked onward across Saglek Bay and beyond the summit of Big Island to a row of twinkling lights. They marked the unmanned radar station on Cape Uivak. This military facility sits right on top of the most prominent cape in this stretch of wilderness, like a power station in Yellowstone National Park. Forget blending it into the landscape or diminishing its visual effect; the installation was visible from fifteen miles out. The whole concept of intercontinental ballistic missiles and the radar installations to detect them seemed incongruous, yet it reminded me that during the Cold War had incoming warheads been detected in time, there was a plan to explode them over Greenland or Labrador or northern Canada before they reached the United States. I don't know what the current policy is. From where we stood, the installation could be seen as a symbol of the low priority given to small isolated populations. From the cities of the United States it could be seen as a symbol of the high priority given to their safety. I had plenty to mull over, and I found some of the associations unsettling. But we turned away and I stumbled to keep upright running across the mossy tundra following Kristin's nimble footsteps in the half-light. Chilled even as I hurried, I looked forward to being warm and cozy in the tent, cooking mushrooms for dinner.

Waking up in the morning was seldom difficult. We slept well, despite thoughts of polar bears, and woke with enthusiasm to the idea of a new day. On a typical morning Kristin would first stretch a hand from the sleeping bag to retrieve her watch, which had a built-in thermometer. When worn under her cuff it usually indicated the warmth of her wrist, but in the morning she could discover how warm it was in the tent. "Forty-five degrees Fahrenheit today!" Next we wrote in our journals, which allowed us to luxuriate together in the comfort of our sleeping bag for a few more minutes. I say "bag," singular, although in truth it was two bags zippered together to make one. Sometimes when it seemed too large for the two of us to keep warm, we bunched it up around us to make it smaller; in the morning the surplus offered room to stretch while we wrote. Often I unfolded a copy of the chart to verify place names. I still had difficulty pronouncing the Inuit names, so memorizing them was a challenge; copying them straight from the chart was the only way I could be accurate in my account. Finally we emerged from the sleeping bag, donned warm clothes, and packed everything in the tent into dry-bags. This did not amount to much. Sleeping bags, the now pathetic sleeping mats that were always deflated before morning, spare clothing, and our journals were usually all we had with us. That part of packing finished, we were ready to grab the rifles, and the little foam mats we knelt on when cooking, and move to the shelter tent.

Espresso, tea, a hot breakfast, such as couscous with scrambled egg, more tea, and then it was time to fold away the stove, clean the pans, and change into kayaking clothing. At this time I often lit a small fire to burn any wrappers from our meals, so we carried no garbage smelling of food that might attract bears. We collapsed the tents and carried the kayaks down the beach to a launching place. To diminish the risk of injury we seldom carried them loaded. Early in the trip they weighed too heavily anyway, and the huge tides required long portages that would have been brutal with even a half empty kayak. Here the tidal range was much less, yet it still made sense to carry several smaller loads than struggle with a single heavy one. We piled our dry-bags into shoulder bags and shuttled up and down the beach with those until all the gear was piled beside our kayaks. That done, loading was swift and easy, since by now we had figured out an appropriate sequence for packing, and our diminishing food supplies left us room to maneuver.

Each kayak had three hatches. The two large oval hatches opened into the main watertight compartments, one in the bow and the other in the stern. Immediately behind the seat was a third compartment accessible through a smaller circular hatch offset to one side of the deck for easy access on the water. Inside this day hatch we kept small loose items and things we needed quick access to: our first aid and repair kits, drink bottles, emergency food, the satellite phone, spare hats, mittens, neck-warmers, and a stove with a small bottle of white gas. We also carried a small stainless steel vacuum flask in case we needed a hot drink in a hurry. We refilled it with boiling water each morning, and since we rarely needed it during the day we used it in the evening for a quick energy-boosting drink of hot chocolate while we prepared to cook.

We each carried a spare paddle that took apart into two pieces. These were protected inside tailored bags that clipped onto our rear decks in such a way that a single finger-pinch would allow quick access to them if necessary. We kept the appropriate charts and topographic maps on the deck in front of us where we could refer to them easily. These were cut into overlapping sections and laminated to make them waterproof, and we pinned them in place under a lacework of bungee cord. I have lost charts from beneath bungee when launching through surf, so this time I punched a hole through the edge of each section so it could also be tethered. I carried my camera on my front deck beyond the charts in a zippered deck bag I designed and Kristin made. This clipped into anchor points on my deck. When open, a stiff panel held its arched shape, making it easy for me to slide the bulky underwater housing in and out. I tethered the camera with a metal cable that re-coiled itself when I stowed the camera. We each had a compass mounted into a special recess in the deck just in front of the bow hatch, and on this trip we used them constantly.

Our float-vests had pockets, which normally held a whistle, a spare compass, sunscreen, candy bars or other food, a towline in case either of us needed that extra help, a laser flare, and a signal mirror. Since coming face to face with a polar bear, each also carried a flare gun and distress flares.

On this Saturday, 21 August, we were afloat by 8:30 on calm water. There were a few fog patches around, but even when we had paddled out from the shelter of the islands into Saglek Bay there was little or no breeze. Apart from a glassy chop and some swell, the sea was unflustered. We planned to cross the mouth of the bay, and as this is one of the longer open-water stretches on this coast, we hoped for a day without strong offshore winds. The aptly named Big Island divides the bay into two at the entrance. We would detour around the island to east or west before making the second part of the crossing. Right now conditions seemed ideal, so instead of steering the longer route west of the island we chose the more direct line toward the steeper east coast of the island with its thousand-foot cliffs. As we pulled from shore, clouds of birds, including puffins, circled and skittered across the water. Behind us the sound of swell crashing on the rocks grew faint and disappeared, leaving us in tranquility, our paddles punctuating the surface with little swirls that were overtaken by our wakes spreading behind us.

We crept past a large iceberg that sat offshore, one end looking as regular as a gigantic sugar cube; it was attached underwater to a shelf that sloped up to a massive irregular island of ice that dwarfed the sugar cube. Icebergs like this look majestic and as immovable as rock, and I guess if you were to bump into one it would be similar to hitting a cliff, but the ice is floating. It is also continually melting, water and ice crystals running down the outside. The sea breaking around it wears away at it at water level. Often the waves erode away the base, undercutting it while leaving a ledge extending underwater; this happens in the same way waves erode rock cliffs, but with ice these shaded undercuts often glow eerily with a blue light. In time the erosion can destabilize a berg, causing it to break, or simply roll over to find a more stable floating position. It is unnerving to be close to even a small iceberg when this happens. The noise and disturbance when the ice churns the water is sobering. We were too distant from this particular berg to even hear the waves breaking against it, but eventually we picked up the shore noise from Big Island.

The cliffs on the seaward side are precipitous. One majestic white wall is split with a single black vertical line from the sea to the summit. The cliffs curve inward to form two large bays, culminating in a steep cape more than a thousand feet tall. We crossed the first of these bays feeling the breath of wind blowing from shore. The farther we paddled the stronger the wind, until in the last bay the gusts were quite hefty. But that is quite common close to high land. When we rounded the final headland and looked across toward Bluebell Island and Cape Uivuk the sea did not look rough. After a pause we began the second crossing. Nevertheless I was alert to any change. As we left Big Island behind the wind dropped away. I could see low areas of what could be spray farther up the fjord, but after watching for a while I concluded it was mist.

Switching my focus to the land ahead, I noticed what appeared to be huts near the shore inland from Cape Uivak. We figured these were probably the remains of the abandoned military site and airfield that was built after the Second World War.

Bluebell Island standing off Cape Uivuk is a stub of an island resembling a gigantic tree stump almost 700 feet tall, shored up with fluted buttresses and surrounded by outliers the size of city buildings. Some, including scientists from the Smithsonian, claim this is the oldest island in the world. I assume it is the rock that is old. As we approached, the current and the arrival of a strong wind combined to push us out of the bay. To gauge the strength of the combined wind and current we angled our kayaks to ferry-glide, lining up the island with the cape beyond. I was astonished to discover how high into the wind we had to aim our bows in order to prevent drift. We could easily make the remaining mile to the cape, but the wind was strong enough to suggest we would have a difficult paddle on the far side of the cape also, and we were unsure how far we might have to paddle before reaching a suitable place to land. We did not know what lay beyond the cape. On the other hand we knew there would be a good beach not far from where we had spotted the huts. To reach that beach we would have to paddle hard against the wind for just three miles from Bluebell Island.

Paddling steadily into the wind to maintain our position, we considered our options and decided in favor of caution. We crabbed across to the base of the cliffs, and slowly worked along into the whitecaps and the spray toward safety. There was no shelter and it was hard work. Each corner of rock we paddled around pointed us into the wind and revealed yet another section of cliff jutting out to obscure our view, so we had almost reached the beach before we could see it, and never had a moment of respite. Finally reaching shore, we ran our kayaks up onto coral-pink pebbles.

Without pausing to unload our gear, we grabbed each end of one kayak and scrunched up the steep stones with it to a level area at the top of the slippery slope. With one secure, we returned for the other. Finally, exhausted, we sat back against the rock in sunshine looking out at a sea of Mediterranean blue. It was warm, and the pebbles were colorful and textured, a lot of them green and black and sparkling in the sun. Kristin fumbled in her pocket and pulled out candy bars, so we continued to relax, eating until our pockets were empty. Comfortably enveloped in waves of warm air that radiated from the rock, I smiled in bliss. I felt as if I were melting into the beach like wax.

CHAPTER 16

Saglek

Saglek, translated from Inuktitut means "shortcut." This is the name given to the saddle that runs southeast between Cape Uivuk and the almost 3,000-foot-high mountains, the Domes. It is a shortcut especially useful in winter for moving north up the coast across the ice, as it halves the distance around the cape. It is also an ideal shortcut for polar bears migrating north in summer. During the Second World War a B-26 Marauder from the 319th Bomb Group, after a layover in Greenland, was heading home to the United States on a route via Goose Bay, Labrador. Flying into cloud, the crew lost sight of the planes flying with them. Although they briefly had a signal from Goose Bay, they lost it again, and on reaching the Labrador coast they turned north, away from Goose Bay. They did not realize their mistake until they were too low on fuel to return. They made a forced landing in the saddle at Saglek. It was December 1942, and Labrador was covered in snow.

One man's journal provides a thin account of what followed. Sheltering first inside the plane, and later in a makeshift lean-to they constructed under the wing, the team tried for days to work their radio with no real success. After nearly two weeks, three of the party set off in the small boat they had in the plane. Although the journal reports they were seen to be making slow progress south, it is doubtful they can have had much open water. The average sea-level air temperatures at that time of year vary between a high of 4 degrees and a low of minus 11 degrees Fahrenheit, all decidedly below freezing. Almost the whole coast of Labrador and Newfoundland would be icebound, with only southeast Newfoundland having water temperatures as high as 30 degrees Fahrenheit. The boat party was never seen again. The remaining four settled in to wait for help. In January, thinking they knew where Hebron was, they made day-trips to look for it, but they were weak from lack of food. Even in good weather and easy snow conditions, they would have been challenged to walk there in daylight. If they had set off at dawn, with nine hours of available daylight they would have needed to walk an average of two miles per hour throughout the day to reach Hebron, about seventeen miles to the south. That is assuming they took a straight-line route. There is no knowing what snow and ice conditions they might have run into on the way, or what pace they could have kept up in their condition. They never found Hebron, and help never came. For them, Saglek turned out to be a shortcut to nowhere. They survived until early February. Inuit from Hebron came across their remains in early April 1943.

The site of the crash-landing was later inspected by rescue forces and thought to be suitable for a runway, so after the war the United States gathered supplies at Saglek for the construction of an airstrip and radar station. This operated from around 1954 until the end of the Cold War period, first as one of the Pinetree stations, then as one of the Distant Early Warning (DEW) stations around the north. After being abandoned in the 1970s and destroyed by fire in 1978, the site again attracted military interest, and in 1986 a North Warning System long-range radar station was erected on the site. During construction, PCB-contaminated soil was found. That soil was containerized and shipped out to Goose Bay in 1990 to be incinerated. Unfortunately this was only part of the PCB story as we were to discover later.

Researching before our kayak trip, I had looked at recent photographs of the remains of the wrecked airplane. Now having lounged in the sun for a while, and with no sign of the wind subsiding, I suggested to Kristin that we climb up to see what we could find. The steep berm above the beach rose as crumbling cliff and piled glacial till, not the most stable surface. We scrambled up awkwardly in our kayaking clothing, dislodging showers of dusty earth and stones that rattled down to the beach. From the brim we could see a number of *inuksuqs* that appeared to have been built recently. Up the hill was a hut, and beyond that other buildings including a tan-colored gas tank and two red-and-white-banded radio towers. The radar installation sat on the distant summit. A fat, silver, reflective-insulated pipe ran down the hill toward the next beach, where we could see signs of what might have been a dock. We began climbing the hill along the pipe toward the buildings. On the door of the first hut hung a sign declaring Pollution Control Center, and we swung open the door to reveal an almost empty room. Yellow fiberglass insulation was peeling away from the walls, and the floor was covered in garbage. We closed the door again and continued up the hill. Now we could hear the sound of a generator.

Cresting the brow we saw several caribou standing around the end of an airstrip; more stood in the shade behind long rectangular buildings that looked like modified shipping containers. There were also yellow earthmoving vehicles. I felt strangely apprehensive. There must be people here. We had not seen anybody since the Inuit hunters three weeks earlier. Suddenly someone appeared from behind a building, walking toward us. It was a short dark-haired man dressed in navy overalls and a bright safety vest. We met amid the scramble of caribou scattering around the corner. The man introduced himself as John and almost immediately produced his walkie-talkie to announce our arrival. Shortly afterwards a truck appeared and pulled up beside us. Several more people piled out to welcome us. I felt happy to see them, as they introduced themselves and shook our hands. They seemed surprised to see us. They explained that a total of thirty-two people were working through summer to complete a cleanup operation to remove PCBs from the site, finishing work started the previous summer. Their aim was to reduce the level of contaminants to that permitted by the government. This newly discovered pollution here was closer to Saglek Bay than that dealt with earlier uphill near the radar installation, where several more buildings had stood. Standing surrounded by a bunch of smiling people, it occurred to me that just minutes ago we had imagined ourselves alone on this coast. Now with more things to focus on than just the plane wreck, and with people to ask, I was full of questions.

So what exactly are PCBs? The letters stand for polychlorinated biphenyls, which are man-made compounds, usually liquid or gas once used in hydraulic fluid, synthetic resins, sealants and caulking compounds. They were also quite commonly used in electrical equipment. Similar to compounds like DDT, the potential adverse repercussions were not realized until they were in common use. PCBs do not break down readily and, if released, remain in the environment for a long time. Releases have occurred during manufacture, through the use of materials containing PCBs, and during disposal. Their use is now mostly banned, but a lot of PCBs are already tied up in stored materials that could be released into the environment in the future. Burning waste that contains PCBs can release them. At Saglek, leaks and fires possibly accounted for much of the contamination.

Once loose in the environment PCBs can travel a long way by air. They can stick to organic particles and in sediments, and they bind strongly to soil. Some remain dissolved in the water where they are taken in by small organisms. Larger creatures that feed on the small ones gather much greater amounts. In this way fish, marine mammals and seabirds can accumulate levels that are thousands of times higher than those found in the water.

PCB levels in vascular plants will show the scale of recent PCB exposure, and may be used as indicators. Soil and sediments, on the other hand, accumulate higher concentrations as contaminants are deposited over time. The so-called short-range spread of PCBs from Saglek has resulted in a halo of contamination more than thirty miles in diameter. Studies have been carried out on nestlings of black guillemots, seabirds that nest on beach sites at Saglek and on islands in the bay. The birds feed their young small fish. The studies showed increased levels of PCBs even in the nestlings. The effects measurable in their livers could be detected even after relatively low PCB exposure. These dose-dependent changes in liver function caused the livers of female nestlings from the beach to be thirty-six percent larger than usual.

Studies like this made me wonder what direct harm PCBs may have on people. We get exposure to PCBs via food and drinking water, by inhaling contaminated air, or through the skin when handling materials such as electrical equipment that contain PCBs. The known effects include acne-like skin rashes and liver damage although there could be worse. Researchers studying animals have seen injuries to the liver, stomach, thyroid gland and skin, and have detected changes to the immune system. PCBs also seem to alter normal behavior and reproduction. On Svalbard, the island group off arctic Norway, polar bears have been found with dual genitalia and possessing no Y chromosome. Scientists have estimated that four percent of Svalbard's population of polar bears is affected in this way, and have concluded that PCBs were the likely cause. PCBs are accumulated in animal fat, and seal blubber forms a major part of polar bear diet. In the case of Svalbard the PCBs likely arrived through both marine and avian food chains from Europe and Russia, accumulating in ever greater amounts with each step up in the food chain toward the polar bear at the top. The only predator to hunt and eat polar bears, the Inuit, did not settle on Svalbard.

Saglek Bay is still a significant area to the Inuit from Nain for harvesting shellfish, salmon, arctic char, and ringed seal. Caribou, a migratory food source, still graze here. That being so, it is fortunate the Department of National Defence was required to test for PCBs and is now minimizing further contamination of the food chain by cleaning up the main source of PCBs at Saglek. Once PCBs are in the food chain there is nothing more that can be done but to monitor the damage.

Our hosts explained they had set up two main sites here for the summer: the laboratory site and the housing site farther inland, where everyone ate and slept. The laboratory had been set up to measure PCB concentrations in soil and sediment samples, and to measure the concentrations in water. The pollutants stick to small particles, so rocks sieved from the soil could be washed and returned to where they had been found. That washing process, carried out in massive water tanks, would diminish the volume of material that would need to be shipped away for hazardous waste incineration, but the water had to be rigorously filtered and the PCBs removed from it before it could be released into the stream Kristin and I had planned to use as our water source. Contaminated soil was loaded into the big gray plastic containers we could see lined up ready for shipment. More than 7,000 of these containers of contaminated soil had already been removed.

The personnel here included laboratory scientists, workers involved in the excavation and loading of soil, engineers, catering staff, administrative staff, and polar bear guards. Because the contaminant is invisible, it was also considered essential that someone kept check to ensure everything was done correctly, so representatives from the Labrador Inuit Association and from the military watched over all that happened. Their brief also included checking the work of the officer in charge of the cleanup. I quickly realized this was a complex operation that must have been extremely well planned for anything to happen at all. If a single inexpensive replacement part for any of the machinery had to be flown in, the flight cost would be calculated in thousands of dollars.

We had come up here to look for a wrecked airplane, and there at the end of the runway was the crumpled mass of a crashed plane, but it appeared to be a small Cessna. This plane had gone missing last year in Labrador, yet although a search was made for it right away it was located only this summer in a lake. It had been a fatal accident. The plane was pulled out and brought here at the request of the insurance company, although no one here knew what would happen to it next. It was not the plane we had expected to see. When we asked about the remains of the bomber, Louis said he'd get someone to run us up to the crash site, which was farther up the saddle to the east side of the runway. He also kindly invited us to stay at the site overnight and to dine with them, and while I recognized his genuine hospitality, I was also informed that while the cleanup was underway, camping on the beach was not an option for security reasons. We accepted, gratefully, and were whisked up the hill past the accommodation complex, a group of long trailers clustered together and accessed by board walks, to the start of the road that wound up the hill to the radar buildings. By a curve in the road stood a memorial to the crew of the Marauder; a simply worded message on a brass plaque mounted to a concrete plinth surmounted by a cross. Beyond lay a sea of big boulders stretching out to a lake. Scattered on the boulders between where we stood and the runway across the valley were pieces of shiny metal debris, the remains of the plane. "It gets blown around by the wind," explained one of our companions as we jumped from boulder to boulder. Then, changing the subject he said, "We're not supposed to go anywhere on the site without an Inuit guard." He nodded toward John, the first man we had met, who had driven down the runway on his ATV to a point opposite and was now making his way across the boulders to meet us. "He's here to watch for polar bears." When I asked, "Do you see many?" He replied, "Oh, we've had a few."

We reached the main wing section of the plane first. It was perched across the boulders like a piece of driftwood on a beach. More sections of wreckage lay closer to the lake, and smaller pieces were tucked down between the striated boulders. The saddle stretched a mile and a half in each direction, with pools of water and flat ground strewn with boulders. The only real color in the landscape came from patches of low bright green vegetation. Above the saddle were sharply detailed mountains with cliffs and patches of snow bright in the sun. April, an attractive Inuit girl employed as an overseer to the PCB project climbed up onto the wreckage and stood on the flat wing, offering me a better idea of the scale of the wreck. I imagined this scene in winter, the lakes frozen solid and the boulders buried in snow. The mountains would have been white with perhaps the steeper scree slopes and crags clear but frosted, the ledges piled with snow. The plane, then intact, would have stood higher on the snow on this open place, leaving room underneath the wing for the crew to live in their improvised tarpaulin shelter. It must have been an anxious time for them all, wondering when or if they would be found and rescued, as they grew weaker. Since then the plane has been blown around for more than sixty years, gradually breaking up. The wing now bears scribbled messages from visitors.

Having fetched a change of clothing and secured the kayaks for the night at the top of the beach we luxuriated in hot showers, me in the men's shower room and Kristin in the women's, apart for the first time in a long time. Afterwards we compared notes, laughing at how we had each stepped out of the shower to the shock of seeing ourselves reflected in the mirrored wall above the washbasins. Both of us were fairly skinny at the start of our trip, but we had been losing weight. The change had been gradual so neither of us had been aware of how our own body had been affected until now, seeing ourselves in a mirror for the first time since the start of the trip. We were both emaciated, bony scarecrow versions of what we had last seen weeks before. But it was now mealtime so we joined the others in the canteen.

The chef offered us the choice of beefsteak or caribou steak wrapped in bacon, or both. We accepted both; together with the mounds of fries and onions, mushrooms and broccoli he piled around them. Enthusiastically we tucked in and cleared our plates, still finding room for the tangy lemon meringue pie, fresh plums, and coffee he then offered. Tonight was Saturday night, and here that meant Steak Night, so we were doubly grateful to not only be invited to dine, but to be invited to the meal of the week.

After dinner the site engineer showed us around the accommodation area. Animals had nibbled into the insulating sheaths around some of the pipes outside, but new barriers made the whole section more secure against bears. One of the trailers held the water treatment plant, with filters and ultraviolet light treatment, sterilizing the water from a more distant lake on the mountain, farther from the PCB contamination. The water was pumped around the buildings supplying the washrooms, showers and kitchens with hot and cold water. The site had its own generators for electrical supply, its own sewerage treatment, and had to deal with issues as varied as waste disposal and refrigeration. Heating and electricity were supplied to all the rooms. Everything here at this site, and at the laboratory down the hill, including all the vehicles, was shipped in and hauled up the hill, assembled and hooked up, wired, plumbed, and turned on ready for the arrival of the main workforce at the direction of the site engineer. This cleanup work at Saglek should be finished and the site cleaned ready for a visit by the Nain elders planned for 16 September. Then the site will be inspected, a drum ceremony held, and everyone will sit down to a meal. Following that last event all the buildings will be dismantled, hauled back to the water, loaded onto boats and shipped out.

Kristin and I were offered a room in one of the cabins for the night, an arrangement I felt less secure about when they told us what happened there last summer. Anchored down with massive straps against the wind, a smaller camper trailer was parked close by the end of the one we would sleep in. One night a polar bear ripped a large hole in the end of that unoccupied trailer in the space of about eight minutes. Everybody from this cabin gathered at the window to watch the activity, but their movements drew the bear's attention. Then someone took a photograph. The glare of the camera flash enraged the bear, and it stood a full ten feet tall on its hind legs and threw itself at the end window. On the second impact the glass shattered, flying the length of the cabin and causing everyone to race from the scene. Although the bear cut its paw and wandered away, it was harried from the scene by trucks with lights blazing, and with firecrackers. After that incident, Louis decided they should take better precautions against bears. This year armed Inuit guards keep watch over the site day and night, spotting and scaring away the bears usually before they reach the trailers. Nobody is allowed to move around the site without an armed guard. Even so, sometimes a bear will catch everyone by surprise. Nobody wants to be the cause of harm to a bear, and as an additional disincentive, there is a heavy penalty for illegally shooting a bear.

Talking with the site workers we learned that many of them were born in Hebron and relocated to Nain with their parents when they were young. They came with us to our room to show us on our charts where we might find good places to camp between Saglek and Nain. One pointed out the route of a good shortcut through the Kaumajet Mountain range, and the position of huts we might use for shelter on our way. They marked the position of the old Inuit village of Okak, and the two areas where we would likely experience the strongest winds. It was fun to hear them talk about their land in a way that was knowledgeable and respectful. They understood its nature and its quirks and knew what we were likely to experience. We especially valued their local knowledge. They also told us we would find a work party restoring the roof on the Moravian mission building at Hebron this summer, so we should bring their greetings to them.

I slept poorly in the bed; I actually fell out onto the floor during the night. There were different noises here. Alert for any sounds of polar bears, I woke at every unfamiliar sound, whether heating or plumbing. I was awake early and by breakfast time I was more than ready to devour another big meal. As we would soon be leaving, Mel, the chef, loaded a box with food for us to take with us. While the medic examined and dressed the wounds on Kristin's hands, the lingering result of torn blisters from the first few days of paddling, Louis ran me up to the hilltop in a truck to see the view. Fifteen miles to the south I imagined I could make out the gleam of light reflected from the roof of the mission building at Hebron. As difficult as it was for me to see anything today, surely nothing much would have been visible under snow in the winter of 1943. Out to the north of us a long-liner was plowing its way into Saglek Bay leaving a broad V of wake behind it. "It's probably one of the Webb brothers," said Louis. "They are about the only people who come up here in that sort of boat." Without its wake the boat would surely have been invisible, an unidentifiable tiny speck in a wide bay studded with islands and surrounded by mountains.

Saglek Bay is one of the bigger fjords in northern Labrador, and one of the few that is relatively free of obstructions and offshore dangers to ships. The cruise ships that occasionally visit can sail more than thirty miles inland here and still find deep water between mountains three thousand feet high, just ten miles from the border with Quebec. The potential for cruise ships was recognized by earlier travelers. Alexander Forbes, writing of his exploration and surveys of northern Labrador by boat and airplane in the 1930s, forecast that Saglek Fjord, along with Nachvak Fjord and Mugford Bay, would afford "abundant scenic splendor for the tourist," and added that the approaches to these three fjords, unlike the many more naturally protected ones farther north are "providentially safe" for larger tour boats. With Saglek Fjord and Mugford Bay positioned south of the proposed Torngat Mountains National Park, it would appear those two areas could become developed for commercial tourism in the future. From my vantage point on the summit of Cape Uivuk I gazed at the steep cliffs, the islands and icebergs, the points of land sectioning off arms of water, and the mountains, and I knew I could be tempted back to explore this fjord. Not only is it spectacular and extensive, it is historically significant to the Inuit.

CHAPTER **17**

Hebron

The weather forecast Louis had printed out for us at Saglek predicted fresh to strong southwesterly winds. It was not our ideal forecast, but we had been kayaking without the benefit of weather reports up till now and were used to making decisions on the evidence the sky offered us. We were well fortified and ready to move on. Determined to try to reach Hebron that night, we slipped rapidly out of sight of our helpers on the beach to skim around the cliffs with the breeze pushing at our backs. Visibility was crisp. From the base of the massive cape it was difficult to see much of the structure on the hilltop above us, but it was not long before we were distracted from looking up by the force of the wind driving at us from the other side of the cape. Soon we were struggling against this wind and working through relentless whitecaps that pitched water into our faces with every wave. It was a push, but not more than we had expected given the forecast and the form of the land.

We reached White Point, three miles beyond the cape, and aimed at the shore three miles farther west, where we hoped to find somewhere to land. Unfortunately this was now directly into the wind which seemed to be getting steadily stronger. We pushed on, aching from the constant exertion and having no opportunity to rest for even a moment without being swept backward again. Eventually I suggested we try to reach a small island not far ahead, where we might shelter for a moment. Perhaps we would find somewhere to land. But reaching that island proved more difficult than it appeared. When we aimed for the island our bows angled across the wind which set us ferry-gliding sideways while pushing us back. Little by little we were drifting toward a second island behind us and farther from shore. For a while I considered cutting our losses and turning to that island instead, but glancing over my shoulder, I could see a pale object on the rocks that looked like a bear. It vanished, but I could not be sure if it had been just light gleaming from the rock or if it had been a bear. Uneasy, I felt determined we should keep to our original plan. Renewing our efforts we gradually made progress forward, and in the end reached the low island. There, gusts snatched at us from either end of the island without warning, then left us for moments of absolute calm.

Swells broke over the rock, which jutted vertically from the water and offered no place to land. Our moment of enjoyment in the partial shelter from the wind was marred by my anxiety that there might be a bear on the rock. There were too many lumps and corners to be able to tell. We were close enough for a bear to leap from the rock to where we sat. After a brief rest we pushed into the wind again. Watching the squalls rip across the water at us, we tried to turn our bows straight into them and clung on until they passed. Then, in even the slightest lull, we sprinted forward to cover as much distance as possible before the next gust hit. Eventually we drew close to land and reached the beach we had been aiming for. But it was a boulder beach, with no obvious place to land safely through the breaking swell. The boulders were too large, and in any case the beach was difficult to scan from the water to check for bears. We searched for somewhere better and found a place where a corner of outcropping rock diminished the power of the shore-break. It was the best of poor alternatives.

I watched the waves and waited for a lull, until the waves were at their smallest in the cycle, then raced in on the back of a wave to minimize the impact with the boulders. That is the best strategy, and one I employed almost daily. Typically I would land first then signal Kristin in, standing ready to grab her bow as she touched shore. I thought I had made a perfect approach this time when I touched rock gently, but I was wrong. I had found a sharp edge. I could feel the gel-coat and fiberglass collapse as the fine edge of the keel was forced across the rock; the noise of the wave drowned any sound of the impact. When I leaped from my kayak to haul it clear I could see the damage underneath where the bow curves to meet the keel. I did not waste time inspecting it, but grabbed the rifle and checked the vicinity for bears. Then I positioned myself to grab Kristin, using hand signals to hold her from shore until there was a suitable lull for a landing. She came in perfectly.

Finally we found respite from the wind. In the last four exhausting hours we had covered only six miles; ordinarily we would have doubled that distance without much effort. The sun was warm. We relaxed and snacked. Then I examined the crushed bow of my kayak. Tidying the hole, I repaired it temporarily with epoxy putty and duct tape, which extended our break to an hour, which was probably good anyway. Then we launched again and continued down the coast. I felt reassured to be close to land, but we now had to choose between weaving between the shoals and small ledges close to shore, where we had shelter from the wind but where surf was breaking over the rocks, or farther from shore where we could paddle confidently but where it was very windy. Neither was satisfactory. The weather made our progress slow and heavy going. We hugged the shore when we could, even though this increased our mileage from twenty to almost twenty-six miles.

As we paddled straight in toward the village site of Hebron the low sun blinded us. It glared from above the hill directly ahead and reflected from the water into our faces, making it almost impossible to see where we were going. When we were within a hundred yards of shore the sun sank below a bank of cloud and we could see the buildings, the long one obviously the mission. Four people walked to the shore and stood there, waiting to greet us. We were tired; they were silent but attentive. As soon as we had climbed out of the kayaks they came down to help us lift them up the rocks. We lay the kayaks side-by-side in long grass by a dilapidated building that apparently used to be the Hudson's Bay Company store. It stood shored up on short wooden posts; the front was boarded up. A makeshift ramp with a handrail led to a gap in the plywood.

"You can camp here if you like." One of the men offered. "There are camp beds in there, in the tent." We looked inside. A white wall-tent had been erected inside, almost filling the building. Two green canvas cots and a pile of boxes stood inside. Tom, a carpenter from Saint Johns, Newfoundland, offered us heating, and when we declined, saying we were used to the nighttime temperatures camping, he hauled in a big gas cylinder with a heating unit fastened to the top into the building for us anyway, explaining, "In case you need it. It can get cold in there." He also left a flashlight and an invitation to come over to the kitchen for coffee when we were ready. We unloaded what we thought we'd need for the night, and discovered that my repair had done a poor job of keeping water out of my kayak. In dry clothes again we walked up the path past the mission building, toward the group of white tents the restoration team was using for accommodation.

Otto, chef for the camp, was employed by the company that provides catering services on the *Northern Ranger,* the ship that serves the Labrador coast. His company won the contract to provide catering for this restoration project, and Otto decided to give it a try. I'm not sure if Hebron turned out to be quite what he expected. The kitchen was in a tent, and the limited food available hampered his creative skills. With nothing more than a cabin or two within a hundred miles, except for the group at Saglek, anything he lacked in the way of seasoning or variety he would have to manage without until the next food arrived from Saint John's, and that would take weeks to work its way up the coast.

Tom sat and chatted with us. He and Otto were both from Newfoundland. All the others working on the project were Inuit, born at Hebron, although most of them now lived in Nain. In 1959 they were still children when the government announced everyone would have to leave their homes and be moved south. Now they had a chance to visit their childhood territory again and be paid by grant to restore the old Moravian mission post. The building they are restoring is one of the oldest mission-built structures in North America, erected with Inuit help by master builder Ferdinand Kruth. It is one of only two Moravian structures remaining in Labrador; in 1976 it was designated a National Historic Site. This year's task was to restore the roof, and Tom said they planned to work from July until September. It is a four-year project, so next year maybe they will tackle the outside walls. Once the roof and walls were finished the building would be weatherproof again, which should stop further decay. Then work could begin inside. Tom said that although nobody knew how the restoration would progress in the allocated time and with the current funding, people hoped work could be done to prevent the Hudson's Bay Company store and other buildings from falling apart. It grew late. We steered into the dark, fortified by hot chocolate and blueberry crumble. Across the hill and down the rutted path we found again the building that would be our home for the night.

Tom was right; sleeping in the big tent in the old building was colder than we expected. The wind blew hard, moving loose boards and making them creak and clatter. If we had needed a haunted house experience, this was the perfect night. Whenever the noise of the wind and the knocking eased we heard the tiny feet of lemmings and mice scuttling everywhere over the roof of the tent and across the floor. The place was alive with them. Waking just before dawn, still sleepy, I stepped outside to chill surroundings and a brightening morning sky that ignited into golden light as the sun emerged from the sea. Light reflected up from the water onto the rocks and the front of the old store. As the sun spread, the cold white caribou antlers that were lying discarded and wet on the grass gleamed almost orange. It was the perfect moment to perch on the entrance ramp with my espresso to reflect how the summer dawn in this place must have always been this magical when the skies were clear.

Sem, one of the roof team and otherwise a lay preacher, whom the others had nicknamed The Shaman because of his eerie sixth sense about what went on, had foretold our arrival and had also forecast when we landed that we would not be leaving the next day. The strong wind racing out from shore confirmed that for us. Offshore winds can be deceptive. From the shore, the water appears calm and the wind manageable. But even half a mile out, where the waves have had time to build, the conditions can be much rougher. The wind, free from the land, can be significantly stronger. We felt we deserved a break from paddling in the wind.

Boxes of books occupied a corner of the tent. They were there for sale in case any cruise ships visited during the summer. Hebron has been of interest to a few small cruise ships, which have begun to make it a port of call in the last few years. In 2001, when the Department of Industry, Trade and Rural Development granted funds for the refurbishment of the Moravian mission building, it stated its long-term goal. The goal, with cruise ships in mind, was to "offer an anchor attraction to an upscale target audience including history enthusiasts and adventure tourists." With the mission house and buildings derelict, gravestones overgrown and sinking into the ground, Hebron has the atmosphere of a ghost town. But this whole bay area has had a long history of occupation. There are said to be abundant tent circles and Inuit graves on the islands. If the density of the native population attracted the Moravians here in the early 1800s, whatever remains will continue to attract visitors. We browsed a book from one of the boxes. Published by the Labrador Inuit Association, *Reconciling with Memories* tells of the involuntary relocation of the people of northern Labrador. Hebron was evacuated in 1959. Inuit who were relocated spoke of their experiences, and those accounts fortify the story of an emotional reunion that took place at Hebron in 1999, forty years later. We bought a copy. It was the first copy sold at Hebron because no cruise ships had visited since the books arrived. We asked the men working on the roof to sign their names on pages where there were photographs of family or friends, or even of themselves. Their agreeing to do so made our copy of the book personal.

Tom explained the roof restoration to us. The dormers that once protruded at intervals along its length had been removed, and temporary level walkways were built; on them the aromatic cedar shingles would be stacked, ready for placement. The old shingles lay in steep heaps on the ground where they had been gathered. A lot of wood was being replaced, and he said the old wood was difficult to get rid of. He had thought burning it would be simple, but the weather here was so changeable, as soon as they lit a fire, the wind came racing over the hill to make it unsafe. They burned small fires to eat away at the waste, but the waste piles were growing, not shrinking.

The mission building is so long it could dominate a city block but here, settled into a sloping meadow beneath a mountain, it appears at once imposing and miniscule. The roofline steps gently down from the tallest section, bearing an ornamental belfry, to the long lower section pointing toward the water. The lower section once housed the families of the brethren, the workers and workshops, classrooms, and medical facilities. To one side stretch the vegetable gardens, which were then enclosed by picket fences against damage from dogs. The uphill section of the main building was the church, a big space where all the inhabitants of the village could gather at once. In April of 1959, everyone in the village was called to the church for a meeting. The population numbered 247. Behind the scenes the Newfoundland government, in liaison with the Moravian Church, had conspired to relocate the families from Hebron farther south. In the church, rather than in the community hall, the church announced it was withdrawing the minister and closing the mission. Next, an official from the provincial government announced that the commercial trade store, at one time run by the Hudson's Bay Company but now run by the government, would close the following year. This would leave the community without its source of supplies and without the means to sell char, on which their economy relied.

With their means of existence at Hebron effectively removed, the families were offered jobs and housing in towns farther south. The families could decide themselves who went where, but five families were to be assigned to Nain, ten to Hopedale and forty-three to Makkovik. The respect for the church, with its teaching that people should never speak out or argue when in church, was so strong nobody felt able to say anything about the evacuation.

The usual place for such a meeting was the community hall; that was where discussions took place. Yet the authorities wanted to prevent people from expressing opinions or posing questions, so this strategy effectively silenced any opposition. The move had been planned in secret for some time with the full complicity of the church, which was concerned about the expense of the Labrador missions and was trying to save money. The head of the Moravian church as far back as 1955 had encouraged the centralization of the people, relocating them farther south, and it was the Hebron minister who suggested in 1958 that they close the Hebron mission. The plan to close it the following year, 1959, was kept secret. The original ethos of the missionaries in the 1700s to carry Christianity to the remote communities had changed. Now it prioritized centralization of the church's financial resources, at the sacrifice of those communities.

With the promise of housing and jobs and a better life farther south, some of the families packed and left right away, fearing they had no option. By fall about half still remained. By now they had heard the news that there were no houses available down south anyway, so they felt they were better off where they were. Then the director of the International Grenfell Association entered the proceedings. He had previously written to the provincial government expressing his concern about the future of the "nonwage" economy of Hebron. He said the Inuit should be brought into a permanent community in one place, instead of allowing them to disperse to make a living by hunting and fishing as they had always done. Now that half of the community had been moved, he withdrew the International Grenfell Association nurse from Hebron. This left one remaining service, the government store. With the store manager as the only official in Hebron, the government decided to close the store in the fall of

1959 instead of waiting until 1960 as scheduled. This last-minute decision left the remaining families with no option but to leave right away. There was too little time to prepare for winter without the store, and almost no time to prepare before the departure of the last boat of the season. We can scarcely imagine the effect on those people; we nowadays take our own relative lack of freedom for granted.

The church building was rotting from within. Boards in the center of the room bubbled with fungus and dark dampness where water dripped from the ceiling. But the structure is being painstakingly reconstructed to look as it used to look. I felt pain for the people who had loved this place. The cuckoo, having thrown out the nestlings, had flown; now the empty nest was being restored. My footsteps echoed as I paced the room, seeing mustard yellow paintwork up to waist-height around the walls with cream paint above, the fallen benches and the multi-pane windows with semicircular arched tops. Then I walked on through the door to explore the rest of the building.

The forty-five years empty from 1959 to 2004 had taken their toll. Everything metal was rusted and crumbling; all the paintwork was peeling, exposing the many different colors of paint layered underneath. Room after room lined the long corridor, the boarded windows making a shadowy system of burrows of the interior. In the dank corners of a few small rooms, oilcans had been fitted with toilet seats, the bare metal corroding to leave only painted sections intact. One advertised Esso. In a larger room, embossed white wallpaper displayed daintily detailed floral posies, and in another the appearance of stenciled red and blue tulips on the linoleum floor caught my eye. People had taken care of these spaces to make them welcoming, to make them their own. Here were rooms used as workshops, or as schoolrooms, but now little distinguishes one from the other. That was part of the genius of these prefabricated buildings. The outer shell could be assembled, freestanding, with the interior rooms and floors added afterwards to suit the current needs. If those needs changed, the interior layout could be altered without compromising the integrity of the structure. Once the frame was completed, the spaces between the timbers were filled with yellow bricks before the inside and the outside were boarded over. The bricks were intended to help insulate the building. I found one of the staircases and climbed up to find Kristin.

Tom had warned us to be careful. Not all the floor was sound, and here and there holes had already been broken through the boards. But we could see well by the light through the open roof where the team worked. I had heard the timbers for the original building were shipped out ready to assemble according to a set of plans. Each timber was pre-marked with identifying symbols to show where it should be slotted into the next, and dowels were driven through drilled holes to lock the joints. When I began looking at the timbers in the roof I saw the name "K E Hettasche" stenciled in black on two adjacent timbers. Could this be for Kate Hettasche, daughter of Labrador missionaries and a teacher herself? On another was stenciled "Bethlehem PA USA," which is where the Moravian church is centered in the United States. Outside, the men rolled out roofing felt and hammered shingles into place, working methodically along the row. Severe winds often made their work difficult, so they were always tethered by rope in case they lost their footing or were blown off balance. Today it was windy, but not raining. Down on the ground a forty-gallon oil drum shimmered with flames that were consuming the old shingles, one load at a time. I brought my head back inside the building and inspected the ornate castings on a heavy iron mangle. Brick chimneys angled up to the ridge, and partition walls sectioned the spaces between. Holes in the roof waited where the dormers would eventually be replaced, but their restoration required tools that had not yet been brought to the site. Tom said the holes will likely be boarded up until the work can be done correctly next year rather than completing it to a lesser standard than the original.

Back in the open air we studied the footings as we skirted the building. A wall several feet high had been neatly constructed of large stone blocks, hewn from the hill behind by the original builders. Unable to manhandle the heavy blocks, the construction team had waited for winter snow so they could haul them to the site by dogsled. The structure was solidly built and has survived well, impressive considering the remote location and that it has withstood the elements here since 1830. We reached the eastern end of the building where a metal plaque nailed to the end wall announced first in English, then in French, and finally in Inuktitut, the words, "Notice. These buildings are part of our national heritage. Your cooperation is requested in leaving everything as you have found it. Leave only footprints, take only pictures. Moravian Mission. Canada." I stared at it, wishing the native language had been placed first, and then imagining: "Notice. This population is our national heritage. Your cooperation is requested in leaving everyone where you have found them...." But of course it's too late for that.

The wider area around the bay revealed the remains of a number of buildings flattened by the wind and scattered. A standing row of three houses had belonged to the Hudson's Bay Company to be rented to Inuit families. Adjacent to the store where we were camped was another building already in a state of collapse. This was probably the first house the Moravians built here in 1831. These meadows, with the windswept grasses, the colorful wild flowers, and the berry patches farther up the hill, would have been sites for sod houses and tents before the European-style houses were built.

From beside the kitchen tent, Otto pointed out an island at the far end of the bay where older Inuit graves could be seen, each the customary mound of boulders enclosing a chamber in which the body would rest on a bed of moss. The boulders gave protection from animals. He said you could see bones, including skulls, but groups from the cruise ships tended to search over there for relics. Changing the subject, he told us about a polar bear that came into the kitchen tent a month ago. He fired a rifle shot between its legs, which startled it. Hearing the shot, everyone came running to scare the bear away. They had only encountered two polar bears here so far, but they thought the dog they brought here later would do a good job of alerting them if a bear was nearby. Otto pointed to the rifle, standing a yard away. "I always keep my gun right there."

We returned to the shore to string up our wet kayaking clothes to dry. We had hoped to leave by late morning, to get in at least half a day of paddling, but the wind that was sending gleaming waves across the grass and wild flowers was also sending whitecaps racing across the bay. On the wooden floor of the Hudson's Bay Company store we placed three yellow bricks to protect the boards from the heat of our stove and brewed hot drinks while the wind whistled between the planks and made the building creak, rattle, and knock.

In the evening Sem came down to talk with us. We sat outside on the grass together in the shelter of the store. Pulled up close by was a little dory, cut out of plywood and roughly fiberglassed together. This was the tender for Sem's boat moored offshore. "I built that," he said proudly. Then he told us he never went to school. "I had a family to look after. When my mother died, I learned from the village elders, not from school. I like to be outside. I like space. I always like to be outside where I can see things, see nature, and the weather, so I listened to the elders and learned from them. That's how we learned before we had school, from the old people. We learned by watching, by listening, by copying. I have a dog team, four dogs: huskies. An old man said, 'Feed your dogs char in the summer.' I asked why. The old man laughed and said, 'You'll see.' He wouldn't say why. He just said, 'You'll see.' So I fed them on char through the summer, and then in the winter their skin and fur was really good. Usually it's patchy, but when I feed them char through the summer, their skin and fur is really good in the winter. Now I know why. That's how I learn, from the older people."

He paused to gaze across the bay. Then he continued, "No, I didn't go to school, but I have 13 children. The oldest son is twenty-eight years old, and the youngest child is two. That's a lot of children, but the oldest daughter, she looks after the youngest ones." Bending over our charts he began to point out details. "Here is a place where there is soapstone for carving. There are three kinds of soapstone white, black and gray... some is quite soft and some is harder to carve. This channel here is a good one for kayaks. There is a portage here, but it's not so far. It's a good way to save time. You'll like it there, and you'll see caribou. If you go around the Kaumajet Mountains, go around in the daytime, not in the morning and not in the evening. But here," he pointed to Cod Bag Harbor and the narrow bridge of land separating it from Lost Channel to the southwest, "This is a good way through. You'll like this. You can carry your kayaks over. It's not far." I asked, "How long do you think it would take us to carry?" He replied, "Not long," he paused to think. "Maybe fifteen minutes."

We asked about Mugford Tickle, but he again asserted the other route was a better one. Taking a pen he marked places on the map that he knew would be good for us to make camp, and places where he knew there were cabins. When we asked him to sign our book, *Reconciling with Memories* for us, he thumbed through the pages to find the photograph of him on his mother's lap. She is smiling out of her fur-trimmed hood while he sits, a solemn-faced baby with dark brown eyes, staring at the camera. He drew a little arrow from the margin to her face. "Mom," he wrote. She had a nice smile. Beneath that he wrote his own name with an arrow to the baby. That baby was Sem, in 1957.

Reading the book brought home to me the injustice that had been done to the people of Hebron when they were moved. There had been neither jobs for them when they arrived at the places they were expected to live, nor adequate housing. They were used to living in small family groups migrating seasonally to hunt and fish, and returning to places where they would overwinter. Some of these families were moved to Hopedale, a place where the population had already become accustomed to living year-round in one place governed by church elders, store managers, welfare officer and police. There the government built five new houses, ten temporary structures, and rented two empty houses for the newcomers. The seventeen houses were to be home for thirty-seven families, a total of 148 people. They were not big houses. That was in 1959. The housing situation was "solved" in 1962 by moving thirty families again, this time to Makkovik, where houses were now available. The Hebron families had to cope with a new language, English, in a town of predominantly English-speaking European or Euro-Inuit people. None of the people who had been moved were able to maintain a living in a familiar way. Nain, Hopedale, and Makkovik are all south of the tree line, so hunting was of a different nature, and local people had already taken over the hunting areas. With a different dialect of Inuktitut spoken in these southern areas, or in the case of Makkovik, English, the Hebron group had little chance to find out anything about local hunting customs, places, or etiquette. Their own land had been taken away from them, together with their self-esteem and their history. Many turned inward, becoming ill, relying on welfare, drinking, and getting into trouble with the authorities. They had no way to pay electricity bills. Their children were taunted at school. They were trapped in one place in contrast to having always been free to move up and down the coast. Their lives were effectively shattered.

For years nothing much was done about the situation until in 1991 the Canadian government established a commission on aboriginal peoples to look into native issues. The commission found the relocation of communities to have been a major problem and sponsored further investigation into their cause and the consequences to the Inuit. Carol Brice-Bennett described in her report how the northern Inuit were continually scorned and neglected after resettlement. The Royal Commission in its final report of 1996 concluded that human rights had been violated, that the government should take responsibility, and that the Human Rights Commission should take further action. Those conclusions led to funding for recovery programs for past abuse in residential schools, but still no remedy for the displaced population. The Labrador Inuit Health commission, aware of the problems relocation had caused, decided to make a start in a healing process by holding a retreat or "healing circle," where Inuit could freely express their grievances to help them come to terms with them. The plan, for which funding was made available, developed into a reunion at Hebron for the people who had been affected by the relocation. Of 418 Inuit relocated from 1956 to 1959, fewer than 200 were still alive; 159 of them gathered at Hebron in 1999 for the reunion. Whatever Hebron meant for those people, it had been the place where they belonged. Within a wide territory they had freely roamed to hunt and to fish, to live with pride. No more.

We met Sem early next morning. He told us he had prayed for us at first light. "But I can only pray in Inuktitut. I speak better in my own language." he said, hoping we would be satisfied with that. "The weather will be good for you today." Looking out, the bay was calm and the weather clear. We loaded our kayaks then walked up to the mission to say goodbye.

CHAPTER **18**

Kaumajet Mountains... the Shining Mountains

It seemed such a long way out of the bay and across Hebron Fjord that I felt we must surely have shrunk, or the landscape must have stretched wide and flat. Kristin thought it was probably just the sun with the lack of breeze making us hot. Also the land was lower. Yet we cruised easily on the calm water and soon were crossing the opening to Napartok Bay. Napartok is Inuktitut for "black duck," or *Anas rubripes*, a duck that breeds in Labrador and migrates south to the United States each winter. To the west, deep in Napartok Bay, is the most northerly patch of trees along this coast. According to Jens Haven, one of the early missionaries, in 1773 there were three settlements there with a total of about 140 people. Inuit from Hebron traveled into the bay to collect wood. The island at the mouth of the bay toward which we paddled was Soapstone Island. During the period known as the Dorset, from approximately 1,000 BC to 1,000 AD, soapstone from this island was carved into lamps. Using wicks made from moss, and burning oil from seal and whale, these simply carved open boxes or bowls provided light and warmth to winter dwellings. I have improvised lamps using kerosene and moss in the same way, and although the flame is smoky, it does provide both heat and light. It surprised me how much I could control the flame, and in that way control the amount of heat and light, by adjusting the moss wick with a stick.

During the period preceding the Dorset, up to perhaps four thousand years ago, the Maritime Archaic people likely used soapstone from here to carve fishing weights. Soapstone was not used for hunting tools, but chert was, for making blades and scrapers; it was dug from outcrops in the Kaumajet Mountains to the south. If you add the nearness of these commodities, plus wood, and the availability of salmon, char, ducks, caribou, bearded seals, ringed seals, and harbor seals, all within easy traveling distances, you find the combination of resources that made Napartok Bay ideal for early human settlement. There were also walrus between Soapstone Island and the mainland, and black bears inland. Polar bears denned in winter on Soapstone Island and were often encountered between Cape Mugford and Nanuktut (White Bear) Island.

Of these animals we saw only caribou, but we collected an escort of two minke whales at one headland, and they accompanied us for a long way, surfacing close to our kayaks each time to breathe. It was wonderful to watch their long bodies cruising underneath the kayaks, crossing our path then vanishing for long minutes before resurfacing close beside, or close in front of us; sometimes so close I was afraid I might hit one with my paddle if I was not watchful enough. I do not know whether these whales gain anything from swimming so close, other than companionship, but they are known for following slow-moving boats. They grow up to thirty feet in length and have a conspicuous white patch on the outer surface of the flippers that helps in identification. The name minke is after a Norwegian whaler in the early 1900s who harpooned one, mistaking it for a blue whale. Since a blue grows to almost a hundred feet, three times the length of a minke, the name made fun of his mistake.

At the northern tip of Soapstone Island we picked up a tailwind that helped us around the head. Then the massive cliffs of the Kaumajet Mountains came into view: substantial wedges of mountain rising up as precipitous cliffs to a ragged skyline of spiky ridges. As the wind increased we were able to surf the waves toward the mountains, spray from the whitecaps chilling our fingers. The cliff of Soapstone Island overlapped the 2,700-foot-high Finger Hill Island, which guided us in turn toward Finger Hill on the mainland, equally high. To our left across the narrowing bay sat Grimmington Island with its close-to-shore mountains reaching 4,300 feet. We aimed our kayaks between Grimmington Island and Finger Hill, into the narrow canyon known as Cod Bag Harbor. The wind funneled into this less than half a mile wide channel, grating the surface into blotches with each gust or downdraft. I was glad the wind was in our favor, but when we reached the bend in the channel the wind gusted erratically, sometimes in our faces and sometimes from behind. High above us a drift of cloud flowed down a hanging valley and launched out into the air over the fjord like a Zeppelin, changing direction abruptly when the eddying wind caught it.

Ahead we could now see the low bridge of land that joins Grimmington Island to the mainland, but it was difficult to gauge the scale of the slopes rising from the sea, the slopes we would have to portage over to reach Lost Channel on the other side. But the closer we got the more obvious the easiest place to land became. The wind was now pressing into our faces with the same ferocity that we had enjoyed at our backs earlier in the afternoon, so I was relieved to guide my kayak between the rocks and run ashore onto sand. I walked up to the top of the beach then laughed out loud. We had been right to trust Sem. The weather had been favorable and the portage was ideal. The confined beach of pebbles here rose to a narrow flat area, dropping down to the water a few yards away on the other side. To either end, this bridge of land rose as a rocky ridge toward mountains.

Although wind was funneling through this saddle right now, it looked as if we could find sufficient shelter at the base of an outcrop. There were already recent tent rings there so we would not even need to search for stones to hold our tents. The view of the mountains and cliffs was stunning; they rose steeply all around us, creating such a feeling of enclosure it was easy to imagine we were camping beside a high mountain lake. Both of us were cold. We pitched the tents as quickly as we could and blocked up the drafts around the bottom of the shelter with pieces of driftwood. I could see we were in a vulnerable position if the wind increased and funneled through the mountains. Wind from any direction, if strong enough, would blow the kayaks into the water. Having had kayaks blown away on earlier trips, I tied each end of our kayaks to boulders as a precaution. With our camp secure, a short walk past more tent rings and numerous Inuit graves brought us to a river of clear water rattling down from the mountains. We had all we needed here for the night, and soon we settled into our sleeping bags, lulled by the sound of the wind around the rocks and the rasp of small waves against the beach.

I awoke abruptly in the dark. There was a slow scrunching sound of pebbles. Heavy footsteps were moving up the beach toward the tent. Quietly I wriggled my shoulders free of the sleeping bag until my arms were free and I could reach for the rifle. A bear? It would be foolish to unzip the tent to look. That would be too much like a seal sticking its head up through a hole in the ice. But if it was a bear, and it was curious, it might pat the tent to find out what it was. Given that warning I could fire the rifle through the end of the tent, and hope it would be enough to scare the bear away for long enough to let us get out of the tent. I lay there listening intently. The slow heavy footsteps continued to sound on the small pebbles, but then I could hear nothing. I listened, and after a while set the gun aside and fell asleep. I awoke again to the light of morning and an unanswered question. Slipping out of the tent I checked the beach. Deeply imprinted in the gravelly shingle were the deep tracks of caribou.

The breeze blowing from the land today was chilly as we strolled toward the river to collect water. Large boulders lay scattered across the ground, maybe the result of rockfalls from the mountain walls surrounding us, or left by the melting ice sheet after the last ice age. Inuit had made use of the shelter beside these big stones for graves.

Smaller rocks had been stacked to form walls beside or beneath each of the boulders, leaving a chamber for a body. Through the chinks between the rocks of some of these graves we could see bones, although some graves were broken open and empty. It did not seem strange to think of all these folk resting here in this beautiful spot. Cliffs, long slopes of scree, piles of fallen boulders and the arms of water reaching in from both sides made it a dramatic location. Ancient tent rings bedded deep into the moss indicated how long this had been used as a camping place. We could see harbor seals resting on rocks in the bay on the inland side, and it was probably fair to assume this was always a good place to find them. Availability of seals and caribou would have been reason enough to camp here. At our feet amid tiny flowers, the unripe berries of bakeapples stood vibrating stiffly in the wind. No, it was a good place for the final resting place of friends and relatives, a place to revisit with joy. I think of our stay here as having been in the company of friends.

Before we left today I wanted to make a better repair to the bow of my kayak, which was still leaking. The first repair had never warmed enough for the epoxy to set. I needed to apply heat, yet in the chill breeze there was little chance of success, so we stuck the bow into the shelter tent and zipped up the entrance. Lighting the stove beside the kayak I boiled water, filled water sacks, and placed them in the forward hatch. Then with another hot bag under the bow I draped a towel over the top to hold in the heat. The combined heat of stove and water bags did the trick. Once dry and warm, the repair set just fine.

The coastal range of the Kaumajet Mountains is considered to have some of the most dramatic scenery south of the Torngats. It was drawings of these mountains that had first captured my imagination and inspired me to further research about Labrador back in the 1970s. Photographs of Cape Mugford, Mugford Tickle, and Bishops Mitre are commonly found in books about Labrador because their precipitous cliffs stand so stark and immense right from the sea. They may not be the most impressive in Labrador, but they certainly convey the image of a rockbound impenetrable land, with classic glaciated features carved out to perfection. From here we would pass to the more sheltered western side of the range, and would remain in waters protected from the east by islands as far south as the Kiglapait Mountains.

I had had mixed feelings about this inland route west of the mountains, via Cod Bag Harbor. I wondered whether the scenery might be more spectacular around the eastern cliffs. My doubts were dispelled when the wind continued to whip across the water toward those mountains without a break for the next few days. Even steady winds here would funnel through the Mugford Tickle and around Cape Mugford to create tough paddling conditions there. With this wind blowing, not even the route we had followed through Cod Bag Harbor would have offered us easy passage between the mountains if we had arrived any later. It was as if a door had closed after us.

CHAPTER **19**

Okak

At this stage in our journey we were definitely getting thinner. Our diet of mostly freeze-dried meals, plus our extras, contained fewer calories than we needed to maintain our weight. As an incidental result, the seats of our kayaks seemed to get harder as our butts disappeared and our bones protruded. That has consequences in paddling a sea kayak.

Paddling straight into a wind is easy. The bow's work of parting the water holds the bow steady; as the water fills in behind, its turbulence makes the stern loose, and the kayak points to the wind like a weathervane. Paddling across the wind is a different matter. The wind on the side pushes the loose stern sideways more than it pushes the secure bow, so the kayak weathercocks, or turns to face the wind. We can compensate with the paddle by drawing the stern sideways at the end of a stroke, but there is another, simpler way: *edging* the kayak, or putting the kayak on edge. By shifting weight onto one hip, we make the kayak sit lower on that side. Lower on the side the wind comes from will anchor the stern and minimize weathercocking. Lower on the opposite side will make the kayak broach, or turn up into the wind. Normally it was easy to edge the kayaks, but now, with our bony butts, it was becoming uncomfortable, and the wind continued to blow hard from the land.

Our target was Okak Island, which we reached a few days later, crossing with light offshore winds. Near the northern tip we saw a swell from the bay and stepped up the pace to reach land as quickly as possible. As we paddled we watched a golden eagle drift in circles high against the cliff, and we jumped when a minke whale broke the water. The 1,600 feet of Tigerschmitt Hill sheltered us from the gathering wind until we rounded the corner and entered the channel that cleaves Okak Island in two. Here the wind swept down the slopes in strong gusts, and we could see turbulence in the air like steam from a kettle.

The wind whipped up whitecaps along the channel. Although our route now lay directly against this wind, neither of us felt anxious about its strength; after all, the channel was narrow, with plenty of landing places. We really wanted to make progress today. At a narrow point five miles into the channel lay the abandoned settlement of Nutak. Surely we could make it that far? I was wrong. A sound like a fast-moving train approached as the first gust roared past, accompanied by lines of flying spray. My paddle wrenched in my hands as I tried to keep it under control. When the gust had passed I looked at Kristin, and she made a face at me. We paddled farther. Creeping along the shore, we made painfully slow progress at the expense of some hard work. Eventually we needed a rest and stopped on the rocks of a tiny beach. Ashore it was hot, despite the wind; we drank, and we each ate a candy bar. The rising tide was fast flooding our beach so we launched again and worked along another mile of shore, but for all our effort we were barely moving. We landed at the next beach that looked suitable for a tent. Here the low cliff and the slope above it offered shelter from the full effect of the wind. We explored the shore in search of fresh water, walking upwind a few hundred yards until we found a deep pool, then returned and pitched the tents.

This was not one of the pristine sites to which we had become accustomed. Pepsi cans lurked in the shrubs and marram grass, along with twisted pieces of plastic melted and blackened by fire, and broken glass. A caribou skull spread wide antlers, from which pieces had been sawn, and when we looked uphill, bones from a carcass were spread over the slope, perhaps dragged there by animals. The shelter tent, with its door away from the wind, filled with deer flies. These powerful insects seemed able to fly low and fast, even against the wind, to find us wherever we were. When we sought refuge in our shelter, they ricocheted rapidly and noisily off the taut green fabric and settled their massive bodies on our unprotected skin. I am not fond of deer flies. Unlike the mosquito, which touches down gently, anaesthetizes the victim, and then draws blood, the deer fly has an irksome bite that feels like the stab of a blunt needle, and it can cause a painful swelling the size of a walnut. The deer fly can bite through clothing. We could do nothing to discourage our unwelcome visitors except zip ourselves inside the tent, away from the sunny spectacle of flying spray and shuddering marram grasses, and burn a mosquito coil.

The Okak Islands have been the site of more than one settlement. The former village of Okak was established near the north end of the western island, squeezed between the sea and a steep slope, by missionaries from Nain in 1776. The first mission house was two stories high, which in winter could be buried to the second floor in snow. Later a hospital was built nearby. Okak was the starting place for the Moravians' boat journey to Kuujjuaq in 1811 that we had been following in reverse.

In the 1800s about 250 Inuit lived in the surrounding area, hunting seals and whales. There was good fishing and a ready supply of wood, even at this northern limit of trees, and the place was capable of supporting a healthy human population. But even then the site attracted voracious biting flies.

The Inuit were encouraged to live around the mission site, so when the supply ship *Harmony* brought Spanish influenza in 1918, the community was devastated. According to the journal of Phillip C. Gordon, 200 died from a population of 253, four out of every five, and the epidemic spread all around the bay. In one settlement, the only adult men to survive were the nonnative minister, doctor, and store man. A woman who survived said the three men dug a huge hole in the ground to bury all the bodies together. It is hard to imagine digging a hole for two hundred bodies.

Many of the survivors moved south, where some of the orphaned children were adopted. Others gathered midway along the western shore of Moores Island Tickle, the channel separating the two Okak Islands. After a fire destroyed buildings in Nain, many of the Okak buildings were dismantled and shipped south to replace them. The mission closed in 1919 and never reopened.

In 1919-1920, a store was established in Moores Island Tickle, and the settlement that grew up around it was named Nutak. With the Okak mission gone, the church considered these people to be part of the Hebron population, and so were visited from time to time by the Hebron minister. In 1951 Nutak was reported to have a population of sixty-six people. Another 171 people, forty-four families, lived in isolated homesteads around the bay; they depended on goods supplied at the Nutak store. These supplies would have included ammunition, by then essential for hunting. The fish and game in the area were certainly capable of supporting a community of that size, for the population had been greater in 1918, but the government had begun discussing the viability of the northern Labrador communities. In the summer of 1956 officials informed the Nutak and Okak Bay residents that the store would be closed and everybody would be relocated. There would be new housing and jobs. Twenty-nine families moved to Nain, others went to Makkovik, North West River, Goose Bay, and Hebron. As far as the government was concerned, once the move was completed the people would settle into their new lives, and they were left to fend for themselves. But there were no facilities for the arriving population, and the government did not inform the receiving communities any more than they prepared the people they moved. The new arrivals from the north were treated as outcasts.

The wind shifted direction in the night and we woke around 5:30 to cold rain driving out of the northeast. I pulled my head back under the covers and fell asleep again, until I was jolted awake by the sound of a whale blowing close by. Kristin stuck her head out of the tent and watched it surface close to shore, moving against the wind. The rain was so relentless that all our gear received a thorough dousing before it got loaded through the hatches. Once we were afloat and paddling, we soon warmed up. I enjoyed the push of the wind at my back, speeding me along the river-like channel amid little whitecaps. Nutak lay inshore of a wide, bleak, exposed beach, with slick boulders and gleaming wet mud. No buildings were visible, and the low tide and the wet, blustery weather discouraged us from exploring. We cruised past trees, the first we had seen on this journey, for we had now reached the tree line, the transition between tundra and taiga. The trees were scrawny black spruce, not very tall, maybe twenty feet, thin, and they grew only on the lower slopes, but they made an impression on me. Trees like this would have provided wood for building sleds and kayaks for Inuit living farther north.

Toward the far end of the channel between the Okak Islands, the waterway spills into Woody Bay. The low shores spread into mud flats studded with boulders, then shallow pools filled with ducks and geese. A pair of peregrines winged heavily past. We could see that at low water the exit dried up into mud flats, even though the chart said it was a clear channel. For a few minutes we sat there, our kayaks resting on the mud, the rain splattering against our backs. Each chunk of rock sitting in the mud around us was draped with scrawny yellow-brown wrack, the bladders bulging from the fronds like cysts. Webbed footprints and probe holes showed that shorebirds had crisscrossed these flats looking for food. Sand worms had thrown up volcano-like cratered mounds several inches high, coated in the gray silt that lay beneath the sand. Although water lay over it, sand broke the surface in drifts and mounds everywhere. I could see how far we would need to carry the kayaks to reach deep water, and it was too far with laden kayaks, yet the water between was too shallow to float them if we walked. So I just sat there, with my energy drained as low as the tide. Kristin was livelier. She rummaged busily in her day-hatch to find her drink bottle and a bag of beef jerky and offered them to me. Then she climbed out of her kayak and began looking for mussels. Kristin has a great capacity to be bright in drab surroundings. With her fingers protruding from her palmless neoprene mittens, she rummaged at the base of the larger boulders, poking beneath the fringe of weed to tease out the blue-black mussels that clung to the rock. The shellfish were scarcely two inches long, but gradually her horde grew until her gritty bag was half full. By then I was wandering around trying to keep warm, splatting through the water in all directions in search of hidden treasures. I found nothing half so appealing as Kristin's mussels. Eventually the rising water began to flow across the sand. The current focused along the deepest channels, and finally we could move, drifting a yard at a time toward the fog banks that clung to the distant water. Rain was dripping down my back. I had dropped my hood to see more easily and had omitted to tighten the neck. I thought, "It's only fresh water." When the incoming tidewater was deep enough we sat in our kayaks with our legs draped out either side, steering, while the wind and current pushed us onward, out toward the big bald rocks in the bay.

There was little to be seen of the coast south of Okak Bay. Fog and low cloud blanked out any landmarks. Instead of crossing right away we edged along the island shore with a crosswind pushing us out sideways past the boulders that protruded from the shallow water. Plump seals, bloated like massive maggots, with head and tail raised as if to keep them from being splashed, capped some of the boulders. Low rocky ridges and green vegetation defined the shore beyond the shallows. I spotted a dark shape moving behind a ridge that ran out to the sea. "Caribou?" I wondered. We were close to shore, and the trees and rocks behind the point appeared to move as we cruised closer. Rain drove against my face. As we rounded the corner we could see a big, lanky, black bear standing on all fours staring right at us, its coat thick and rich and dark, twenty yards away. We stopped paddling and drifted, watching. If the Barren Grounds brown bears had not been hunted to extinction

I would have imagined this to be one of them on account of its bulk, yet it did not seem intimidating in the way a brown bear or polar bear would. A polar bear would follow us into the water from curiosity; I didn't expect a black bear to do that. It turned and paused, displaying its full bulk, then trundled away up the slope, making the diminutive trees look tiny. Effortless strides carried it over the hill and out of sight. We resumed our weaving line between the rows of rocks and the shore, peering into the fog for any glimpse of land to the south. We turned and headed from land on a compass bearing. Somewhere out there, fairly close, was our next target.

CHAPTER 20

Cabins

Sem, at Hebron, had marked a cabin on our chart about ten miles south from Okak Islands. With wind driving us forward we looked for it, hoping to find shelter from the rain. So much water had run down my neck and through my fleece that by now I was sitting in a cold pool inside my waterproof pants, and my arms were wet and cold. It reminded me of my early paddling days. When I paddled from Baffin Island to Labrador I did not have the luxury of latex wrist seals, so water poured into my cuffs to hang in my sleeves as I paddled. When I raised an arm, that water would rush down my armpit to my seat, where it would leak out from my pants into my cockpit. Now, on the steep shore beside us, the trees hugged the lower slopes and fog clung to the trees like shreds of wool. Loud waterfalls cascaded from the mountains and vanished behind the trees. We scrutinized the shore, determined that even if the cabin was not penciled-in accurately on the map, we would still not pass it. At last we spotted its shadowy shape on a low flat treeless corner between a small lake and a bay.

We hopped out of the kayaks in shallow water onto an eroding peaty bank, sliding the kayaks right up onto a field of ground-hugging blueberries. "So this is a cabin?" I said sourly. From where we stood the hut looked as if a bear had savaged it. When we stepped closer we realized that, yes, a bear indeed had mauled it. Much of the outer covering had been ripped away, and the yellow insulation had either been dragged away or had leaked out and lay scattered across the ground. Broad claw marks scratched the cladding on the corner of the building. The doorframe had been ripped off, but a cover had been nailed roughly across it, and when we lifted that aside and looked in it was to a scene of chaos, with pans, broken glass from the window, and an overturned table scattered across the floor. A few yards inland, work had been started on a new log cabin. Head-high walls had been built around a neat concrete floor. Beside it a deep carpet of bark shavings surrounded some workhorses, in recognition of someone's hard labor. There wasn't a roof yet. We pulled out our tents and pitched them on the low springy berry bushes nearby, the poles sticking to the wet fabric and challenging our cold fingers. All around us were short stumps where trees had been cut to make this clearing. Inside the shelter tent we eagerly peeled off our wet layers and replaced them with dry, fired up the stove, and heated water for chocolate, cradling the steaming bowls until our fingers warmed.

The twenty-eighth of August began with rain, so we were reluctant to leave our sleeping bag. Around 8 o'clock it eased, so we got up. It sounded so different to hear birds chattering in woodland after so long without trees, and we could hear the thunder of water falling in the distance. Small waves burst one after the other along the shore. Kristin strung our dripping wet gear out to dry while I filled a pan with berries. We had just begun cooking breakfast when rain suddenly hit, driven ferociously hard against the tent by a squall. Neither of us had the inclination to run out to gather in the wet gear, as it was obvious we would be soaked almost instantly, so we resigned ourselves to wearing wet kayaking gear later and relaxed over breakfast. When we had eaten and the time had come to change and pack, we reconsidered our decision. Perhaps instead of starting our day cold and wet in the rain we should try to dry our clothes first. We decided to look at the old cabin to see if we could maybe dry everything there.

Yes, but it would take work. The cabin was trashed. Rain had driven through the glassless window to pool on the torn linoleum with the rusty nails and broken glass. Empty food cans and tools lay scattered across the floor, but a sheet iron woodstove stood intact near the corner where we had squeezed inside. A note on the wall said that Eli and Hulda, Bony and Sybrilla had come to clean the logs on 8 May. "Wet and windy old day." Another visit by Eli and Hulda was recorded on 16 May. They were most likely from Nain; hunters occasionally visit Okak Bay, which is only about 75 miles from Nain by open boat. We scraped up the broken glass from the floor, upturned the table, and cleared the stove. Kristin tied line between nails in the roof beams and hung our gear, while I lit a fire in the stove using wet cardboard, candle wax, and wood shavings. Once it was alight I added ends of wood and stacked wet wood near the stove to dry. Kristin had soaked the mussels she had collected yesterday in fresh seawater, changing the water periodically. Now she cleaned a cast iron pot in the cabin, filled it with water and sat it on the stove. I went out and collected more berries, discovering a patch of bakeapples in the process, and also *boleti*. The wind continued to blow hard, and rain came intermittently all day. While whitecaps chased across the bay we relaxed, cooking mushroom soup, collecting more mussels, heating our collected berries, and watching the birds darting between the narrow trees.

Between Okak Islands and the Kiglapait Mountains there are several cabins, mostly used in winter by hunters. A winter snowmobile shortcut from Nain across lower-lying land to the west of the Kiglapaits is a less dangerous alternative to the summer journey by open boat, which involves a long haul around the exposed coast east of the mountains. Skirting these "Sawtooth Mountains," as they would translate into English, is regarded as committing and potentially dangerous unless the weather is stable. We had made a detour to visit one cabin on our way to the Kiglapait Mountains. We reached that cabin in the middle of the day when the mountains stood clear and bold, like a hand of cards held up to the sky. Landing was not easy. The tide was low and the beach encumbered with slippery rocks covered in weed. Had we arrived at high tide we could have landed easily on a pebble beach instead of picking our way across the slick surfaces.

The cabin, built far enough up the saddle to be clear of the roughest seas, was small and cozy. Someone had gathered boulders from between the beach and the cabin, heaping them into mounds to clear the ground. Boulders had been heaped into a substantial rock wall against the back of the cabin, whether for protection against the wind, weather, or bears I don't know. The door of the cabin gaped open. Inside were two bed frames, one of iron, the other of wood. A wood stove made from a slice of a forty-gallon oil drum stood in the corner with a simple metal chimney pipe leading straight up through the roof. Stretched above were poles over which cloth was draped to dry. Little shelves held books, scissors, and candles. I sat down. The walls had been used to record messages. Most offered names and dates, but one simply said, "I love you! I hate you! And Smile and Laugh!" Another reported: "Too windy on the sea to do much hunting, storm bound 3 days." Another: "Seen polar bear this morning 4 a.m. by the tent Aug 7th 02." From where I sat looking through the door, the view across Snyder Bay revealed all the twisty jagged mountains of the Kiglapaits with their long rock faces and slopes reflected in the bay. Kristin perched herself on a plywood board on one of the beds and leaned back against the wall to read the messages written on the ceiling.

This was Jako's cabin, and we had met Jako at Saglek. He was one of the men who had marked the position of cabins on our chart for us. We wrote a short message on the wall, hoping he would see it someday and realize we had stopped by and thought of him. Then we walked up to the brow of the hill to look down at the water in the little bay on the other side. If one side were rough, there would surely be a more sheltered landing on the other. Up here the lichen-dark pebbles clung to the ground like eggs in a nest. Plants nestled low in tight clumps. A few circles of stones were bedded deep in the ground. Here was a good place to find a breeze, good for camping if the flies were bad, but not good if the weather grew wild!

We had no plans to stop so soon for the night. We returned to our kayaks, crossed the bay toward the mountains, and tucked into the shelter of Kiglapait Harbor. We made it just in time. Behind us a westerly squall slammed down from the mountains to furrow the water. At the end of the harbor, as the bay is named, stood another cabin above a flat, yellow sand beach beside a stream. Clustered beside and behind it on the low ground were pencil-like conifers and dense alder shrubs, from which golden slabs of rock soared up to the mountain ridges and peaks. Long waterfalls and cascades threaded the steep faces.

The cabin looked like a little plywood barn. Inside were bunks for at least six people, with a wooden ladder leading to a sleeping loft. A stove lacking a stovepipe or chimney, two tables, a bench and chair, a few kitchen utensils, and a discarded jacket offered us a stark welcome. We glanced around again to see signs that children had been here: a tiny plastic record player. A ceramic heart hanging on the wall read; "I love you mum!" On another nail hung the Fisherman's Prayer. Outside in a dense clump of trees that rose to maybe fifteen feet was a den, in which we found pots and pans and the remains of an oil lamp. Someone had created it as a shelter for play. The mosquitoes were formidable, so we cooked inside the cabin on a table in front of the window where we could watch the sea slowly inundating the sands until it lapped against the blue grass.

Slowly the sun sank, to cast a mellow light across the mountains and stretch out the shadows. Our gear dangled from drying racks around the hole in the roof where the stove once had an outlet. With the wind whistling through broken windowpanes and through holes in the walls and roof we decided to sleep in the tent, which we pitched in the middle of the cabin floor.

To ward off bears I wedged a chair under the door handle, hoping it would at least give us warning, but the wind rattled the building so much I woke up frequently. I got up during the night to try to identify the noises. Outside the door in the chill of the wind the full moon shone so brightly I could hardly look at it. In the morning the ground around the cabin was indented everywhere with fresh caribou prints.

CHAPTER **21**

Kiglapait Mountains and Village Bay

As the sun climbed from the horizon, its fiery light reflected from the bay up onto the mountains, until we seemed to stand at the focal point of the amber glow radiating toward us from the slopes all around. Then, almost as quickly as the warm orange light had arrived, the colors cooled again to greens and blues to reveal a normal sunny day. With a light breeze at our backs we skirted the Kiglapait Mountains. We saw many more potential landing spots than we had anticipated, so if the weather did turn bad we could surely find somewhere to land. Up on the hill above one of these landings was a huge radar installation, part of the same defensive shield that includes the Saglek radar.

We had perfect cruising weather and an interesting coast, with long sweeping slabs of gray rock that sloped down to the water. Minke whales surfaced around us through a large part of the day. Finally we passed the surf beach at the northern end of a finger of land that extends south toward South Aulatsivik Island. Behind it was Medusa Bay. To reach our target for today we had to paddle five more miles or portage nearly a mile through sand over a saddle from the surf beach. We opted to paddle.

Swells trundled heavily across the shoals at the north side of the narrow channel that ran into Medusa Bay. Although the south side appeared clear of breakers, we threaded our way between the rocks and breakers for the fun of it, finally running onto calm water, appropriately full of plankton, including jellyfish. This was a significant moment on our journey. We had already decided that from here to Nain we would follow the sheltered route between the mainland and South Aulatsivik Island, so at this point we left the open ocean shore for the inland passage. We expected our remaining days to be on calmer water without the potential for large swells, risky surf landings, no-landing zones, or sudden weather changes. We relished the idea of slowing down and relaxing from here to the end of the journey, and right now the water was glassy.

We rounded a full 180 degrees to paddle the western shore of the finger of land that sheltered Medusa Bay from the sea. The rocky promontory beside us was the site of an ancient settlement where chert flakes have been found. It could be a natural place to call home. Ahead were slopes of sand; on the far side of these lay the surf beach we had passed. Our destination for the night was a cabin belonging to Jim Anderson and Helena, in the corner called Village Bay or Port Manvers. The cabin stood beside a teepee-shaped log pile. All the logs stood on end leaning inward. This arrangement makes firewood easier to access in the winter snows. Cruising forward on the glassy water we struggled to make sense of what we finally realized was a boat floating in front of the rock, and then, closer still, we caught sight of something moving. We were close enough to see it was a figure walking along the shore toward the boat. We changed our course slightly to intercept him.

The man in blue denim jeans and a short-sleeved shirt introduced himself as Jim. He was retrieving his boat, now that the tide had risen high enough over the sand banks for him to bring it closer to his cabin. He and his wife were visiting from Nain to spend time hunting and fishing. Helena was in the cabin, he said. He encouraged us to paddle ahead. We floated the last few yards, following directions from Helena, who was now standing on the beach guiding us in.

She suggested a place farther down the beach from the cabin, where the beach was steeper, and narrow from water to shore. It took only moments to lift the kayaks the short distance to the grass. Then we joined them.

Jim was a round-faced man with slightly graying hair, mustache, and bushy dark eyebrows. He had a cheerful calm about him that matched that of his wife. Helena had thick black wavy hair and a ready smile; they seemed close and well suited. Their cabin seemed too much like a home to be called a cabin. Jim had built it in 1998. There were photographs on the wall. Blown eggs and amulets, such as rabbit paws and feathers, hung from a beam. In the corner stood a double bed, and a homebuilt ladder led up to a sleeping loft above one end of the room. A broad woodstove burned vigorously in the center throwing heat into the room. Helena pushed a kettle of water across the stovetop to heat and immediately it began to steam. Jim gestured toward the chairs by the table at the window, and we sat down. He poured hot water into cups at the table. Teabags, instant coffee, and powdered chocolate clustered alongside the salt and pepper shakers at the end of the table. Yes, this was more than a cabin, but I realized it was neither the decorations nor the resources that made it a home, it was Helena and Jim. This was their world, and they were deeply content to be here. Jim worked at the diesel power station that supplies electricity to Nain. Helena worked as a nurse in Nain. Jim said it was expensive to buy gas for their boat for the short visits their jobs allowed. The expense could only be offset by what they could catch or hunt, which would feed them when they returned home. They loved to be out here at Port Manvers. It was close to the ocean, with mountain views across Medusa Bay. "We all grew up subsistence hunting." Jim explained. "It's what we're used to, what we like to do." They always stayed as long as they could, but they were in the wage economy and needed their jobs to survive.

This trip, Jim had shot seals and caught char. He said it was late in the season to catch char in salt water, for by now they should be heading upriver to spawn. The cabin was in a good location for summer, but they used it in winter too, traveling by snowmobile. Helena's snowmobile sat behind the cabin; a bear had ripped off the seat cover and chewed it up. "Probably a black bear," Jim explained. "Last winter a black bear holed up in the snow in a bank just over there." He indicated the edge of the bay where the grass gave way to a rocky hill. Bears can cause a lot of damage, especially when they're marking their territory. "My family doesn't like to eat bear meat, so we leave them alone." He elaborated "Some people don't like the flavor; they find it too strong. I'm going to build a shelter for the snowmobile to protect it better."

We talked about kayaking. Jim said they had hosted kayaking visitors once before, a group from United States on a three-week trip. One week into the trip they were rounding the Kiglapait Mountains when they spotted a polar bear at the cape that seemed to take interest in them. Fifteen minutes later they spotted it again, this time in the water quite close and swimming right for them. They turned away from it, and after a time paddling back south they seemed to lose it, and after ten hours paddling they stopped to set up camp. Next day they returned to Jim's cabin to await better weather. Jim said he thought they went back to Nain to pick up a gun before heading out again. We thumbed through his guest book to read their brief entry.

Jim's cabin stands at the base of Tikkegaksuak Peninsula, which points out like a thumb to almost reach South Aulatsivik Island. This was the peninsula we paddled around to reach this bay. It offers the most obvious route north for polar bears, and since there are frequently seals in the shallow Medusa Bay, one might expect to see bears here. In March this year (2004), several polar bears came to the cabin while Helena was staying there with an elderly woman friend. The women managed to scare the first few away with gunshots. One bear wasn't scared by that and walked right up to confront them. Helena had no option but to shoot it with the last of her ammunition. More bears arrived shortly after, and when Helena was finally able to call the authorities on the radio, they flew out in a helicopter with more ammunition for her. Seeing so many polar bears had scared the older woman. With the helicopter standing there, she took the opportunity to ask for a ride home. Helena, now alone in the cabin, said she felt safer sleeping upstairs in the loft.

Although the incident did nothing to dampen Helena's enthusiasm for the cabin, Jim built an enclosure outside around the cabin windows. "We had a window down to here," he said, indicating a low point by the table, "but a bear broke in, so now we have this smaller window with the fences outside." The tops of the railings bristled with galvanized nails, as did the plywood sheets on the ground, which made me think of a fakir's bed of nails. "The bears don't hurt themselves on the nails, because they can feel the sharpness and don't step on them."

Wires ran across the cabin to photoelectric cells on the roof that kept batteries charged inside. Antenna wires ran all over the walls and roof, but still they could not pick up any radio signals. "It would have been useful for the weather forecast. But we have enough electricity to play music cassettes, and to run some lights at night."

When the couple left along the beach to check their fishing nets, we unloaded our kayaks, pitched our tent near the cabin, then changed and strung out our paddling clothes to dry. We declined their invitation to sleep in the cabin; we were accustomed to the cool of our tent at night and the cabin was exceedingly warm. But when Jim returned with an arctic char and invited us to eat with them, we readily accepted. Jim said char doesn't freeze well, as it often takes on a different flavor, so it is best smoked or dried or eaten fresh. The fishery at Nain had not found a market for it. Helena fired up a white-gas stove and began to fry the char. Talking with Jim, I mentioned mushrooms, and he said he was not familiar enough with them to recognize the edible ones. I guessed there would be plenty in the area as the ground seemed suitable for caribou, so Kristin and I quickly scouted around, and we filled a pan with *boleti*. I showed Jim how to identify them, and how to check for worms, before we chopped them. Helena fried them up with onions in the pan once the char was cooked. On the plate before us the char opened to a rich pink inside its silvery skin. The oil in the fish was just what we needed, and it tasted so good.

Jim asked us to sign their visitors' book, and in return we asked if they would sign our Hebron book. Jim was born at Hebron and spent his childhood there. After his family was relocated he never returned. "I've hunted as far north as the Kaumajet Mountains, but never went back to Hebron." I asked why not and he replied, "There's nothing left there any more to return to." I thought for a long time about his reply.

Helena came from Nutak, the settlement on the channel between the Okak Islands. Her family had been relocated to North West River. "Most of the relocations happened in September, but it was October or later before anyone was housed. By then there was already snow and it was very cold. They were hard times." Kristin asked whether they thought the Inuit were capable of governing themselves nowadays. Jim's attitude was, "We'll see." He had concerns about jobs, about the young people, and about drinking problems in the towns. A clock on the wall had the grandfather's name at the top, Jim and Helena in the middle, and their daughter and two sons at three, six, and nine o'clock. "We sometimes foster children, too," Jim said. But right now it was time for their evening stroll along the shore, and so they left, arm in arm. Kristin and I walked only as far as our tent. The evening dampness had left the fabric sagging, so we tightened the guy lines before turning in. We could hear seabirds calling and the small waves breaking along the gravelly shore sounded like gentle breathing. I felt particularly relaxed and secure.

In the night I awoke to the sound of laughing, clapping, and whistling, and Helena's ringing calls, "Nigel! Kristin! Come outside!" The dark sky glowed in the north with a deep emerald green, which spread outward then snaked across the sky as curtains of green light. At times the lower part of the bands glowed red, but mostly the dancing lights were green as the spectacle wandered across the sky. Helena related a story her father had told her when she was young. "When the lights dance in the sky at night, you may whistle to make them dance, and when they reach down close to the earth, clap your hands and they'll go back up again. Show respect to the lights!

Once there was a little girl who taunted the lights, and when they reached down she didn't clap her hands to tell them when to stop. The lights cut off her head before she could run inside to escape."

The lights faded and quite abruptly vanished. The show was over for tonight. I became aware of the big fat moon hanging over the cabin, and an intense pattern of stars, but everything seemed so still, so dull after the aurora.

CHAPTER 22

Port Manvers Run

Jim was up early cutting wood for the stove. We heard the clack of axe against wood and the thunk of the split pieces falling, carrying crisply through the air. The dawn was bright, and I stood gazing across the calm water of the bay that reflected the clear blue sky. The sun lit the rocky summit of the peninsula and the mountains of South Aulatsivik Island with a warm glow that had not yet reached us. It was a serene moment to stand and stare, to savor the cool air and the clarity of every tiny sound. With my head against Kristin's and her body clasped to mine there was no need to speak. It was sufficient to simply watch and listen and feel the strange sensation that every cell in my body was stretching outward from me into the new day. When Kristin moved away I pulled off the tent rain sheet, threw it inverted over the tent to dry the condensation, then followed her into the cabin. Helena, tired from a week of working the night shift, was still fast asleep, her peaceful brown face sticking out from under the covers. I brewed espresso for us all, but when I stepped outside to empty the grounds I spotted an open boat speeding across the bay. Jim said it was Helena's aunt Sarah, with Timothy and Eugene and some boys. They soon burst in through the door carrying snacks for the table, bustling with energy. Sarah chatted cheerfully in Inuktitut. I retrieved my book about Hebron and showed it to her, and her eyes lit up. She knew this book. She thumbed through the pages excitedly, pointing to people she knew, bursting out with spontaneous comments and laughter. Occasionally Jim or Helena would translate something for us. Sarah pointed out the place she used to live at Hebron. It was the middle cottage of three rented by the Hudson's Bay Company to Inuit families. She brushed her finger across the slopes above the house in the photograph as if stroking fur, sighed warmly, and elaborated. On translation we heard, "Fantastic berry-picking area!" Our book was gaining life. We asked if she would sign it for us, and to mark where she used to live. She did so, but kept finding pictures of more people she knew and had stories about. I encouraged her to write their names down where she could. The others clustered over her to add their comments.

Sarah has a cabin farther down the run and asked if we would stop to sign her guest book. "The door is nailed shut," Jim said, translating, "but there are claw hammers hanging there to pull out the nails. They've had trouble with bears breaking in so they've nailed boards over the windows and planks across the door, but you should be able to open it. Just close it back up when you leave." Sarah stood and everyone bustled outside like a crackling ball of energy. The boys fishing at the shore were called back and everyone climbed into the boat. They were heading home to Nain. The engine fired, they turned slowly, and then they were off, the boat spreading spray as it accelerated onto the plane. When it turned out of sight and the sound of the engine dropped away it was time for us to load our kayaks to follow.

The tide had narrowed the sand to a strip a few feet wide below the deep grass, and the mosquitoes by now were dense. We were stowing our bags quickly and deftly with our backs to the lapping waves and our feet wet when I heard Helena call from the cabin, "Nigel! Kristin!" We stood up to look. "Nigel! Kristin! Polar Bear! Out there, coming toward you!" Sure enough, there was the now familiar sight of a swimming bear. We walked back to the cabin, where Jim was standing with his gun. The bear, possibly in response to being spotted, changed direction abruptly and began diving, then surfacing with a big splash, as if it was leaping up from the bottom in the shallows. It headed toward the nets. Jim and Helena hurried over in that direction to warn it away, and we heard the report of gunshot. The morning was once again tranquil when soon afterwards our kayaks glided almost silently across the reflections from shore, but we were alert. Our eyes followed every ripple on the water and every movement on the shore.

Traveling south along Port Manvers Run we felt we were truly on the home stretch to Nain, and in a way we were. We just did not realize how long it might take us to get there. The waterway resembled a broad river with cliffs, but with mountains rising to almost three thousand feet and trees on the low land, it was also like a fjord. We stopped at the beach below Sarah's cabin and strolled up to pull out the nails and sign the guest book behind the door. The cabin was tucked into the island near a promontory that juts out across the run. Jim said the cabin was used most often in winter. It was built in a great place for heading out across the low land that runs northward to the inland side of the Kiglapait Mountains. It is also within easy reach of the mountains themselves. In winter, Inuit travel out there to hunt caribou. We nailed the cabin shut again and nibbled the bannock Helena had packed for us. As if by summons Jim and Helena buzzed by in their boat, headed toward Nain, and motored gently inshore to see that we were OK. After they had gone, we felt alone, almost lonely. We had enjoyed their company.

There are two narrows in the Port Manvers Run that are marked on the chart as First Rattle and Second Rattle. We approached Second Rattle first, paddling against the wind and the tide, and found the tide running too strongly against us through the narrows. We sprinted from eddy to eddy, but the current was so strong we pulled ashore to wait for it to slacken. The rock was smooth, water-carved, and as curvaceous as if Henry Moore had sculpted the whole cliff. The rock was eroded into pillars that defined the now-dry channels. Beds of mussels lay exposed on the flats between the cliffs in these little canyons. We secured the kayaks and walked across the sweeping surface at the top of the low cliff, nestling down together in a hollow for a time to rest. But Kristin, eying the dense, blue-black, prickly carpets of mussels, thought they looked like too much of a good meal to waste. She grabbed a bag and began gathering. By the time the tide had slackened Kristin had a bulging bag of mussels.

We paddled against the wind along the wooded island shore, scanning for landings but seeing nowhere suitable at this low level of tide. Above the dispiritingly large boulders that littered the water's edge were patches of sand that would offer easy landing at high tide. From shore the mountains rise to more than 2,000 feet on either side of the channel. We pressed on, watching cloud build up. We nominally agreed to target Igloo Island as our destination, but when Kristin spotted a cabin on the mainland shore we crossed the channel and discovered an easy beach landing. There were actually two cabins; we chose the larger because it had a better stove. We scoured the shore for driftwood until we ran out of energy. Everything seemed to take twice as much effort as usual. Later, sitting by candlelight in front of a hot bowl of tender steamed mussels, with a tiny ceramic tumbler of whisky at hand and basking in the warmth of the stove, I looked across the table and watched Kristin's quirky smile make her whole face change, flashing furrows between her dodging eyebrows and changing in a moment from a serious look to one of elfin mischief. It was interesting to reconcile that playfulness with her tenacious character. I was so happy to be traveling with her.

With only nineteen miles farther to paddle, it seemed certain we would reach Nain the next day. But in the night, mice ran around constantly, disturbing our sleep, so although we got up with the sun we were slow to get moving. To appease our hunger, Kristin cooked extra food, including thick pancakes, and since a night of rain had swollen the little stream that ran across the beach, I took the opportunity to rinse some clothes and dry them in front of the stove. While we waited for the pancakes to cook I idly flipped through the pages of a guest book lying in the corner. It had been filled with comments and journal entries. With the book full, visitors had taken to writing their reports on the walls. "Jim and Helena stayed over," began one account. They were heading for their own cabin, but there was too much ice for them to reach it. One entry ruefully described the plight of a group stuck for an extended period because of bad weather with "only caribou meat to eat." Whereas Jim and Helena's guest book at their cabin consistently recorded sightings and encounters with both polar bears and black bears, the entries here seemed less dramatic. As if to make up for that, when I turned to leave I caught my head on the short doorframe, and very efficiently laid myself out on the floor.

The water was calm, so calm we took photographs of the perfectly reflected clouds. Utter stillness. But the weather here can change rapidly, and before we had paddled a mile, dark cloud had moved in from the west and was spilling rain on us. The breeze that had picked up with the rain rapidly pushed up a chop. We aimed across Webb Bay with the rising wind deftly embroidering the water with whitecaps. Angling across the storm, side by side, we fought toward the southwest shore of the bay and potential shelter from this sudden blow. Kristin was paddling strongly but looked apprehensive. Then I noticed the gathering darkness of a deeper rain cloud low over the hills at the end of the bay. I anticipated stronger winds arriving with it.

"Kristin, can you paddle faster?" She replied that she was already paddling as hard as possible. Our kayaks pitched through the chop, throwing water into the wind. So relentless was the onslaught it was difficult to tell if it was even raining at all, or whether it was just spray that soaked us. We struggled closer and closer to land, first feeling the effect of the diminished fetch shrinking the wave size, then finding the wind more gusty and fluky but weaker. Finally we reached shallow water. A foreshore of sand and mud interspersed with rocks and seaweed stretched up toward a narrow sand edge, tide-lined with dead seaweed. A peaty bank bordered the top of the beach and a forest of short conifers stood above a carpet of yellow-green lichen so pale it seemed to glow. The rain was driving hard. Kristin said that right now she wanted to cry, but did not see the point: "There's too much still to do."

There was no point in waiting on the water so we carried the kayaks up to rest them on a bed of blueberries and pitched the shelter tent by the trees. The bay was now a furrowed frenzy of white foam streaks and crashing crests. While the wind howled and whistled through the treetops and rain lashed at us, we scooped up fresh water from a pool in the marshy ground and gathered mussels and mushrooms before retreating to shelter. Completely drenched, we were relieved to light the stove and boil water for a drink. The mist from our warming clothes shuddered with each pulse of wind against the tent. Our faces, close in the narrow space, broke into smiles over tumblers of hot chocolate.

The barometer on Kristin's wrist showed the pressure falling fast. We could evidently expect more wind, so I ran out and pitched the sleeping tent a little distance away. It was far enough from the shelter and our cooking smells in case of black bears. Only then did we change into dry clothes to warm ourselves again and prepare to cook. From our buffeted shelter the wind through the trees sounded like heavy surf. We were fourteen miles from Nain.

The weather settled in for a good extended blow, so we busied ourselves in the following days collecting mussels whenever the tide dropped, and *boleti* and berries from the land when the tide was high. In view of our dwindling fuel supplies, I built a tiny fireplace on the beach, and we prepared a pile of short sticks. Then I discovered pebbles of Labradorite on the beach. These gleamed with a startling blue, or blue-green, orange or red iridescence. It was as if the aurora borealis had been captured in pebbles that could be clasped in the palm of a hand, and twisted to turn the lights on and off. Dull gray rock sprang to blue fire as light played across the surface. So special is this iridescent property that it has been given its own name, Labradorescence. It is as magic as rainbows, bioluminescence, mirages, and the northern lights.

Labradorite is the provincial stone of Newfoundland and Labrador. A quarry on an island near Nain cuts huge blocks of Anorthosite, a gray igneous rock that contains blue flecks of Labradorite, for shipment mostly to Italy. It is used as decorative stone for counter tops, memorials, and other stone finish work. Small pieces of Labradorite are used as gemstones in jewelry. Soon we could spot the dull gray feldspar pieces from a distance by their color and the way the light played on their flat surfaces, although sometimes the pearlescent gleam from inside a blue mussel shell would deceive us.

After a few days of strong winds, the sky cleared and the wind dropped. It was evening, and everything seemed quiet. It was then we heard the urgent buzz of an engine from the south, and soon a boat laden with people appeared around the low headland. The arcs of spray from the bow gleamed white in the low sun. The boat had passed us, when it turned abruptly and headed straight for our camp. Closer to shore it slowed. "Nigel!" I heard a man's voice call. We made our way across the slippery beach, leaping over the pools, until we reached boulders at the water's edge. It was John, the first person we had met at Saglek, the Inuk employed as a polar bear guard—and Helena was with him!

With the engine lifted and the boat poled in close, everyone clambered out onto the rocks, bundled deep in clothes. Without ceremony they handed us a food package. John introduced his wife, two sons and a daughter. Then, while the children ran off to the woods to gather berries, we talked. He had six days leave, so he was heading off with his family and Helena in Jim and Helena's boat to do a little hunting. They would stay with Helena in the cabin. John said he'd like to hunt caribou and geese, and added with a smile, "Hopefully, no bears." He asked if we had seen any more south of Saglek. I listed them: "One black bear at Okak, one polar bear at Helena's cabin." He said they had not seen any more at Saglek since we left. Kristin chatted with the two women, telling them about our journey from the cabin and the strong winds.

We could have talked all night, but evening was coming on and our visitors still had a distance to go before dark. One by one they leaped from the rock to the boat. Last to board, John's daughter handed Kristin the bag of chips she was eating, saying, "These are for you." Then she, too, hopped into the boat. With the craft coaxed from shore, all took their seats huddled together behind the little windshield and they were off again, the spray flying, the sound fading as they crossed Webb Bay. I felt warmed by their kindness. Their gift of food was welcome, but more touching was that they stopped to say hello and to check we were OK.

The break in the weather held overnight, and we awoke to find a crisp frost coating everything in a shimmering white layer, its sparkle as intense as the glitter on a Christmas card. Suddenly transported to childhood, I recalled sprinkling sparkly glitter onto the glue my teacher spread around the edges of the Christmas cards I had so painstakingly crayoned. I could now almost smell the card, the crayon, and the glue. These were cards I proudly carried home to mum and dad, my little hands gritty with the shedding silver fragments.

I carried dry twigs from the shelter tent to kindle the fire, startling a jay into noisy flight across the treetops. The sun crept up behind the mountains of South Aulatsivik Island, casting rich color across the beach and melting the frost where it touched, leaving it untouched in the shadows. The hills were white with early snow. Two small boats roared along the waterway heading north.

Searching for breakfast fungi, I spotted a single parasol mushroom, *Lepiota procura*, one of the largest mushrooms I know and a full ten inches in diameter. I was excited. Possibly my favorite of all the mushrooms, I find them least often. Kristin had never tasted one. The cap almost perfectly filled our pan and I tended it with care over the tiny fire. The firm flesh, with its rich, nutty flavor, was worth waiting for.

Relaxed, and paddling in good weather, we made easy progress. A cluster of houses on the slope above a narrow bay told us we had reached Nain. There was no reason to hurry now. We rafted our kayaks together for a moment at the mouth of the bay, staring across the calm blue sea at the town. It was a good time to pause and reflect. For Kristin, this moment was confirmation that she had been capable of tackling a trip of such magnitude and duration. When she agreed to come she had little idea of what to expect. I had watched her face the dangers and overcome the difficulties. She trusted me to know what I was doing. Unable at first to visualize the scale of time and distance ahead, she had tackled the journey one day at a time. I felt immeasurably proud of her, and intensely close.

At the beginning of this trip I wanted to complete the journey I had begun in 1981. Now I realized that as wonderful as Labrador and Ungava Bay had been, my greatest reward had come from traveling with Kristin. Tipping our kayaks on edge, we threw our arms around each other and kissed. When we resumed paddling, the sea was still calm and blue, but I was smiling even more broadly than before. We were here.

We idled past an airstrip to a small harbor to a steep beach of angular stones by a fish plant. Construction workers were building a second dock close to the existing one and I could see them watching us. I hope they saw the slender woman hop nimbly onto the stones and lift her kayak ashore as if she did it every day, which she did. I hope they were amused to see the bearded man behind her climb out stiffly, lose balance, and fall backward over his kayak into the water. Laughter seemed an appropriate closure to such a wonderful kayak trip!

CHAPTER **23**

Nain

A modern fish plant, clad in vertical unpainted wooden boards, stood a few yards from the beach where we landed. Outside, a woman in waterproof dungarees stood hosing buckets. Through the wide entrance we could see layers of large shellfish, in big stainless steel tray tables, being rinsed under fast running water. "Scallops," the woman explained. A boat had just brought in the catch they were preparing. She said scallops were the only profitable catch that came to town nowadays. "The cod's gone. Over-fished by Newfoundlanders. Now the salmon's unprofitable too, and char just doesn't keep well." Listening to her talk it seemed strange to me how natural it seemed to be here. Yet we had only just arrived. Although it was interesting to hear about the fish, we were looking for somewhere safe to leave our kayaks for a few days until the arrival of the coastal steamer, the *Northern Ranger*. She suggested we ask someone inside the plant.

Pleman Cooper, the engineer in charge, came striding out to our aid. "You don't want to leave anything out in the open," he advised right away, his voice suggesting he had said this before. "It'll disappear before you get back. I can lock them in there for you if you like." He pointed to a white-sided shipping container parked on a trailer beside the plant. Dropping everything to help us, Pleman even reversed his pickup truck to the shore for us to load our gear inside to save us carrying it the few yards. Everything we would not need while in Nain we passed into the container and then, hoisting each kayak shoulder-high, we slid them in on top. Pleman then jumped down and shut and locked the heavy tailgate.

Coming from Newfoundland, Pleman said he found Nain out of the way, but the pay was good, twice what he could expect back home. He smiled and turned his palms up for emphasis as he added that accommodation and unlimited phone use was thrown in extra. Trained engineers are difficult to find in a town of 1,400 people, when half of those are of school age or younger. The issue of skilled workers in a place with a small population is a dilemma. If you are born into a small community and wish to stay there, how can you possibly succeed as a specialist? Specialized jobs are so few you have to go elsewhere to gain experience. In a small community it is easier to find a job if you are a jack-of-all-trades. But then people from outside the community who have the training and experience fill the occasional jobs that require special skills. Even when that employment is only short-term, it is often the highest paid work in town. Anyway, it worked in Pleman's favor. "I expect I'll stay for a while," he said, "unless it drives me crazy."

Pleman drove us slowly along the dusty gravel roads through town, pointing out the tiny stores, the police station, the school, and the diesel-fueled power station up the hill where Jim worked. In front of the houses lay *komatiks* (sleds), fluorescent fishing buoys, caribou antlers, and all-terrain vehicles. There were also snowmobiles scattered in the long grass around the houses. With just a few hundred houses Nain is not a large place. It would have been easy for us to walk but for our clumsy array of bags. We had gear we wanted to rinse and dry to make ready for the next stage in our travels. Overhead, wires looped back and forth across the streets, clumping together occasionally at a leaning pole, only to spider-web outward to the low clapboard houses. Rusted oil drums lay at the side of the road.

We pulled up outside the only hotel in town, the Atsanik Lodge. Inside, the white-haired man behind the counter, Tom, puzzled over his bookings and wondered softly to himself in his faintly Scottish accent how he would fit us in. Normally we would require a reservation. Surprising to us, the hotel was fully booked. As it happened, one guest would not arrive until tomorrow morning, when someone else would leave. By switching their respective rooms he could free up a room for two consecutive nights for us at the quiet end of the building. When I asked what he meant by that, he looked up at me, smiled wryly, and said it was Friday night. Evidently the bar got pretty rowdy as the evening progressed.

Eyeing our mound of bags he added that he had better put us in a room on the ground floor too. The quiet end of the building on the ground floor sounded great. Pleman patiently waited behind us. Only when he was satisfied that we had a place to stay did he head back to the fish plant, leaving us to find our way around the long corridors of the lodge.

As soon as we were in our room, I drew back the curtains to throw open the window for air. I recoiled. The outside window ledge was densely spiked with galvanized nails protruding points-up, presumably to discourage bears. Beyond stretched a patch of bare dirt laced with animal tracks and boot prints, the only barrier between the building and the coniferous woodland beyond.

We left our bags in an untidy heap on the floor and collapsed onto the bed. Our normal onshore routine after kayaking was now useless. Even if taking a shower was the obvious next step, anything that required such effort seemed impossible. Our energy had vanished. But realizing we could soon eat, we stripped off to shower, laughing loudly at each other, ridiculing our skinny bodies.

Clean and trim, my skeletal frame inadequately filled the seemingly cavernous clothes I had carried for this moment. My pants would not stay up until I put on and tucked in an extra T-shirt. Kristin, too, was emaciated. But our appearance was of little concern; we were hungry. We hastened down the corridor to the dining room only to find service was over for the evening because all the known guests had been fed. Almost begrudgingly the woman clearing tables offered us one plate of fish-and-brewis and one of lasagna. Neither was warm but we ate everything eagerly. Kristin skipped across the room to gather some untouched bread rolls she spotted on a table not yet cleared. She could not bear to see them go to waste.

When the server returned, Kristin asked for a second helping and explained why we were still so hungry. The woman went to check if it was OK for her to serve more, then came back with two heaped plates of lasagna. Although we cleared the plates, we left the dining room still hungry, so we carried cups of coffee to our room. There, sinking onto the bed, we switched on the television to surf the few channels we could find for news. If we had missed something significant in the last few weeks, we failed to discover it, for we found the food channel first. With our stomachs fuller than they had been for some time, it was pleasing nonetheless to view food on the screen.

At this point in our journey we felt elated at having reached Nain alive and unscathed. Kristin said she felt amazed that we had been close enough to make eye contact with so many polar bears without coming to harm. She kept bursting out in wonder about the rocks we had seen, the mountains, navigating through the fog and spotting the rim of a cliff way above us, or how every place we landed seemed to be an old camp site. I shared her joy, but at the same time I could not help but compare the last stages of this trip with others, when I had paddled powerfully to shore feeling fitter and stronger than when I set out. Now, instead of feeling physically fit and ready to celebrate our success, I felt depleted. We were clearly in worse shape than when we set out. We had not only lost any body fat we had started with, but our muscles also had visibly shrunk. We had underestimated the burden of powering our heavily laden kayaks for twenty miles a day across cold seas. As we watched a chef prepare a rack of lamb, we fell asleep in front of the TV.

Nain nestles at the side of a bay overlooked by mountains all around. The dirt roads run in random directions, shrinking without warning toward the edge of town into footpaths that climb into the sparse coniferous woodland. The stores disguise themselves as houses; everyone knows where they are, so there is little to be gained by setting up a sign outside. The official buildings carry signs. A crisp board with a white background displayed against the clean wooden siding of one tall building announced the location of the Voisey's Bay Nickel Company. That is the newcomer to town, a subsidiary of the Inco Corporation, and poised to become the world's largest producer of nickel.

Now that Canada recognizes there is value to Labrador, there is a conflict of interest between the government and the indigenous people who never ceded their lands to Canada. Land settlement agreements are under way. The broad Labrador territory, and all it held, was the dominion of the Inuit and the Innu, but it would be naïve to presume all this would be placed on the table by Canada at the start of any negotiation regarding land settlement. Voisey's Bay was part of the land offered to the Inuit in a land settlement package until January 1997, when the Newfoundland government, realizing the potential value of the nickel deposits there, withdrew that area from the offer. The Labrador Inuit, after years of negotiation, have been offered 6,100 square miles of designated territory in Labrador that would become "lands owned by Labrador Inuit and governed by the proposed Nunatsiavut government." Less than six percent of the area of Labrador, it is easier to visualize it as a patch roughly seventy-eight miles by seventy-eight miles.

Kristin wanted chocolate, but it was Sunday. We had spent our last Canadian dollars on fuel and flares in Kuujjuaq, and there was nowhere in town to use our cash cards or credit cards. Pausing outside a small store, on impulse we climbed the broad wooden steps to enter a cramped dimly-lit space inside. I could already smell the chocolate that Kristin lusted after, but first we had to find out if we could use our few remaining American dollars in a place where Canadian dollars were the legal tender. At first the shopkeeper refused, saying he did not know the exchange rate. Kristin pleaded. She argued that although it was Sunday, and the bank would not open today, she was certain the American dollar was worth more than the Canadian. "We don't need change. You can charge us what it is in Canadian and we'll give you that many American dollars." Maybe he was not prepared to overcharge us. Perhaps he misunderstood or was reluctant to get saddled with foreign currency. Kristin tried again, holding up our remaining twenty-dollar bill. "Here, if we give you this, can we take these? You can keep the change." She pointed to four candy bars and a bag of double-chocolate cookies.

He relented. I felt we were getting the best deal even if what we paid for the chocolate far exceeded its normal retail worth. Back in the bright daylight Kristin, grinning, held up our prize, then clasped the treats close to herself and looked at me as if to say, "Mine!" Instead she teased, "Shall we eat them all now?" We did.

We strolled onward down the dirt streets toward the green-steeple church near the dock. People rode past on ATVs while others sauntered in the warm sun with their kids, but the flies were biting. Down at the dock a small ship was being unloaded. This is where the *Northern Ranger* would berth. A temporary building on the dock served as the office. On its semitrailer close by stood the shipping container holding our kayaks. We stopped to look. A group of youngsters sat on the ground below the church overlooking the dock and the dark blue water. They were smoking and talking, huddled close together in a row. A small twin-engine plane floated down toward the airstrip, its bright wings contrasting against the dark blue water. The idling engines sounded clear in the still air, like a lawn mower heard from a long way off. As my eyes followed the plane I spotted a twenty-foot-long wooden boat sitting upside down on trestles, awaiting repair. Close by, in a wire-netting enclosure surrounded by tall grasses, a group of sandy colored sled dogs lazed in the sun. When I looked up again the plane had landed.

As we stood absorbing the scene, I heard the race of a motor approaching down the road and looked up to see a bright red ATV roaring toward us. It stopped abruptly beside us in a cloud of dust and gravel. There, looking out from her parka, was the smiling face of April, the Inuk girl we had met who was overseeing the work at the Saglek site. She had time off from work and had come home to Nain to spend it with her child. Nain is a town of children. In 2004 the average age in Nain was 14.7 years. April beamed at us. She seemed delighted we had completed our journey safely. She was concerned about us and surprised to see us already here. News usually travels fast, she explained, so she expected to hear as soon as we arrived. April said she would like us to meet her boyfriend. "He's not the father of my child." She added, "But he lives in Nain, too."

Walking around town talking to people left me with a lot of questions. Later at the Atsanik Lodge, as we perched on tall stools at the bar sipping Canadian beer from bottles with the owner, Tom, we were able to find answers to some of them. First we were curious about Killinek. Tom lived there in the 1960s and '70s working on behalf of the federal government. Killinek, or Port Burwell, was at that time part of the Northwest Territories, not Quebec or Labrador. Their borders reached only as far as McLelan Strait. In those days the town had 100 to 150 people, including five white people. Tom considered Killinek to have been a model socialist community in those days—that is, socialist with a small S.

The men hunted seals, especially when they migrated through the straits, harvesting perhaps 6,000 per year. This left plenty of skins to be treated and sold, while the meat went into the community freezer. He said there was always plenty of seal meat so people just took what they needed from the freezer. In addition, people traveled south by boat to hunt caribou, and that meat also went into the community freezer. Besides the hunting, there was reliable fishing for char and cod right there, off the rocks by the village. "You just had to drop a line in the water to catch fish," he said.

Then, during the 1970s, animal rights activists lobbied for a boycott on the use of seal furs. Their media campaign pivoted around images of seal pups, "helpless baby seals," clubbed to death on the ice off southern Labrador and Newfoundland for their soft white fur. It was easy to gain indignant support from the public by showing close-up film of the wide-eyed fluffy white pups lying on the ice, followed by the starkly contrasting bloodstained snow. It was not a good time to wear fur, so the value of furs dropped drastically. The hunters from Killinek, far from clubbing seal pups for their skins, hunted the larger free-swimming adults for meat. The media campaign did nothing to reduce the killing of seals for meat, but the cash reward from the byproduct, sealskins, dwindled. In the 1980s prices dropped to $5.00 per sealskin and less. Many hunters lost their only source of income, which for some families had reached several thousand dollars a year. It was a nail in the coffin for those Inuit communities that relied on seal hunting. Whole communities became dependent on welfare. "But Killinek," Tom said, "was a good community right up until the government relocated everyone south in 1978."

In 1995, in an attempt to help the Inuit become self-supporting again using traditional resources, the government in the Northwest Territories began buying furs to sell in Ontario. Five thousand ringed-seal skins were sold in 2001 and the annual number has since more than doubled. With more reasonable market prices, the need for welfare has dropped. In Labrador, too, seals are said to be in healthy supply, so communities here are discussing ways they might market seal products.

Life in the north must be pretty bleak for much of the year. I asked Tom what attracted him there in the first place. He said he saw advertisements posted in Edinburgh, Scotland, where he then lived, for jobs with the Hudson's Bay Company. He went for an interview and signed on as store manager in the 1960s at Iqaluit (called Frobisher at that time). I asked if anyone else he knew had left for Canada like that, and he said there were about five recruits from his part of Edinburgh. He had asked his interviewer, who was from Manitoba, "Why do you come to Scotland to get people? Why don't you get people from Canada?" The interviewer said they couldn't get people to go up north to work, "Only Newfies and Scotsmen." I recalled that in 1981, when I visited Iqaluit, I met the HBC manager there. He was Scottish.

Tom now manages his hotel in Nain, and runs his small boat,

the *Spirit of the Torngat*, up the coast, dropping hikers, kayakers, and archaeologists farther north and collecting them when they are ready to return. He also owns a cabin near Cape Mugford. "Most cabins are on Crown land" he said, "but with the land settlements the control will go to the Inuit, so there may be changes coming." He expected the national park to become a reality, and with it limited access and compulsory permits for travel in the north. He said we were fortunate to see the area as a wilderness before the new controls took effect.

The national park will need rangers, guides, and administrative staff, so it might offer employment to people from here. Tom said employment in Nain tended to be seasonal and often took people out of town. "It's really not seen as a problem. Moving around seasonally is the Inuit tradition. It used to be for hunting and fishing, so the people are used to doing it." The current construction phase at the Voisey's Bay mine now offers employment with good pay, but when the construction is complete, those jobs will dry up. The company then will be seeking skilled operators for the mining. Perhaps local people could be trained for those jobs, but the company might look elsewhere for workers already experienced. Last summer and this summer the PCB cleanup operation provided summer jobs, as did the restoration work at the Hebron Mission, which was likely to continue for a few more summers. But these were typical of local job opportunities: short-term and seasonal.

I had heard about a museum in Nain, but Tom said we were too late; it burned down a few years ago. "Was everything in it burned?" we asked. A woman, sitting nearby and listening to our conversation, suggested that some items had been saved and were stored in a vacant house, since boarded up. Nobody had assumed care of it. She said there used to be handwritten accounts by the Moravians, written in German, from their time of arrival in the 1700s. There was also the first printing press in North America, albeit a small one brought in to "print the Word." My attention was piqued when she mentioned a skin kayak and a second kayak with a man-made cover, possibly of canvas. "They might not have survived the fire."

She added. She suggested someone should take charge of whatever was left and make something of it. This was their heritage after all, and tourists would also be interested to see that sort of thing. She sounded doubtful anything would be done; someone would have to take the initiative.

The Voisey's Bay nickel mine is hugely significant to Nain, not only because of employment possibilities but also in the way it must change the way the community views wildlife management. Inuit representatives have been employed to look into the environmental effects of the mining, but that is a big challenge. Individual natives have never, for example, had to measure or record the number of shellfish harvested and eaten in a season from a particular location, or had to record which years they harvested from a particular section of coast, or how many caribou they shot in a particular area and in which year. With no historical records it is difficult to establish the baseline from which to monitor any changes that might be due to the effects of the mine, beyond the immediate effects of digging. Any mining operation will obviously affect Inuit hunting and fishing and will modify the behavior of the caribou, ducks, and other wildlife. But will mine effluent affect the shellfish in Voisey's Bay? Nobody knows, and in this case nobody knows what shellfish are there. If this mine is just the first of many to come, then in future perhaps Inuit hunters and fishermen will be forced to record what they harvest in order to better safeguard their resources. Increased regulation and bureaucracy is a trend we all see in our lives nowadays.

Another point of significance to Nain concerns the way in which nickel will be transported from the mine. With no road or rail access, the only option at the moment is by sea. Winter ice limits sea navigation to just half of the year. Even within that navigation season, coastal supply boats have not proved immune to ice damage. The ferry *Carson* sank in heavy ice off Labrador in 1977. Environmental risks could increase if the shipping seasons are extended. Another alternative under consideration is to build a road up the coast from Goose Bay to connect the remaining settlements as far as Nain. This would permit year-round transportation of ore from Voisey's

Bay. The infrastructure might also make mining farther north viable. With a road in place it would also be easy to extract timber. Another option could be a railroad.

When nickel was discovered at Voisey's Bay, the prospectors were actually looking for diamonds, which often occur in deposits that may contain nickel and chromium. Nickel occurs in igneous rocks, when minerals solidify from molten rock or magma; although it may be found scattered throughout the rock, sometimes it clusters in clumps near the margins of formations. It must have been exciting to drill for diamonds and discover such a rich mineral deposit. Tom said he was given a core sample that had come from Voisey's Bay. He described it as a shining silver-white cylinder of what looked like pure metal. He set it on the mantelpiece in the foyer of the lodge along with other rocks he had collected, but someone stole it.

Kristin and I had begun to appreciate how popular geological prospecting is here. Almost all our fellow lodgers at the Atsanik Lodge introduced themselves as either geologists or helicopter pilots responsible for transporting geologists. Nowadays, despite the inaccessibility, any rich new mineral discovery in Labrador could become feasible for a mining company to exploit. Nearby South Aulatsivik Island is being test-drilled, and farther north there is a lot of prospecting activity and excitement around the Kiglapait Mountains, where the geological formations are considered favorable for diamonds. Significant mineral deposits have been found at Okak Bay.

The three big resources recognized here by the government are hydroelectric power, minerals, and timber. All three require a certain amount of infrastructure, roads, that by definition will destroy the wilderness. But a road as far as Nain would also be an access route for tourists. Increased tourism could help the economy of the otherwise isolated communities, no doubt changing life there in other ways too. The government controls road building, but according to new guidelines the Inuit and Innu may be able to take a part in future decision-making. Any road to Voisey's Bay and Nain will surely be extended to future mine sites, at the expense of the remaining wilderness, but road or no road, mining has already started on the doorstep of Nain.

Later, in his office, Tom let us browse through the precious photograph albums given to him by Duller Alfred, a man from Innsbruck, Austria, who had visited Labrador every summer for many years. His albums combined wonderful photographic images of scenery and wildlife with candid captions and tight essays. In this way he effectively captured the essence of Labrador. We turned the pages slowly to reveal mountains and lakes, islands and beaches, calm fjords and wind-racked fjords, fog trails and snowdrifts, and caribou and foxes. Here, too, were polar bears and the inside-out carcasses of seals and black bears they had eaten. Tom saw our enthusiasm and offered, "Take them back to your room with you to look at if you like." I staggered out carrying a two-foot pile of the big volumes. Later, lying on the bed, I studied a photograph of a large black bear. The caption below it was handwritten in black ink. It read, "They are not harmless black clowns. I barely got away in the kayak from a determined black bear fast swimming toward me."

Tom ferried Duller Alfred up the coast every summer in the *Spirit of the Torngat*, dropping him with his camping gear and food and sometimes with his take-apart kayak. Alfred enjoyed the peace and isolation the wilderness of Labrador offered him. He usually traveled alone. Photography being his main hobby, he typically camped in one area for the whole summer, hiking in all directions from his base to view the surrounding area. His camp inevitably attracted attention. Polar bears checked him out, sometimes returning daily, which perhaps explains how he managed to take so many excellent photographs of them.

I learned from his albums things that would have been useful to know before we set out on our journey. Alfred explained, for instance, how he circled his tent with a tripwire as an early warning system in case bears approached while he was asleep. He was visited repeatedly by both bears and arctic foxes and soon learned to raise the wire just enough so the foxes would not keep waking him up. When approached by polar bears he found that if firing his rifle into the air or at the ground near the bear had no effect, firing directly at the bear with plastic rounds was usually a sufficient deterrent. He carried lead bullets too, just in case the plastic ones were not enough. Despite his precautions, his sleep was broken one night when a polar bear dragged him bodily from his tent by the foot of his sleeping bag. As I drifted into sleep that night I felt more secure knowing our windowsill had been spiked.

CHAPTER **24**

Northern Ranger

Until Tom drove us down the hill to the dock in his pickup I had no idea how different the arrival of the *Northern Ranger* could be from that of the cargo ship a few days ago. The dock now crawled with people. It seemed the whole town had come out to watch or participate in a social event. Children ran and cycled around the dock, racing underneath the pallets loaded with goods as the ship's crane lowered them from the hold to the dock. ATVs cruised around slowly, one towing a small wooden box-trailer containing a crowd of small children. Youngsters competed to see who could climb the farthest up the massive braided mooring lines before either falling off or judging their height to be enough and retreating.

On deck, crewmembers chased a youth who had climbed on board surreptitiously without a ticket. The chase ran round and round the vessel until they finally cornered him and sent him ashore. He strutted down the gangway grinning to his friends. Tom said the last time *Northern Ranger* stopped here, a week ago, kids got on board and threw all the lifejackets and floats off the back, so the crew this week were trying their best to keep troublemakers off the ship.

While Kristin hurried off to make arrangements for our passage, I stood with Tom to watch the fun. A forklift carried loaded pallets to the dock to be hoisted on board, returning with goods that had been offloaded. As the driver did not have a clear view of the way ahead, older siblings rushed in to snatch toddlers to safety, while bicycles swerved and raced in anticipation of the forklift's abrupt changes of direction. The aluminum gangway was packed with kids from five to fifteen years old, pushing their way steadily up only to be turned back by the crew at the top. Genuine passengers had a difficult time squeezing past the children, who draped themselves across the railings on both sides of the narrow gangway. At the side of the ship where the bulwark dropped lower to the dock near the cargo hatch, teenagers were giving each other a leg up and a shoulder to stand on to scramble aboard.

All the while, one little boy hurtled around the crowd on the rear wheel of his bicycle, sustaining a wheelie most of the way along the dock before applying his heel to the rear wheel to brake and bring the front tire back to the ground. It was chaos. "Drives you cuckoo," was Tom's short comment before he took his leave. He was needed back at work, or at least that was his excuse to escape. He edged his pickup truck slowly away through the crowd.

Kristin returned with our paperwork completed, and we carried our kayaks to the dock ready to have them hoisted aboard. As soon as we set them down, kids started removing the hatches to see what was inside, crawling into the cockpit, and burrowing into our gear with endless questions about what we had, where we were going, and whether we needed help. I was relieved when the kayaks were lifted like slender pencils into the air and lowered into the hold, leaving us free to talk.

April came down with her boyfriend to see us off. Jerry, one of the men we met working on the roof of the mission at Hebron, also came to wish us a safe journey. He said the restoration team had run out of materials for the roof, so he had hitched a ride back to Nain on a fishing boat. Last week he had stepped on a rotten plank and had fallen through the roof. He landed on his feet on the floor below, unhurt. I looked at him with admiration. He looked strong and wiry and weathered, but ten or twenty years older than I was. He looked like a man accustomed to landing on his feet.

Jerry asked if we had encountered any more bears, and I told him of our final sighting and of the black bear we had seen. Had he seen any? He said their camp had been visited by what he described as a "really big polar bear," the biggest he had ever seen. He said the paw prints it left behind were bigger than our oval kayak hatches. He had been impressed.

Finally the last ship-bound freight items, a motorcycle and an ATV, were hoisted aboard and the cargo hatch was closed. It was time for us to board and watch the antics of the children on the dock from above. As the *Northern Ranger* eased away from the dock, the water churned white bubbles deep into the clear blue water and the bright sunlight enriched the colored clothing of the crowd on the dock. We gathered speed, leaving Tom's boat, the *Spirit of the Torngat,* rocking at its mooring in the bay.

The *Northern Ranger* serves partly as freighter, partly as passenger vessel. She is no cruise ship, but we found ourselves in a cabin with a bathroom, four bunks, and a porthole and with plenty of storage cupboards and drawers to stow all our gear. We visited the canteen as soon as it was open, to feast on calorie-rich food. Later that evening we docked briefly at Natuashish, and then moved a short distance away to anchor for the night. Our first night on board was punctuated by visits to the deck to see the northern lights and by strange dreams probably caused by overeating.

Early in the voyage we scanned the islands we passed, hoping perhaps to see a bear or a whale. It made me think of the cruise ships that visit Labrador. As far back as the 1930s Grenfell saw the potential for cruise ships. By 1941 at least one of the great steamship companies had accepted the idea of running summer tourist steamers to Labrador, with fishing and spectacular scenery as attractions.

Forbes, on the other hand, noted in 1938 that the Clarke Steamship Company did not dare send its larger ships farther north than Battle Harbor in southern Labrador. After the HMS Challenger from Britain surveyed the area around Nain, a sea chart was produced, but the area was still insufficiently mapped for safe passage. However, Forbes identified three areas in northern Labrador where the shore was both spectacular and easily approached in safety, namely, Nachvak Fjord, Saglek Fjord, and the Kaumajet Mountains via Mugford Tickle. He suggested that steamship companies should sponsor aerial surveys to chart safe routes, and added that Nain should be added to the places that would be worth visiting. A safe route through the island chain that extends north, south, and east from Nain could be identified and then marked with buoys. Presumably the route would have to be re-marked each season after the ice had cleared.

Much has changed in the steamship industry since then. A modern cruise ship can carry thousands of passengers, but the established size categories include: boutique, carrying fewer than 500 passengers; small, between 500 and 1,000; large, between 1000 and 1800; and so on up in size. Currently the Canadian Border Services Agency requires vessels arriving in Canadian waters to clear customs at their first port of call. The CBSA designates Saint John's and Corner Brook on the island of Newfoundland as the ports of arrival for cruise ships (cruise ship operations or CSO ports) where customs procedures can be followed. For destinations within the Great Lakes or southern Canada these two ports are appropriate, but for a cruise ship from Europe planning a northern voyage to visit Iceland, Greenland, and Labrador, they are ridiculously distant. A detour to clear customs at Saint John's Newfoundland could easily entail 1,500 miles of extra sailing.

To illustrate the distances involved using examples in perhaps more familiar territory, imagine a cruise ship sailing the relatively short distance from Alaska to Vancouver, British Columbia, being required to clear customs in California first, or a ship sailing south from Canada being required to clear customs in South Carolina before being permitted to visit New York. There is clearly a case for a CSO port much farther north than southern Newfoundland. Perhaps

Forbes's suggestion of nearly seventy years ago that Nain would be a good port of call for cruise ships might still be valid. If Nain were a CSO port, this would make Labrador much more practical for cruise ship operators, and bring benefits to the population of Labrador too.

In addition to the required visit to south Newfoundland prior to landfall in Labrador, there is a regulation requiring cruise ships carrying more than 200 people to have all their passengers processed at every subsequent port of call. Evidently this regulation discourages cruise lines to offer Labrador as a destination except for the smallest boutique-class ship. Still, it is difficult to imagine a town like Nain, with its population of 1,400, being visited by a small-category cruise ship with 1,000 passengers, or one in the large category carrying 1,800. Maybe there is a better way for Labrador to benefit from tourism.

Pressure from big cruise ship companies and financial factors could lead to changes in policy. The overall economic benefit generated from the cruise industry in Newfoundland and Labrador in 2004 was estimated at $3.5 million dollars, with thirty-nine ports in the province hosting cruise ships and more than 44,000 guests. That is 12,000 more visitors than 2003, and a 400 percent increase in port calls since 1998. The percentage of this traffic that will visit ports in the north of Labrador will depend in part on whether the decision is made to create a northern CSO port.

Kristin and I were on a budget cruise. Our voyage on *Northern Ranger* went southeast from Natuashish to Postville, to Makkovik, into Hamilton Inlet, then west and south via Rigolet to Goose Bay; it took three days.

CHAPTER **25**

The Road of Progress

A road now reaches from the Saint Lawrence River inland to Fermont and Labrador City, then onward as far as Goose Bay. In southern Labrador a road runs north from L'Anse-au-Loup to Cartwright. The road under construction will soon connect Cartwright to Goose Bay, a section now connected only by car ferry. As it becomes easier for visitors to access this area, there likely will be an increase in tourism. Kirk, who works on the *Northern Ranger*, talked optimistically about the changes. He comes from a small village in southern Labrador. When the Newfoundland fisheries collapsed, the economy in southern Labrador suffered.

Last year, the new road reached Kirk's home village, linking it to the rest of the south Labrador coast. That road already brings tourists. Farther down the coast where the road arrived earlier, new businesses, hotels, restaurants, and tourist services have injected new cash into the economy. He expects the effect to spread all along the road. Although it is mostly people from outside who set up the new businesses, he thinks local people benefit, too. He has concerns about the forest, because the road also opens the way for logging companies to extract timber, and the trees grow very slowly here. If the trees were cut, it would take a lifetime before any more logging jobs returned, and the landscape would look torn and ravaged, with nothing to attract a tourist. Logging roads open vehicular access to the little lakes and rivers that are at the moment havens of wildlife. Road access, together with power boats, will inevitably cause pollution and noise. The very things that tourists want to see, the reasons they would travel to a place like southern Labrador, could be destroyed in a flash. He says that right now the changes brought by the road seem good, but, "I don't know how things will turn out." The sequence Kirk hints at, of progress like a wildfire surging up the coast along the road, leaving behind logged land and ravaged scenery, is thought-provoking. But what would become of the trees from Labrador if they were felled? Most likely they would be used for paper pulp, for trees do not grow large enough here to make them a source of commercial timber.

In 1911, in his book, *Among the Eskimos of Labrador,* Hutton said the Inuit preferred to travel long distances to cut a Labrador tree rather than use imported timber. The tough local wood better suited their needs. In northern Labrador the trees take centuries to grow to a useful size, so the growth rings are tightly packed and the timber needs no seasoning. Hutton related the story of a fir seedling planted in a sheltered place near Nain to celebrate the birth of a child. The tree grew knee-high in twenty-one years. With that perspective, it is difficult to regard the northern forest as a renewable resource, except for the occasional taking of a tree by a small number of people. The alternative is a less than once in a lifetime clear-cut for paper pulp. That is, unless the climate continues to grow warmer.

The *Northern Ranger* forced its way west into Hamilton Inlet against a wind that sent plumes of spray high into the air after every thudding impact. The sun lit the spray and lit the rolling crests of the frenzied water. It was fun to stand at the bow, to be lifted high by every swell without being soaked, as we would have been in our kayaks. Soon we were docking at Goose Bay.

As the ship's derrick lowered our kayaks one at a time onto the dock, a local radio reporter approached us. She agreed to drive me to collect our car from the airport before interviewing us, prompting Kristin's plaintive plea, "Oh no, I don't want you to take him away from me. We haven't been separated for weeks!" The next day we drove in sunshine from Goose Bay, with a plume of pale brown dust marking our progress. In dry weather even the slowest vehicles throw up a dust storm, so it was easy to spot oncoming traffic in time to slow down. One reason to slow down was, there was so little traffic drivers became mesmerized and did not notice us until the last moment. With nobody on the road for mile after mile, it is easy to drift into driving on the left side, or on the right, or down the middle, wherever the potholes and boulders are smallest. Another reason was that visibility dropped abruptly to a yard or two after passing. Until the dust dissipated it would be too easy to tumble off the steep berm into muskeg, trees, or boulders, or to end up stuck on the pale yellow floor of lichens between the trees.

We had two objectives that day: to visit the Churchill Falls hydroelectric power station and before that to visit Muskrat Falls. We eased off the main road and down a short, narrow track to parking. A short hike along a snaking muddy trail took us to the slabs of rock that overlook the river midway down Muskrat Falls. The falls are not a single vertical pour-over, but rather a series of drops over a distance, so the effect is a huge river rapid, a white, heavy, heaving display of raw energy, a big volume of water on its way downhill. The noise rumbled through my body, shaking me, as I watched, mesmerized. Muskrat Falls is at the lower end of a natural lake, where the water squeezes through a gap in the bedrock, like a draft through a partly opened door. The falls could provide an immense amount of power for Labrador if a hydroelectric plant were built here. We made our way back through the woods, plucking plump blueberries as we went. We had made a reservation for a tour around the Churchill Falls power station, so we needed to keep to schedule. Even so, we misjudged the time it would take to drive the 250 miles from Goose Bay to Churchill Falls on the gravel road, and we missed our rendezvous.

It took only a short drive around Churchill Falls to find the tour minibus parked outside a hotel. We pulled up alongside and joined the group in the hotel, late, but in time for a drink of hot chocolate and a very slick public relations lecture. Here we learned about the hydroelectric power scheme, the aims, the challenges and how they were overcome, the smooth operation of the plant, and more facts and figures anyone less demanding than an accountant might wish for. As I listened I scrutinized the map on the wall. Grand Lake stretched northwest from North West River near Goose Bay, with the Nascaupi River threading inland as a fine blue line, linking small lakes as far as the amoebic Smallwood Reservoir. The reservoir extends its tendrils north to the Labrador watershed border with Quebec, branching south to touch Churchill Falls.

I oriented myself to trace Mina Hubbard's 1905 canoe route up the Nascaupi River to Lake Michikamau and north to George River (Kangiqsualujjuaq) close to Ungava Bay. I felt a swell of pride, knowing we had been there. It had been a long time since I first read Mina Hubbard's book. The thin blue lines on the wall map reflected the corrections she had made to the maps she took with her. Her map might have been accurate enough to endure, except that now, a hundred years later, Lake Michikamau has vanished beneath the Smallwood reservoir, and the magnificent Churchill Falls of mystery and native legend has been calmed into a quiet, water-worn cliff. Water that once fell almost a thousand feet over the falls is now diverted underground, channeled through pipes (penstocks) to eleven huge turbines mounted almost a thousand feet underground. Once past the turbines, the water is released into daylight to run back to its original riverbed downstream. So the maps have been redrawn to reflect the new landscape, and the diverted water rushing through the turbines generates up to 5,428 Megawatts of power, equivalent to six nuclear power stations. This is productivity of which Canada is proud.

The project began in the 1950s. As many as 6,300 construction workers were flown in and housed in trailers and metal buildings at the peak of construction, but only a small team was needed to run the plant when it was finished. The town of Churchill Falls was built to house those people. Approximately 650 people, 230 families, now live there in company-owned houses. Everybody is associated with the power plant because the company owns the town. There are no retired people here; anyone leaving their job or retiring must relinquish their company-owned home, and since the company owns every house in Churchill Falls, the only option is to leave town.

Our tour guide drove us to the power station. Beginning that week, new security measures called for photo-identification of all visitors and a rule of no photographs. When we descended underground, the scale of the operation amazed me. I had visited other underground hydroelectric plants before but this one was significantly bigger than any of them. It made me wonder how so many essential component ideas can be brought together to make a project so huge work as smoothly as a pendulum. We walked down roads leading through broad tunnels in what at first appeared to be gray rock, but on closer inspection of the walls revealed thin alternating streaks of black and white sparkling crystals. Here was a mix of clinical scientific cleanliness and dusty bare blasted rock, with a group of tourists wearing colorful hard hats walking through underground tunnels hundreds of feet beneath the ground, at a power plant that cleanly produces the same average electrical output as a conventional oil-powered station burning 93.8 barrels of oil per minute. From our lowest viewing point we gaped at the thundering water of the river as it emerged after its fall of more than a thousand feet.

The road out leads past the twin mining towns of Labrador City and Wabush, the largest concentration of people in Labrador. Established in the 1960s, the combined population of these two adjacent towns amounts to around 11,400 people, and the only reason they are here is iron ore, lots of it. Everyone here makes a living either directly or indirectly from the mines. When we drove into town the mineworkers had been on strike for more than six weeks, and the depressed mood affected everyone. That is, perhaps everyone but a man named Gary Shaw, and his son, also named Gary Shaw. They had just returned from a summer helping raise a plane that had crash-landed sixty miles away. The plane, a Boeing B17G search and rescue aircraft, was returning from Greenland via Resolute Bay in Arctic Canada toward Goose Bay when it ran out of fuel and made an emergency landing on a frozen lake. That was on 23 December 1947. It sank during the following spring thaw and lay beneath twenty-five feet of water in Dyke Lake for fifty-seven years.

A salvage team worked for seven years to complete the necessary paperwork to legally raise the plane and ship it home to the United States. This summer they floated it to the surface using airbags. Reducing its wingspan to about ninety-five feet by removing the wingtips, they towed it sideways sixty-five miles downriver to the Smallwood reservoir. There they dismantled it and lifted the sections by crane onto flatbeds for trucking to a railway yard in Labrador City. We were eager to see the plane, and Gary was excited to show us.

Gawping at the dismantled sections I marveled at how well preserved everything appeared to be. Gary pointed out where yellow stickers remained on the fuel tanks. The instructions were intact and as readable as if they had only recently been applied. Then he drew our attention to the wheels. They had been retracted for the landing for fear they might break through the ice. The tires were still inflated. If all goes to plan the parts will be trucked to Georgia in the United States where work will start to restore the plane, ultimately to fly again. It could be in the air again within the next ten years.

So here we were on the border between Labrador and Quebec, at the site of the biggest concentration of people in the whole of Labrador, anticipating another day of driving on the dusty gravel road before hitting paved highway. Until fifty years ago this place was uninhabited but for migrating Innu and Métis people. (The Métis are the descendents of marriages between native people and Europeans). The changes here have been rapid, within my lifetime, and have depended on road and rail. It was so very recently that the road reached Goose Bay. Soon it will link up with the road that skirts the southeast coast of Labrador. After that, who knows where the road will lead next?

For us, the road ahead will lead to Seattle, and our journey will be a time for reflection. As we traveled into increasingly developed country, we saw an accelerated vision of what might befall Labrador and Ungava in the twenty-first century. We crossed from gravel road to tarmac. The single road began to branch with increasing frequency. We followed logging trucks, passed dams for hydroelectric power stations, and drove across land ever more sectioned off for specific uses. Perhaps that will be how the Labrador wilderness will be tamed: by building an access road, then logging roads, by improving the road surfaces, and sectioning the land. That familiar development process has crept across the world and is advancing here. Perhaps in a generation or two the native people will have blended into the incoming population, as appears to be happening at Labrador City, where they represent a tiny minority within the flood of arrivals from outside. But perhaps by negotiation they will retain enough of their historic identity to shape the way Labrador develops into something unique and special.

Soon we will be telling our friends stories about polar bears and Second World War airplane wrecks, of winds springing like vengeful spirits from the dark mountains, of forty-foot tides and fog. Our families will ask how our trip went and we'll blurt out stories they will perhaps believe but barely comprehend. We will have too many stories to tell, and still more beyond our skill to relate, but already our shared memories can be triggered by a word or a phrase, to conjure up images and emotions far deeper and richer than any of the stories either of us could tell in words.

"Remember the beacon bear?" one will say, or, "Remember David and Suzie?" Already they bring to mind places and people and events and weather and smells and sounds that will forever connect us. At either end of the stepping stones, we discover we speak the same language. I glanced at Kristin; she smiled. We were going home. With our two kayaks strapped to the roof rack above the Jeep, we cruised comfortably above the staccato beat of the tires on the washboard of the gravel road. The fine dust billowed up to obscure the road behind us like a closing curtain.

Index

N.B. A bibliography may be found at www.nigelkayaks.com

LaVergne, TN USA
29 April 2010
181053LV00002B/1/P

9 781432 745288